Buddhism in Five Minutes

Religion in Five Minutes

Series Editors
Russell T. McCutcheon
University of Alabama
Aaron W. Hughes
University of Rochester

Volumes in the **Religion in Five Minutes** book series are each an opportunity for novice readers to benefit from the expertise of scholars, all addressing common questions about everything from Hinduism and Buddhism to Paganism and Indigenous religion. Students and general readers will find here questions that they might ask—What is the oldest religion? Do all religions have scriptures?—all answered in a readable manner. Because each chapter can be read in about five minutes, the books offer ideal supplementary resources in classrooms or an engaging read for those curious about the world around them. And, sooner or later, the assumptions entailed in the questions themselves take center stage for the contributors. With recommended readings in each chapter, the Religion in 5 Minutes book series meets readers where they are and invites them to entertain just how fascinating the world might be.

Published

Religion in Five Minutes
Edited by Aaron Hughes and Russell T. McCutcheon

Forthcoming

African Diaspora Religions in Five Minutes
Edited by Emily D. Crews and Curtis J. Evans

Ancient Religion in Five Minutes
Edited by Andrew Durdin

Atheism in Five Minutes
Edited by Teemu Taira

Christianity in Five Minutes
Edited by Robyn Faith Walsh

Hinduism in Five Minutes
Edited by Steven W. Ramey

Indigenous Religious Traditions in Five Minutes
Edited by Molly Bassett and Natalie Avalos

Islam in Five Minutes
Edited by Edith Szanto

Pagan Religions in Five Minutes
Edited by Suzanne Owen and Angela Puca

Buddhism in Five Minutes

Edited by
Elizabeth J. Harris

SHEFFIELD UK   BRISTOL CT

Published by Equinox Publishing Ltd.

UK: Office 415, The Workstation, 15 Paternoster Row, Sheffield, South Yorkshire S1 2BX

USA: ISD, 70 Enterprise Drive, Bristol, CT 06010

www.equinoxpub.com

First published 2021

© Elizabeth J. Harris and contributors 2021

All rights reserved. No part of this publication may be reproduced or transmitted in any form or by any means, electronic or mechanical, including photocopying, recording or any information storage or retrieval system, without prior permission in writing from the publishers.

British Library Cataloguing-in-Publication Data

A catalogue record for this book is available from the British Library.

ISBN-13 978 1 80050 089 1 (hardback)
         978 1 80050 090 7 (paperback)
         978 1 80050 091 4 (ePDF)
         978 1 80050 122 5 (ePub)

Library of Congress Cataloging-in-Publication Data

Names: Harris, Elizabeth J. (Elizabeth June) 1950- editor.
Title: Buddhism in five minutes / edited by Elizabeth J Harris.
Description: Bristol : Equinox Publishing Ltd, 2021. | Series: Religion in
   5 minutes | Includes bibliographical references and index. | Summary:
   'In Buddhism in Five Minutes, academic specialists offer answers to
   questions about Buddhism that people curious about Buddhism might ask'--
   Provided by publisher.
Identifiers: LCCN 2021023276 (print) | LCCN 2021023277 (ebook) | ISBN
   9781800500891 (hardback) | ISBN 9781800500907 (paperback) | ISBN
   9781800500914 (pdf) | ISBN 9781800501225 (epub)
Subjects: LCSH: Buddhism. | Buddhism--Popular works.
Classification: LCC BQ4022 .B835 2021 (print) | LCC BQ4022 (ebook) | DDC
   294.3--dc23
LC record available at https://lccn.loc.gov/2021023276
LC ebook record available at https://lccn.loc.gov/2021023277

Typeset by Witchwood Production House Ltd, Sheffield

Contents

Preface   xiii
    Cathy Cantwell

Introduction   1
    Elizabeth J. Harris

Part One: Buddhism as a religion

1. Is Buddhism a religion?   6
    Denise Cush

2. What is the role and focus of faith in Buddhism?   10
    Asanga Tilakaratne

3. What is the role of ritual in Buddhism?   14
    Asanga Tilakaratne

4. Are relics important to Buddhists?   19
    Kevin Trainor

5. What are the holy texts of Buddhism?   24
    Asanga Tilakaratne

6. What is the place of images in Buddhism?   29
    Sarah Shaw

7. What is the role of narrative in Buddhism?   35
    Brian Black

8. Is Buddhism atheistic, non-theistic, or theistic?   40
    Peter Harvey

Part Two: The Buddha

9. What do we know about the historical Buddha?   46
    Dhivan Thomas Jones

10	How is the nature of buddhahood to be understood? *Christopher V. Jones*	50
11	How does one "read" a Buddha-image? *Ronit Wang*	55
12	Who is the fat Buddha figure? *Paulina Kolata*	60
13	What is a bodhisattva? *Jiancheng Shi*	63
14	How do Buddhists show their devotion to the Buddha? *Paulina Kolata*	68

Part Three: What the Buddha taught (1)

15	Can we know what the historical Buddha taught? *Rupert Gethin*	76
16	What part does belief in rebirth play in Buddhism? *Peter Harvey*	81
17	Does Buddhism see the mind as separate from the body? *Peter Harvey*	86
18	Do Buddhists see all that happens to one as due to karma? *Peter Harvey*	91
19	What is seen as reborn, according to Buddhism? *Peter Harvey*	96
20	To what extent does Buddhism "deny the self"? The non-self teaching. *Christopher V. Jones*	99
21	What are the "Four Noble Truths" about? *Arjuna C. B. Ranatunga*	104
22	What is non-attachment in Buddhism? *Dhivan Thomas Jones*	108
23	What is nirvana? *Arjuna C. B. Ranatunga*	112
24	What is it to be "enlightened" or "awakened"? *Peter Harvey*	116

25	What kinds of "saints" does Buddhism have? *Arjuna C. B. Ranatunga*	120

Part Four: What the Buddha taught (2) — Meditation

26	Why do Buddhists meditate? *Sarah Shaw*	126
27	What is "mindfulness" in Buddhism? And does it differ from modern secular "mindfulness"? *Tse-fu Kuan*	130
28	What kinds of meditation are there in Buddhism? *Dhivan Thomas Jones*	136
29	What is the role of chanting in Buddhism? *Xiaoqi Tang*	141

Part Five: Monasticism and lay people in Buddhism

30	What is the role of monasticism in Buddhism? *Ann Heirman*	148
31	How does one become ordained? *Ann Heirman*	153
32	What rules do monastics follow? *Alice Collett*	157
33	What is the position of nuns in Buddhism? *Ann Heirman*	163
34	What is the role of lay Buddhists? *Alice Collett*	168
35	Does Buddhism support gender equality? *Alice Collett*	172
36	What is the role of preaching in Buddhism? *Mahinda Deegalle*	176

Part Six: Development of Buddhism — Mahayana and Vajrayana Buddhism

37	How did Buddhism relate to the Brahmanism of the Buddha's day, and later Hinduism? *Christopher V. Jones*	182
38	What splits were there in Buddhism in the early centuries? *Peter Harvey*	188
39	What are the main contemporary divisions in Buddhism: Theravada, Mahayana, and Vajrayana? *Christopher V. Jones*	193
40	What is Hinayana? *Elizabeth J. Harris*	199
41	What is Zen Buddhism? *Hiroko Kawanami*	202
42	What is Pure Land Buddhism? *Wendy Dossett*	207
43	What is the role of the Dalai Lama? *Cathy Cantwell*	212
44	What is the bodhisattva vow? *Nick Swann*	217
45	What is Buddha-nature? *Christopher V. Jones*	220
46	What are the meanings of "emptiness" in Mahayana Buddhism? *Christopher V. Jones*	223
47	Is Tantric Buddhism just about sex? *Nick Swann*	228
48	Why are there so many different celestial beings in Tibetan Buddhism? *Cathy Cantwell*	232

Part Seven: Buddhist art and material culture

49 What are the main buildings and symbols of Buddhism? 238
   Arjuna C. B. Ranatunga
   with a contribution from Cathy Cantwell

50 Why do Buddhists make art? 248
   Christian Luczanits

51 What is a mandala? 254
   Christian Luczanits

52 How is Buddhism influencing contemporary art? 259
   Tim Stephens

Part Eight: Buddhism and other religions

53 How has Buddhism been influenced by other religious traditions? 266
   Sophie Barker

54 How do Buddhists view other religious traditions, and what kind of interreligious encounters are Buddhists involved in now? 272
   Elizabeth J. Harris

Part Nine: Buddhism and ethics

55 What vows do Buddhists take? 280
   Nick Swann

56 Are Buddhists pacifists? 284
   Peter Harvey

57 Are Buddhists vegetarian? 289
   Dhivan Thomas Jones

58 Does Buddhism have rules for marriage and family life? 293
   Alice Collett

59 How do Buddhists view suicide and self-immolation? 297
   Peter Harvey

60 What is engaged Buddhism? 302
   Manu Ato-Carrera and Tim Stephens

61	What is the relationship between Buddhism and politics? Brian Black	307
62	How important is compassion in Buddhism? Pyi Phyo Kyaw	313
63	Is non-attachment compatible with compassion? Elizabeth J. Harris	318

Part Ten: Buddhism and contemporary issues

64	What do Buddhists think about sex? Amy Langenberg	322
65	What do Buddhists think about those who are LGBTQI? Sal Campbell	327
66	Should Buddhism be taught in schools? Denise Cush	332
67	Are alcohol and drugs ever acceptable to Buddhists? Wendy Dossett	337
68	Are human rights compatible with Buddhism? Damien Keown	341
69	What does Buddhism have to say about race? Tim Stephens	346
70	Are Buddhists active in ecological movements and protecting the environment to mitigate climate change? Alex Owens	352
71	How do Buddhists relate to the methods of science? Tim Stephens	356
72	What is the Buddhist attitude to modern technology? Nick Swann	360

Part Eleven: Emergent Buddhism

73	What is secular Buddhism? Tim Stephens	366
74	How do Buddhists view artificial intelligence? Ralph Quinlan Ford	370

75 Is Western Buddhism a new form of Buddhism? 374
   Sarah Shaw

Index 379

Preface

Cathy Cantwell

The idea for this book came out of a meeting in 2017 between Janet Joyce of Equinox Publishing and myself, along with Peter Harvey. Peter and I were representing the UK Association for Buddhist Studies (UKABS; https://ukabs.org.uk), and the meeting concerned our association's journal, *Buddhist Studies Review*, which is published by Equinox. However, in the course of our discussions, Janet brought to our attention their "Five Minutes" series, suggesting that *Buddhism in Five Minutes* could work well.

The purpose of these books is to tackle a number of typical questions that people outside the subject area might ask of a specialist, so that the answers are simple and succinct, yet remain academically rigorous. The book should thus serve as a highly accessible introduction to the field. We took the proposal to the next UKABS Committee meeting, where it was adopted. We then began to formulate the list of possible questions, and asked our esteemed colleague, Elizabeth Harris, if she would be prepared to act as editor. Fortunately, she agreed, and she has succeeded in gathering an excellent group of contributors, most of whom are specialists in the topics they have written on. As a scholar with many years involvement in a wide range of areas in Buddhist Studies, Elizabeth Harris has been ideally placed to edit the contributions, and to meld them together in the book as a whole.

We hope that this work will effectively answer readers' questions about Buddhism and will stimulate interest in Buddhist Studies.

Cathy Cantwell, President, UK Association
for Buddhist Studies, 2015–2021

Introduction

Elizabeth J. Harris

Buddhism in Five Minutes answers seventy-five questions that people might ask about Buddhism. Each answer should take about five minutes to read! Each has been written by a specialist in Buddhist Studies, who has aimed to make Buddhism accessible to non-specialists. So there are no footnotes, nor long bibliographies and lists of references. Some technical words have been included— Buddhism would be the poorer without them—but these are kept to a minimum. Inevitably, though, given the diversity of the questions, some answers are more complicated than others and need more work from the reader.

This book could be read from beginning to end, but there are also other ways to approach it. For instance, readers could begin with a question that interests them personally from any part of the book. They could then move to the other questions mentioned at the end of the one they have chosen, in the "further reading" section. All of these connect in some way with the question, and create a web of answers that support and illuminate each other. Each answer also lists further reading outside the confines of the book, including texts and sources used in the answer. It is important to remember that no single answer gives all the information needed to understand how Buddhists practice and live their religion. To build up a more comprehensive picture, readers will need to move from section to section, question to question, perhaps using this cross-referencing method.

The book is divided into eleven sections:
1. Buddhism as a religion;
2. The Buddha;
3. What the Buddha taught (1);
4. What the Buddha taught (2): meditation;
5. Monastics and lay people in Buddhism;
6. The development of Buddhism: Mahayana and Vajrayana Buddhism;
7. Buddhist art and material culture;
8. Buddhism and other religions;
9. Buddhism and ethics;
10. Buddhism and contemporary issues;
11. Emergent Buddhism.

The sections, therefore, move through what Buddhists call the Three Jewels or Gems, namely the Buddha, the Dharma (the truth that the Buddha taught), and the Sangha (the community, usually interpreted as the monastic community), before focusing on the historical development of Buddhism, art, ethics, and issues of contemporary concern, such as Buddhism and sex, Buddhism and those who identify as LGBTQI, and Buddhism and race. The limitation of a single book has meant that the questions in some sections are illustrative rather than absolutely comprehensive. For instance, had there been space we would have liked to have included Buddhism and disability, or Buddhism and conversion.

Buddhism in Five Minutes demonstrates that Buddhism is not only about beliefs or the practice of meditation, although both are important. It is also about devotion, ritual, art and materiality, institutions, embodiment, ethics, and engagement with contemporary issues. Within these categories, there is diversity across Buddhist communities and geographical areas, and the different answers demonstrate this.

With over thirty contributors from different countries, with different specialisms in Buddhist Studies and different experiences of Buddhism, the answers, therefore, differ in emphasis, although overall consistency has been the aim. Some answers, for instance, give more emphasis to Theravada Buddhism, found, for example, in Laos, Myanmar, Thailand, and Sri Lanka. Others emphasize Mahayana Buddhism, found, for example, in China, Japan, Korea, and Tibet. In line with this, when using technical terms, some answers give priority to Pali, the foundational language of Theravada Buddhist texts, and some to Sanskrit, which became the foundational language for most Mahayana texts. The two languages share many words in common. For instance, the teaching of the Buddha is called the Dharma (Sanskrit) and the *Dhamma* (Pali). These differences in emphasis, however, are an integral part of the dynamic and changing world of Buddhism.

It has been a privilege to edit this book on behalf of and in cooperation with the UK Association for Buddhist Studies (UKABS). I have been grateful for the support of the UKABS Committee and would like to give particular thanks to: Cathy Cantwell, who read the whole text before publication and created consistency in our use of Tibetan terms; Alice Collett, with whom I discussed stylistic matters; Peter Harvey, who assisted in editing some questions; and Janine Nicol, who made sure the representation of Chinese and Japanese terms was consistent. I am also grateful to those who supplied photographs: Cathy Cantwell, Nicolas Chong, Nicholas Cope, Christian Luczanits, Yuka Itawaki, and Ryofu Pussel.

Practical notes on the style of the book

Some technical Buddhist terms have entered the English language and can now be found in the Oxford English Dictionary: for example, nirvana, sutra, Pali, arhat (one who has attained nirvana), Mahayana Buddhism and Theravada Buddhism. We have not placed these words in italics or used diacritical marks to indicate how they are pronounced. Other technical terms have been italicized with diacritics. Diacritics aid the transliteration of Pali and Sanskrit terms into Roman lettering. They are necessary because

Pali and Sanskrit have a more extensive alphabet than Western languages. The most common diacritics are these:

- ā   a straight mark over a vowel indicates that the vowel is long: e.g., as in *star*;
- ī   pronounced as the vowel in *seek*;
- ū   pronounced as the vowel in *lute*;
- ñ   pronounced as the *gn* in the Spanish *signora*;
- ś/ṣ   pronounced as the *sh* in *shut*;
- ṭ   pronounced as the *t* in *teach* (without the dot, it is pronounced as the *th* in *thatch*)
- ṃ   pronounced nasally as the *ng* in *sing*;
- ṅ   pronounced nasally as the *n* in *think*;
- ṇ   pronounced as the *n* in *name*.

Hanyu Pinyin is used for Chinese names and terms, with the exception of Taiwanese names where Wade–Giles is maintained. The Revised Hepburn romanization system is used for Japanese names and terms. As regards Tibetan terms, although Tibetan letters can be transliterated into Roman script, this produces combinations of letters that cannot be pronounced by those unfamiliar with Tibetan. It is not possible to create phonetic spellings that consistently indicate the original Tibetan spelling; nonetheless, several phonetic systems have been widely used in recent years. Here, we mostly use the Rigpa Phonetics (English) system, although some words had to be modified, and it is discarded if a name or term (such as Dalai Lama) is established in English-language sources.

Capitalization is used sparingly in line with current usage in English. We have made an exception for the Triple Gem. Because of the importance of the Buddha, the Dharma, and the Sangha in Buddhism, these are capitalized throughout.

Elizabeth J. Harris, Edward Cadbury Centre for the Public Understanding of Religion, University of Birmingham, UK
February 2021

Part One
Buddhism as a religion

1
Is Buddhism a religion?

Denise Cush

It depends what you mean by religion, and what you think of as Buddhism, or which Buddhist or scholar you ask. Some definitely want to call Buddhism a religion (see, for example, the title of David Brazier's 2014 book *Buddhism is a Religion: You Can Believe It*) and others prefer to position Buddhism as more of a philosophy or "way of life," such as the secular philosophy, proposed by Stephen Batchelor in his 1997 book *Buddhism without Beliefs*, which emphasizes the practical relief of suffering in this life. This is very much a live debate—for adherents, scholars, university and school students, and the general public.

We use the word "religion" in everyday discourse as if there is an unproblematic and shared understanding of what it means; but, once you start to examine it further, it becomes more complicated. The meaning of the word has changed over time, contemporary usage is varied, and, in some languages, there isn't even a word to translate it, or wasn't until recently. Most scholars would agree that the concept of "religion" as generally understood today is a modern and "Western" construction, dating back to the European Enlightenment of the eighteenth century, especially the notion of "a religion" as a unified system of beliefs or metaphysical truth claims, separate both from other such systems and from the secular world. So people tend to see religions as monolithic and static, rather than as dynamic and changing, downplaying the complex interactions between individuals and traditions, and relationships between traditions. This can lead to dangerous generalizations: for example, that "Muslims" or "Hindus" are competitors set against each other. A further development of seeing religions as a series of separate and competing entities is what scholars call the "World Religions Paradigm"—a list of "isms" that ignores the internal diversity of and connections between the so-called religions, and also marginalizes smaller traditions or newer developments. Such lists of "world religions" tend actually to reflect parochial and colonial concerns. For example, the list that has become somewhat fixed in British schools since the mid-1980s is (alphabetically) Buddhism, Christianity, Hinduism, Islam, Judaism, and Sikhism.

Scholars differ on whether we should ditch the term "religion" as unhelpful and replace it with terms such as "faith," "tradition," "culture," or "worldview," or if we should separate out this dimension of human experience at all, or should continue to use the term as a conceptual tool while remaining aware that it is only that, and doesn't refer to a reality "out there." A further problem is that the Enlightenment notion of religion was modeled on the tradition most familiar to Europeans—Christianity—and presumes that every religion must have its equivalents to elements such as God, scripture, revelation, or creeds. But this is particularly inappropriate when exploring traditions such as Buddhism, Hinduism, or Jainism.

In recent decades, scholars such as Linda Woodhead have noted the sharp increase in people self-identifying as "non-religious" (the "nones") in the Western world. Research reveals that they are often dissociating themselves from religions understood as institutions—often discredited by scandals, holding illiberal social attitudes, causing conflict and wars, and preaching unthinking obedience—as well as the concept described above, namely metaphysical beliefs and truth claims. It is unsurprising, then, that people from many different traditions prefer to talk about their "philosophy" (which has a better public image and sounds more sophisticated and rational than "religion") or stress the existential and practical, ethical importance of their "way of life."

If the concept of religion is a "Western" invention, it is not surprising that it is problematic when applied to Buddhism. If religion is defined as being centered on belief in and worship of God, on the model of Christianity, then this excludes Buddhism. If religions are viewed as exclusive traditions with distinct boundaries, then this is difficult to maintain in relation to traditions of Indian origin. In many Buddhist contexts, deities, beliefs, and practices that some others might label "Hindu" or "folk religion" feature not only in popular practice but also in official institutional settings. The neat divisions expected by the "Western" concept of religion do not always apply, as in the story of the Nepali who, when asked whether he was "Hindu" or "Buddhist," answered "yes."

"Buddhism," of course, is not one monolithic thing; with such a long history and wide geographical spread through many countries, cultures, and languages, it is very diverse. It might be argued that some forms of Buddhism are (or are perceived/perceive themselves to be) less "religious" than others, such as the tendency of some Theravada modernists or some Western Buddhist groups to play down elements such as faith or ritual, and emphasize the philosophical, rational, and scientific. Others, such as some forms of Tibetan Buddhism with many colorful rituals, or Pure Land's faith in Amitābha Buddha (more commonly known by his Japanese name, Amida), might seem to conform more to a popular understanding of "religion."

However, if the category of "religion" is used in a more flexible and fluid way, as a useful tool we fashion for ourselves and define according to context, rather than an actual object (as scholars such as Jonathan Z. Smith and Russell McCutcheon suggest), and if it can be freed from the negative associations, colonial assumptions, and the hegemony of the Christian model discussed above, the complex and changing tradition(s) to which we apply the label "Buddhism" does seem to fit here. Buddhists, varied and diverse as they are, identify with a tradition, follow teachings that provide an overall approach to life and give meaning to human experience, strive to live by ethical guidelines, have a variety of texts, stories, and non-verbal ways of eliciting and expressing ideas, emotions, and experiences, have created a variety of institutional organizations and material items (from Buddha-images and temples to prayer flags), have interacted in different ways over the centuries with wider communities and cultures (including at times gaining considerable political power), and claim transformative personal experiences. These seem to be the sorts of things we mean when we employ the term "religion." I prefer to include Buddhism in the category of religion because doing so actually challenges and broadens the concept itself: religion does not have to center on God. And so, if I am only allowed to say yes or no (rather than "it depends what you mean by religion"), I'd opt for yes.

About the author
Denise Cush is Emeritus Professor of Religion and Education at Bath Spa University, UK. Her research interests include religious education, religion and worldviews, Buddhism, and Paganism.

Suggestions for further reading

In this book
See also Chapters 2 (faith), 3 (ritual), 5 (texts), 7 (narrative), 8 (Is Buddhism atheistic, non-theistic, or theistic?), 42 (Pure Land Buddhism), 49 (buildings and symbols), 53 (influence of other religions), 61 (Buddhism and politics), and 73 (secular Buddhism).

Elsewhere
Cush, Denise, and Catherine Robinson. "'Buddhism is not a religion, but Paganism is': The Applicability of the Concept of 'Religion' to Dharmic and Nature-Based Traditions, and the Implications for Religious Education." In *Religion and Education: The Forgotten Dimensions of Religious Education?* edited by Gert Biesta and Patricia Hannam, 66–84. Leiden: Brill | Sense, 2021.

Hughes, Aaron W., and Russell T. McCutcheon (editors). *Religion in Five Minutes*. Sheffield: Equinox, 2017.

Smith, Wilfred Cantwell. *The Meaning and End of Religion*. London: SPCK, 1978.

2
What is the role and focus of faith in Buddhism?

Asanga Tilakaratne

In Buddhism, faith is a prerequisite for the practice of the path taught by the Buddha. Buddhists see it as meaning trust and a sense of admiration. So faith is the trust a Buddhist has in the Buddha, as the teacher, in his teaching (Dharma), the path capable of leading its practitioner to the goal, and in the monastic community (Sangha), those who are following the path fruitfully. Without this trust in the Triple Gem, to use the traditional mode of reference, religious life is not possible for Buddhists. Accordingly, faith is the most precious treasure a Buddhist can have, and the foremost motivating factor behind his or her religious life. Although faith is not the sufficient condition for final awakening or enlightenment, it is certainly a necessary condition that is present all the way through the path. To understand the role and focus of faith in Buddhism, we need to know why and how Buddhists should generate faith in the Triple Gem.

In order to see why Buddhists should have faith, we could imagine what it was like during the time of the Buddha, when people had to choose among religious alternatives. When the Buddha started teaching in ancient India, his was one of many teachings available to his listeners. Most probably, his listeners already had accepted religious beliefs. In such a situation, why should they give up their existing beliefs and opt to follow what the Buddha said? Clearly, they had to be convinced that the Buddha was a reliable person, who was teaching a viable path leading its practitioners to the goal of freedom from suffering. Without this initial conviction, they would not have opted to follow the Buddha. Although this process is not likely to happen where people are born into Buddhist communities, it cannot be denied that any meaningful practice of religion has to have this conviction as a prerequisite.

How should one develop this conviction? Buddhists have to have an inquiring mind to do so. The Buddha often encouraged his listeners to question, examine, and inquire before making up their minds to accept what he said. What is revealing is that this openness was meant not only for his first-time listeners but even for his immediate monastic disciples. Addressing them, the Buddha once said that they should investigate whether or not he was fully enlightened. Furthermore, he asked them to observe his behavior to see if there was any inconsistency between what he said and did, or any possibilities of the presence of defiling factors in him. If they failed to find anything objectionable, they should go even further, the Buddha said, to question him personally on any matters of doubt before they made up their minds definitively. The faith generated at this level of understanding is what the Buddha considered ideal.

Even with such an exercise, there is a point in the Buddhist path when practitioners lack the knowledge that comes only with practice, and, in order to practice, they need to make up their own mind. It is at this difficult point that the practitioners' "informed" faith plays its role: they take a calculated "risk" and undertake to practice what the Buddha said. Once practitioners reach the first of four stages of purity—that of "stream entry"—it is said that they are in a position to "see" their destination (although they have not yet reached it). From this point onwards, they cannot go astray. It is said that only at this stage will doubts disappear and they will reach a state of firm faith. Proceeding in the path, they reach the fourth and final state of the arhat, at which point they know with their own knowledge that "the Buddha is truly enlightened, the Dharma leads to nirvana, and the Sangha has properly entered the path." With this knowledge arising, there is no further need or room for doubt because faith has now culminated in knowledge/understanding.

An interesting question is how far this ideal practice corresponded to actual practice. Although the Buddha expected his disciples to exercise their faculty of inquiry in generating faith in him, there is evidence that, in actual practice, this didn't always happen. Once the Buddha asked a monastic disciple, who was mesmerized by the Buddha's physical personality, to stop looking at his filthy body and see him through seeing the Dharma. Nevertheless, the Buddha is recorded as saying that, by mere faith and mere love toward him, people are bound to escape hell and be reborn in heaven. This idea occurring in early discourses has been given utmost prominence in some East Asian Buddhist traditions with their belief in the saving power of the buddhas and bodhisattvas.

It is not easy to cover the role and focus of faith in all the traditions of Buddhism that have evolved over more than two millennia in different geographical locations. What is shared by all traditions, however, is that faith is essential in the path, whether it leads directly or in a roundabout way to the ultimate goal.

About the author
Asanga Tilakaratne is Emeritus Professor of Buddhist Studies, University of Colombo, Sri Lanka. His research interests include the theory and practice of the social application of Buddhism.

Suggestions for further reading

In this book
See Chapters 3 (ritual), 14 (devotion to the Buddha), 21 (Four Noble Truths), 24 (enlightenment) and 25 ("saints").

Elsewhere
Rahula, Walpola. *What the Buddha Taught* (2nd edition). London: Gordon Fraser, 1967: Chapter 1.

Tilakaratne, Asanga. *Theravada Buddhism: The View of the Elders*. Honolulu: University of Hawai'i Press, 2012: pages 24–28.

3
What is the role of ritual in Buddhism?

Asanga Tilakaratne

In order to answer this question, we need to make a distinction between two types of followers of Buddhism: those whose sole aim is to make an end to suffering by realizing nirvana and those who are happy to enjoy being in the round of birth and rebirth, which is *saṃsāra*, until they reach nirvana some day in the future. For the former, the path is quite straightforward. They would be satisfied with a bare minimum of possessions and be singularly motivated by the goal of nirvana. Rituals would not be necessary. For the members of the monastic Sangha in this category, ordination ceremonies and recital of disciplinary rules would be part of their lives—from a Theravada perspective, they would be considered legal requirements of the *Vinaya* (their code of disciplinary conduct) and not ritual. The second type comprises householders who have their families to look after, wealth to enjoy, and social duties to perform. The need for ritual basically came from this group.

Although the widespread use of ritual is a later development, the introduction of rituals into the Buddhist life seems to have started at the time of the Buddha himself. There are early references to rituals such as protective chanting, veneration of Bodhi trees (the kind of tree under which the Buddha gained enlightenment) and relic worship. According to one story, when the great city Visala was stricken by famine, disease, and non-human interference, the Buddha asked his closest companion, Ānanda,

Ritual devotion, Shwedagon Pagoda, Myanmar
Elizabeth Harris, 2018

to sprinkle water in the city, while chanting verses detailing the virtues of the Buddha, Dharma, and Sangha. This is considered the origin of a text called the *Ratana Sutta*, a highly popular discourse which is still chanted for protection and blessing in the Theravada tradition. Another similarly popular discourse used to invoke blessing on pregnant women is attributed to Aṅgulimāla, a murderer turned saint. According to another tradition, veneration of the Bodhi tree was initially introduced to satisfy people who visited a monastery to pay homage to the Buddha only to find that he was not there. A reference to relic worship is found in a text that tells the story of the Buddha's last days, the *Mahāparinibbāna*

Sutta, which is believed to have been compiled not long after his passing away.

Although the historicity of some of these stories may be doubted, what cannot be denied is that the formation of two groups within Buddhism goes back to its early beginnings. Interestingly, for the lay practitioners, a somewhat lesser degree of practice was accommodated. This suggests that rituals were not later introductions to a system that was first meant for monastics. The Buddha's path was never meant for monastics exclusively, although they were considered the ideal.

Today, after two millennia, Buddhism is a global phenomenon, finding its home in different cultural settings, influencing those cultures by its message of universal loving kindness, and being influenced by them at the same time. All three Buddhist traditions are rich with their own ritual practices, some performed individually and domestically, and others publicly in groups. In the Buddhist world, it is quite commonplace for people to observe religious rites and rituals daily in their own domestic shrine rooms. Among daily household rituals are such practices as burning incense, lighting oil lamps, and the offering of flowers, fruits, other food items, and even meals before a Buddha statue. In addition, people spend a considerable part of their daily life in chanting religious formulas directed toward the Triple Gem (Buddha, Dharma, and Sangha), personal protection, and meditation.

Public rituals range from simple gatherings at monasteries on religiously identified days to complex and elaborate events held on special occasions, accompanied by music, dancing, and chanting. Among such public rituals, those inspired by devotion to the Buddha and to bodhisattvas, particularly in Mahayana and Vajrayana traditions, are universal in the Buddhist world. The Theravada Buddhist world—Sri Lanka, for instance—celebrates Vesak, marking the birth, enlightenment, and passing-away of the Buddha, with processions that include dancing, singing, and music, and displays of lights, in addition to silent religious observances. Another example is the annual *Kaṭhina* ceremony in South and Southeast Asian Theravada countries, marking the end of the monastic rains retreat, which is celebrated with much religious zeal, accompanied by colorful processions of music and dance. Vajrayana Buddhism, in particular, is known for its elaborate system of rituals performed by both monastics and lay alike.

In this manner, the presence of ritual has become an important aspect of contemporary Buddhist religious life among both monastics and lay people. It is no longer a lay activity that monks and nuns simply tolerated. Instead, monks and nuns initiate rituals and guide their followers to perform them properly. An average Buddhist monk's life today is dedicated to attending to multiple rituals associated with the life of his lay followers, such as conducting last rites for the dead, officiating at religious functions, and chanting to bestow blessings at times of misery or at auspicious moments. So an important question is how far the distinction we made at the beginning of this discussion—between meditating monks and worldly lay people—remains valid today. The ideal of the forest-dwelling monk or nun totally dedicated to inner purity is far from over; it is very much alive in many Buddhist countries, although the actual numbers have diminished. It is interesting to note, however, that even such practitioners, from time to time, will take part in pilgrimages to pay homage to bodily relics of the Buddha, another very popular religious practice in the Buddhist world.

Over the time, in this manner, rituals have evolved to become part and parcel of Buddhist life, both lay and monastic. In adopting rituals, Buddhists have not so much deviated from their nirvanic ideal as they have found more creative and aesthetically pleasing ways to express their religiosity.

About the author
Asanga Tilakaratne is Emeritus Professor of Buddhist Studies, University of Colombo, Sri Lanka. His research interests include the theory and practice of the social application of Buddhism.

Suggestions for further reading

In this book
See also Chapters 2 (faith), 4 (relics), 6 (images), 8 (is Buddhism atheistic, non-theistic, or theistic?), 14 (devotion), 29 (chanting), 30 (role of monasticism) 48 (celestial beings in Tibetan Buddhism), 49 (buildings and symbols), and 53 (influence of other religions).

Elsewhere
Cabezón, José Ignacio (editor). *Tibetan Ritual.* Oxford and New York: Oxford University Press, 2010.

Gombrich, Richard, and Gananath Obeysekere. *Buddhism Transformed: Religious Change in Sri Lanka.* Princeton, NJ: Princeton University Press, 1988.

Lopez, Donald S. (editor). *Buddhism in Practice.* Princeton, NJ: Princeton University Press, 1995.

Tilakaratne, Asanga. *Theravada Buddhism: The View of Elders.* Honolulu: University of Hawai'i Press, 2012: Chapter 7.

4
Are relics important to Buddhists?

Kevin Trainor

Given the great diversity of Buddhist traditions, it's not surprising that the relative importance of relics has varied over time and within different communities of Buddhists. And the term "relic" itself has a range of meanings and associations, both in English usage and in the words to which it most closely corresponds in the diversity of languages used by Buddhists. What is a relic? Put simply, Buddhist relics refer to material objects that connect Buddhists with departed buddhas and other awakened beings. Relics "re-present" these powerful figures, in both a temporal and physical sense, overcoming their "past-ness" and making them tangibly present to those who physically interact with them for the purposes of spiritual transformation. Such ritualized interactions have, from the earliest centuries of Buddhist tradition, been regarded as "skillful" deeds whose karmic effects advance Buddhist practitioners toward their religious goals.

There are many references to Buddhist relic practices in Buddhist scriptural sources, including a widely referenced account in the *Mahāparinibbāna Sutta*, which recounts the final days of Gotama Buddha's life (Sanskrit: Gautama). This text provides an extended account of his death, cremation, and the enshrinement of his physical remains in stupas or "relic monuments." There is also substantial inscriptional and archaeological evidence that relic practices were central to the dramatic expansion of the

Buddhist tradition during the reign of the Indian emperor Aśoka in the third century BCE, and to the wider spread and development of Buddhist traditions throughout Asia.

Despite the historical importance of relic practices in ancient Indian Buddhism, nineteenth-century orientalist accounts of Buddhism tended to downplay the significance of Buddhist ritual practices in general and relics in particular, perhaps reflecting the largely Protestant and implicitly anti-Catholic ethos that informed early Western scholarship on Buddhism. This scholarship characterized the development of relic practices as a debasement of the rarefied, atheistic philosophy of the Buddha, which was seen as more authentically embodied in the textual and meditational practices of the monastic community. In contrast, the Buddhist laity were represented as clinging superstitiously to the Buddha's physical remains, as if unable to grasp his authentic teachings, which in their true form supposedly rejected the value of ritual, and encouraged emotional restraint and sensory detachment. More recent Buddhist Studies scholarship over the past several decades has increasingly questioned such approaches, highlighting instead the importance of materiality, emotion, and human embodiment across the great diversity of Buddhist traditions.

What sorts of objects count as relics? One common classification distinguishes three categories: "bodily relics" (hair relics and cremated remains); "relics of use" (objects used by buddhas and arhats during their lifetimes, including clothing, Bodhi trees, and even particular physical locations linked to the buddhas); and "relics of indication," objects that point toward departed buddhas and awakened beings, including Buddha-images. This third category of relics, in contrast to the other two, gains its authority through visual resemblance rather than any claim to a physical connection with those they represent, and consequently the objects in this category are in principle endlessly reproducible (although there is evidence that some early Buddha-images had bodily relics enshrined within them). All three categories are typically present in Sri Lankan Buddhist temples in the form of a stupa, Bodhi tree, and image house, which together serve as primary locations for

Temple of the Tooth Relic (Daḷadā Māligāva), Kandy, Sri Lanka
Elizabeth Harris, 2010

devotional offerings. Sri Lankan Buddhists also recognize a circuit of sixteen major pilgrimage sites linked to the tradition of Gotama Buddha's three visits to Sri Lanka; each is considered a "relic of use" through its historical connection to the Buddha, and most are also sites of later bodily relic enshrinements.

This is not to suggest that bodily relics have always been considered the primary means through which the transformative power of buddhas and other awakened beings are made present to later communities of Buddhists. The emergence of Mahayana traditions was closely tied to the centrality of authoritative Mahayana scriptures, and passages in some early Mahayana texts—for example, the *Perfection of Wisdom in 8,000 Lines*—explicitly assert the superiority of texts over bodily relics. Nevertheless, the spread of Buddhist traditions into Central and East Asia was supported by two important developments: the translation of Sanskrit texts into Central and East Asian languages, and the relocation and enshrinement of relics as new Buddhist communities were established. The complementarity of texts and relics was reinforced, as well, by the common practice of enshrining Buddhist texts alongside bodily relics in stupas.

Following the exemplary practice of the great emperor Aśoka, many Asian rulers have displayed and reinforced their political authority by building monumental stupas and, with the support of local Buddhist monastic communities, by enshrining relics within them. The materiality of relics and their centrality to merit-making activities, along with the ease through which relic monuments can symbolically expand and reinforce the boundaries of religious and political authority, have enhanced their attractiveness to Buddhist rulers even into the present day. The circulation of relics across Buddhist traditions and national boundaries can likewise be seen as both reflecting and accelerating globalized expressions of Buddhist tradition.

It will be interesting to see how Buddhists' increasing internet use will affect Buddhist relic practices. On the one hand, digital virtualization can be seen as fundamentally contrary to the essential logic of physical embodiment that lies at the heart of Buddhist relic practices. On the other hand, the internet's potential to visually connect local Buddhist communities around the globe promises to further extend the seemingly limitless expansion of the Buddha's presence that emerged with images as "relics of indication." It likewise remains to be seen how internet-mediated donations and exchanges may stimulate the physical movement of relics and create new possibilities for Buddhist pilgrimage.

About the author
Kevin Trainor is Professor of Religion at the University of Vermont. His research centers on Indian and Sri Lankan Buddhist traditions, in particular the role of material religion and religious practice.

Suggestions for further reading

In this book
See also Chapters 2 (faith), 3 (ritual), 6 (images), 14 (devotion to the Buddha), 61 (Buddhism and politics), and 72 (modern technology).

Elsewhere
Strong, John S. *Relics of the Buddha*. Princeton, NJ: Princeton University Press, 2004.

Trainor, Kevin. *Relics, Ritual, and Representation in Buddhism: Rematerializing the Sri Lankan Theravāda Tradition*. Cambridge: Cambridge University Press, 1997.

5
What are the holy texts of Buddhism?

Asanga Tilakaratne

Buddhism has a variety of collections of holy texts. They differ depending on the school or tradition. In this discussion we will look at holy texts belonging to three traditions of Buddhism: Theravada, Mahayana and Vajrayana, referred to here according to their chronological order.

Theravada holy texts

Theravada holy texts are collectively called the "three baskets," (Sanskrit: *tripiṭaka*; Pali: *tipiṭaka*), referring to three collections determined by the early members of the monastic community, who traced their origin to the Buddha. The three baskets are: Discourses (*Sutta Piṭaka*), containing doctrinal and philosophical discussions as well as narratives; Discipline (*Vinaya Piṭaka*), covering the disciplinary dimension of the Buddhist monastic life; and Higher Doctrine (*Abhidhamma Piṭaka*), exclusively devoted to doctrinal and philosophical matters and considered to be somewhat later than the other two. These texts are in the Pali language, which is believed by Theravadins to be close to the language spoken by the Buddha. The texts were transmitted from generation to generation by oral memory, until they were written down on palm leaves by Sri Lankan monks just before the beginning of the Common Era.

The Sutta Piṭaka
This contains the record of what the Buddha taught to his various listeners during his career of forty-five years. They are arranged into five collections: the *Dīgha Nikāya* (Long Discourses), the *Majjhima Nikāya* (Middle-Length Discourses), the *Saṃyutta Nikāya* (Connected Discourses), the *Aṅguttara Nikāya* (Gradual Discourses), and the *Khuddaka Nikāya* (Short Discourses), a collection of fifteen texts of varying sizes, which include the very popular *Dhammapada* (a set of verses about doctrine), the *Sutta Nipāta* (a collection of early discourses, including a popular one on loving kindness), the *Theragāthā* (verses of the early monks), the *Therīgāthā* (verses of the early nuns), and the *Jātaka* (stories of the previous lives of the Buddha when he was a bodhisattva).

The Vinaya Piṭaka
This contains the rules of behavior prescribed by the Buddha to his male and female monastic community. They are classified into three categories: disciplinary rules for *bhikkhu*s and *bhikkhunī*s (monks and nuns), collections of conventions for proper behavior, and explanatory details related to rules and ecclesiastical functions. It also contains much narrative material: for instance, stories about when each rule was laid down.

The Abhidhamma Piṭaka
Contained in seven treatises, *Abhidhamma* deals with the analysis and classification of the doctrines found in the discourses, with the exception of one work detailing Theravada responses to the views developed by the later Buddhist sects.

Mahayana holy texts
The texts of Mahayana Buddhism were written mainly in Sanskrit. They began to appear in India from at least the first century BCE. Among the earliest texts were the *Prajñāpāramitā Sūtra*s (the perfection of wisdom discourses), which became fundamental to Mahayana. They vary in size, from eight thousand lines to one

hundred thousand lines, and concentrate on the bodhisattva path and insight into the truth of "emptiness." The well-known *Diamond Sutra* is a very short text belonging to this category.

Some Mahayana texts, owing to their extended size relative to the early Buddhist discourses, are known as "large sutras." Nine are singled out as belonging to this category. One of the most popular of these is the *Saddharmapuṇḍarīka Sūtra* ("The Lotus Blossom of the True Dharma Discourse"), known as the *Lotus Sutra*. This is also an early text and versions exist in Sanskrit, Chinese, and Tibetan. Its message that all can become buddhas is presented through story and dialogue. Another popular Mahayana text is the *Laṅkāvatāra Sūtra*, which particularly influenced Chinese Buddhism.

Although not included among the nine texts, there are many other texts, both extended and short, which are considered very important within the tradition. The *Heart Sutra* is particularly significant. In only a few lines, it summarizes Mahayana teaching on emptiness and is often chanted and used in ritual settings. Also important are the *Avataṃsaka Sūtra* and the *Sukhāvatīvyūha Sūtra*.

Chinese holy texts

Numerous Buddhist texts, mainly in Sanskrit, were brought from India and translated into Chinese to form the Chinese "Great Store of Scriptures." Other texts originated in China. An interesting new development is that, in China, particular schools chose to have just one or two Mahayana texts as their central, holy texts. For example, the *Avataṃsaka Sūtra* ("The Garland Discourse") was the basis for the Huayan school, whereas the *Sukhāvatīvyūha Sūtra* ("The Land of Bliss [Pure Land] Discourse") and the *Saddharmapuṇḍarīka Sūtra* respectively provided the doctrinal basis for the Pure Land and the Tiantai (Tendai in Japan) schools. The *Platform Sutra* of Huineng, the Sixth Patriarch, a sutra of Chinese origin, became the holy text of the Chan or Zen Buddhist tradition.

Vajrayana holy texts and Tibetan Buddhism

The Vajrayana holy texts, containing esoteric or tantric teachings, developed within late Indian Buddhism, were written originally in forms of Prakrit and Sanskrit and subsequently taken over the Himalayas and translated into Tibetan. However, not only tantric texts were brought to Tibet but also texts from other schools of Buddhism, such that Tibetan Buddhists claim that their textual heritage covers all schools.

The Tibetan Canon is divided into two: *Kangyur* (translated words) and *Tengyur* (translated treatises). The former contains the translations of the sutras and the Tantras, considered to be the word of the Buddha. The latter comprises, among other works, the translations of commentaries and annotations written by Indian masters on the words of the Buddha. Different editions of the Canon contain different versions and some altogether different texts, and there is also an additional canon of tantric texts transmitted in early times (*Nyingma Gyü-bum*). Tibetan Buddhism also includes *terma* (treasure) literature. These are texts, which are believed to be hidden, await discovery by a *tertön* (treasure revealer), considered to be a rebirth of one of Padmasambhava's followers. The so-called *Tibetan Book of the Dead* is a *terma*.

Holy texts in Buddhism, in this manner, are found in three traditions, Theravada, Mahayana, and Vajrayana, and in four main languages, Pali, Sanskrit, Chinese, and Tibetan. These holy texts are revered as "the word of the Buddha," in spite of the fact that many were compiled well after the death of the historical Buddha.

About the author

Asanga Tilakaratne is Emeritus Professor of Buddhist Studies, University of Colombo, Sri Lanka. His research interests include the theory and practice of the social application of Buddhism.

Suggestions for further reading

In this book
Chapters 7 (narrative), 15 (can we know what the historical Buddha taught?), 32 (monastic rules), 39 (contemporary divisions), 41 (Zen), 42 (Pure Land Buddhism), and 47 (Tantra and sex).

Elsewhere
Tilakaratne, Asanga. *Theravada Buddhism: The View of the Elders*. Honolulu: University of Hawai'i Press, 2012: pages 159–164.

Warder, A. K. *Indian Buddhism*. Delhi: Motilal Banarsidass, 2002: pages 493–532.

6
What is the place of images in Buddhism?

Sarah Shaw

If you go to a Buddhist temple or monastery, or a practitioner's house, you may see a shrine, on which are placed one or maybe several buddha figures. As the Buddha said, "Who sees me sees the Dharma (the teaching), who sees the Dharma, sees me." People respond intuitively to a buddha figure, seeing there the calm, wisdom, and humor they would like to find for themselves.

Throughout the history of Buddhism, images have been made, created, and honored in places to remind practitioners of the Buddha, his teaching, and his community—though it appears that representations of, for instance, the Buddha's footprint, were used for several hundred years instead of his bodily image. So, if you visit Buddhist temples, in any part of the world, you can see many different kinds. Traditionally, three material objects are said to give a connection to the historical Buddha, and act as a reminder of the Triple Gem of the Buddha, the teaching (the Dharma), and the Sangha (community). They are: (1) a representation of the Buddha, (2) a stupa, sometimes known as a pagoda or a *dāgäba*, with relics of the Buddha, and (3) a Bodhi tree, the same species under which the Buddha attained his awakening. Offshoots from the original tree are said to flourish at sacred sites, including Bodh Gaya in India and Anuradhapura in Sri Lanka, and are accorded great respect as landmarks, symbols of the awakening, and as a living thread of connection back to the Buddha's awakening itself.

All of these three symbols are found in Buddhist countries: many or even most Asian temples have all three. They become a focus for devotion, worship, and meditation. So many temples have a special place for the Bodhi tree, whose branches are sometimes decorated with banners and flags; special *pūjas* (acts of devotion) are chanted for it. Stupas offer a chance for circumambulations, a traditional Buddhist practice, accompanied by chants and devotions to the relics inside.

In Buddhist homes, the Buddha-image is the one you are most likely to find. It is usually raised slightly so that the figure is in an honored space. Practitioners offer flowers, candles, and incense to the image, and sit in front of it for devotions, chanting, and meditation. The image represents the fully awake mind, and the potential the human body has for transformation and wisdom. By becoming aware of the Buddha, Buddhists hope to find qualities that are associated with the figure in themselves: the Buddha-image becomes a kind of text, that we can all read. One ancient list describes thirty-two marks found on the body of a fully awakened being. Several of these are usually shown on Buddha-images. Some of the marks are straightforward and easy to see and try for oneself in meditation: the straight back for instance, the evenly rounded shoulders, or the lion-like chest are all helpful guides to someone meditating, to show how to hold the body. Others seem more mysterious, and even esoteric, such as the *anulom*, the fine cotton-like filament between the eyebrows, or the turban-crowned head. These have symbolic and meditative meanings. The whole of the Buddhist path is felt to be known within the body: the body of the Buddha, shown in a statue, is felt to embody this. "In this fathom-long body, with its perception and mind, arises the world, the arising of the world, the ceasing of the world and the path that leads to the cessation of the world," the Buddha is reported as saying.

Buddha-images in Asia undergo ritual consecrations; many feel that the figure becomes a living embodiment of the Buddha. Special ceremonies accompany the empowerment of a Buddha-image, with particular emphasis on the last act that completes the

Buddha images, Shwedagon Pagoda, Myanmar
Elizabeth Harris, 2017

image: painting in the eyes. Chanting, festivities, and offerings are given to welcome a new Buddha-image. Once this has been done, the Buddha-image is felt to be "awake" and should be treated with the utmost respect and devotion.

But is this some sort of idol worship? As the image represents both the Buddha, who said he was one of a line of many buddhas, and the teaching too, it is not seen that way. The body is felt to be an enactment of the path to liberation, as it can be known and experienced in the human body. So, to illustrate diversity, there are many different postures shown on such figures. Some are sitting, some standing, some lying down, and some even walking. Each posture represents a different part of the Buddha's life story. So, for the awakening, the concentration (*samādhi*) pose, with the Buddha's hands resting on one another in meditation, is often shown. For the moment before the awakening, the "earth-touching" gesture is shown, with the seated Buddha placing his hand on the earth to call it to witness his great generosity in past lives, to rout the "demons" of Māra, the lord of delusion. There is a complex language of gesture in Buddhism, and each buddha enacts awakening in a different way, evoking different qualities. A standing buddha, for instance, has quite a different presence and authority from a sitting one: at Polonnaruwa, Sri Lanka, there is a strikingly authoritative and serenely reassuring standing buddha. Walking buddhas became particularly popular in sixteenth-century Siam, perhaps a symbol for the way that Buddhism was traveling and adapting in different regions: the figure shows the stillness possible within movement and change. The lying-down posture is also frequently depicted, as it represents the final moments of the Buddha's human life, before he finally attains what Buddhists call *parinirvāṇa* (final or highest nirvana). There is a vast reclining buddha at Wat Pho, Bangkok, which is particularly impressive in this regard. The black feet have beautiful mother-of-pearl inlays, representing the auspicious symbols that characterize buddha footprints, found elsewhere in other Buddhist regions, too.

Buddha-images, footprints, and other symbols are there to suggest and inspire the path to follow: they are not idols. They are certainly considered inspirers of devotion and a deep sense of reverence. Alongside that, they are meditative and practice aids: the recollections on the Buddha, the teaching, and the Sangha, inspired and helped by such images, are ancient and constantly practiced meditations and chants. Such recollections are regarded as full meditations, intended to arouse confidence, calm, cheerfulness, and a sense of one's own individual contact with the teaching and potential for change.

In many forms of Buddhism, images occupy a specific and technical role within other forms of meditation, too. In Tibetan or Northern Buddhism, for instance, many aspects of awakening are represented, and many deities and bodhisattvas are invoked and evoked within visualization practices, particularly in the Vajrayana or Tantra traditions. They are painted with scrupulous care and in accordance with long-established guidelines on *tangka*s: ceremonial wall hangings. Such representations are often kept hidden much of the time, behind a silken veil, which can be lifted for the time when the practitioner wishes to conduct their tantric meditation. Then, the deity or bodhisattva is felt to be both invoked and evoked, as their energies are felt and found within the practitioner. Postures, chants, rosaries, and the ringing of the handbell signal the practitioner's readiness and strength to receive the power of the deities or bodhisattvas. At the end of the ceremony, the deities are thanked, and visualizations are dissolved—the cloth placed over the *tangka*, so to speak. Many Vajrayana lineages show their most revered teachers (gurus) in this way.

Images of all kinds are found in the Buddhist tradition. Often with precise meditative or ritual purpose, they are celebratory, too—artistic outflowings expressing through material objects a sense of the Buddhist path.

About the author
Sarah Shaw is the Khyentse Foundation Reader in Buddhist Studies at the University of South Wales, UK, a fellow of the Oxford Centre for Buddhist Studies, and a member of the Faculty of Oriental Studies, University of Oxford, UK. She researches Buddhist meditation, ritual, narrative, and chant.

Suggestions for further reading

In this book
See Chapters 2 (faith), 3 (ritual), 4 (relics), 11 (reading a Buddha-image), 12 (fat Buddha), 26 (why Buddhists meditate), and 50 (Buddhist art).

Elsewhere

Beyer, Stephen. *Magic and Ritual in Tibet: The Cult of Tārā*. Delhi: Motilal Banarsidass, 2013.

Matics, K. I. *Gestures of the Buddha*. Bangkok: Chulalongkorn Press, 1998.

Swearer, Donald K. *Becoming the Buddha. The Ritual of Image Consecration in Thailand*. Princeton, NJ and Oxford: Princeton University Press, 2004.

7
What is the role of narrative in Buddhism?

Brian Black

Narrative is an integral part of Buddhism. Although many textbooks focus on core teachings, such as the Four Noble Truths, dependent origination, emptiness, or the ideal of the bodhisattva, stories are one of the main ways that Buddhists through the centuries have communicated and explored their ideas, beliefs, and values. Narratives create a shared Buddhist world among its followers and ground otherwise abstract teachings in the relatable experiences of everyday life. They also demand an engagement from their audiences and remain open to a variety of different readings and interpretations. Additionally, stories are memorable, often engaging audiences on an emotional as well as an intellectual level.

Beyond the story of the Buddha
Despite the importance of the story of the Buddha (his early life, quest for enlightenment, and long career as an enlightened teacher), some of the most popular Buddhist narratives are about his previous lives as a bodhisattva—a buddha in the making. In these stories, known as *Jātaka*s (birth stories), the main characters are not the present Buddha and his followers, but rather the various personae that the Buddha and his followers were in previous lives. These stories often explore ideas such as karma and rebirth,

35

as well as Buddhist values such as generosity and self-sacrifice. The *Jātaka*s contain a number of stories that also appear elsewhere in ancient Indian literature (such as in the *Mahābhārata* and *Rāmāyaṇa*), and many feature prominently in Buddhist art. Perhaps the most well-known *Jātaka* story is about the Buddha's previous life as the prince Vessantara, who personifies the Buddhist ideal of generosity by giving away all his possessions, including his wife and children. This story, which appears in many different versions across several languages, has circulated widely in South, East, and Southeast Asia.

Another genre related to, but distinct from, *Jātaka* literature is called *Avadāna* (Noble Deeds). Like the *Jātaka*s, *Avadāna* stories are considered to be the words of the Buddha and were part of the moral education of both the monastic and lay communities. Many of them are hagiographical accounts of great monks or kings. Like the *Jātaka*s, *Avadāna* stories are widely represented in Buddhist art.

Although the vast majority of Buddhist texts were composed by men, a notable exception is the *Therīgāthā*, a collection of poems composed by nuns, which is widely regarded as the oldest extant book composed entirely by women. Although some poems consist of only a single verse, others are poetic narratives that give accounts of women who renounced their household lives to become followers of the Buddha. Muttā, for example, writes of giving up her domestic drudgery and leaving her unhappy marriage to join the monastery. Meanwhile, Sumedhā is a beautiful princess, who gives up her life of luxury to be a Buddhist nun. A recurring theme in the *Therīgāthā* is the emancipatory potential of the Buddhist path for women.

One of the most well-known poets of the *Therīgāthā* is Kisā Gotamī, who writes about her experience of losing both her husband and her son. A popular narrative about Kisā Gotamī is that, when her son dies and she is desperate with grief, she meets the Buddha, who promises to revive her son, but only if she can collect a mustard seed from a house that has experienced no deaths. Although she visits every house in the village, she cannot collect such a seed. Through this experience, Kisā learns that every household has experienced the death of a family member. As a consequence, she learns to accept the death of her son and subsequently becomes a follower of the Buddha.

Mahayana narratives

With the emergence of Mahayana Buddhism came an explosion of new Buddhist texts, many of them composed in a narrative style. While earlier sources were most likely composed and transmitted orally, most of the new Mahayana literature was written. This was an important development because, once writing was accepted as a mode of preserving texts, it opened up the possibility for new texts to be included in the Buddhist canon. Another important development of Mahayana literature was that it began to place emphasis on the text as a physical object. There were sutra cults, in which reading became a devotional practice and individual copies of books were worshipped with flags, incense, and bells.

The *Lotus Sutra* is perhaps the most important scripture in Mahayana Buddhism. It is the foundational text of both the Tiantai and Nichiren schools, while also significant in other schools such as Chan in China, which in Japan is Zen. It is also widely represented in Buddhist art. Throughout the text, the Buddha's teachings are demonstrated through short stories or parables, which are used to illustrate central Mahayana doctrines, such as skillful means, emptiness, and the ideal of the bodhisattva. Perhaps the most famous parable is the "Burning House," in which a man saves his children from a burning house by promising toys if they come outside. Although the man lies about the toys, his actions are a demonstration of skillful means because he compassionately saves his children from a horrible death. Another theme developed throughout the sutra is the doctrine of Buddha-nature—the idea that everyone has the capacity to be a buddha. In one story, for example, Devadatta, whose conspiracy to kill the Buddha is recounted in earlier sources, becomes enlightened. In the final chapter, an eight-year-old *nāga* (serpent) princess achieves buddhahood after changing from a woman to a man. Through these examples of a murderer and a young girl who attain the highest wisdom, the Buddha teaches that anyone can achieve enlightenment.

Another popular Mahayana Buddhist narrative is the *Gaṇḍavyūha Sūtra*, which comprises one section of the larger *Avataṃsaka Sūtra*. The *Gaṇḍavyūha Sūtra* is a quest story about a merchant, Sudhana, who reaches the highest knowledge through a series of encounters he has with good friends, each of whom offers a different perspective as he progresses along the Buddhist path.

Buddhist narrative in East Asia

Although both the *Lotus Sutra* and *Gaṇḍavyūha Sūtra* were likely composed in India, they reached their height of popularity in East Asia. As Buddhism flourished in East Asia, many Buddhist texts began to be composed in China, Korea, and Japan. The Chan (Zen in Japan) school, in particular, was prolific, producing more texts than any other school of Buddhism outside the Indian subcontinent. Many Chan texts feature stories of teachers who convey their teachings in strange, non-linguistic ways—sometimes through actions like subtle gestures, or through surprising behavior such as shouting or hitting. When speaking, they employ paradoxical words and non sequiturs. In many cases, these strange teachings and surprising episodes became the basis for koans, which are enigmatic riddles used as a teaching device to nudge students toward enlightenment. One of the most important Chan texts is the *Platform Sutra* (*c.* 900–1300), which is the oldest known sutra not to claim to be the words of the Buddha himself. The *Platform Sutra* recounts the life story of Huineng, a simple, illiterate man from humble origins who achieves enlightenment based on his own innate qualities.

These are just a sample of the rich and varied narratives of the Buddhist tradition. One of the best ways to learn more about Buddhism is not through textbooks, but rather through its wonderful stories.

About the author

Brian Black, originally from California, earned his doctorate at SOAS (University of London) and now teaches at Lancaster University. His research interests include the Upaniṣads and the *Mahābhārata,* and the relationships between Hindu and Buddhist texts.

Suggestions for further reading

In this book
See also Chapters 2 (faith), 5 (texts), 10 (buddhahood), 13 (bodhisattva), 33 (nuns), 41 (Zen), and 50 (Buddhist art).

Elsewhere
Appleton, Naomi (translator). *Many Buddhas, One Buddha: A Study and Translation of Avadanasataka 1–40.* Sheffield and Bristol, CT: Equinox, 2020.

Hallisey, Charles (translator). *Therigatha: Poems of the First Buddhist Women.* Cambridge: Murty Classical Library of India, 2015.

Reeves, Gene (translator). *The Lotus Sutra: A Contemporary Translation of a Buddhist Classic.* Boston, MA: Wisdom Publications, 2014.

Shaw, Sarah (translator). *The Jatakas: Birth Stories of the Bodhisatta.* London: Penguin Classics, 2006.

8
Is Buddhism atheistic, non-theistic, or theistic?

Peter Harvey

Buddhism is not focused on the idea of an eternal creator God, but from its beginning has included belief in a range of mortal gods (*deva*s), who are seen as part of the round of rebirths along with humans, animals, ghosts, and beings in hell. None of these rebirths is seen as lasting forever, although some are seen as very long-lasting. The Buddha did not see himself as an incarnation of a god, but as a human who had been radically transformed by becoming enlightened, and as a "teacher of humans and *deva*s."

Although Buddhists do not believe in a creator God, they do believe in an ultimate, transcendent reality: nirvana. Nirvana is beyond time, change, and death—a transcendent reality the peace of which is beyond that of even the subtlest heaven. Like the God of theistic religions, it is eternal, at least in the sense of being beyond time, rather than lasting forever in time. It is not seen as creating the world, and is a seen as a state to be experienced rather than a being.

The gods

Life as some kind of *deva* in one of a variety of heavenly rebirths is seen as a fruit of past good actions such as generosity, helpfulness, kindness, and attaining meditative calm. But, without liberating insight, those reborn in the heavens are still seen as subject to future rebirths, which might in time even include rebirth in hell.

There are said to be twenty-six heavens. The four most subtle and refined are four "formless" ones, purely mental realms, beyond the senses, which last many eons. They include realms such as the realm of infinite space and the realm of infinite consciousness.

Less subtle are the sixteen heavens of the realm of pure, elemental form (*rūpa*). The top five "form" heavens are known as the "pure abodes," and are attainable only by persons known as non-returners, who are almost enlightened arhats. The remaining eleven "form" heavens parallel states of deep meditative calm, which "tune" a person's mind into a certain level of existence. Of the beings of these heavens, perhaps the most significant is Great Brahmā, who dwells in the third up of the lower "form" heavens, and whose life span is one great eon. This being is said to be rich in loving-kindness and compassion, but prone to the delusion that he is the eternal creator of the world.

Great Brahmā

One story in a text called the *Brahmajāla Sutta* recounts why Great Brahmā had this belief. According to Buddhist cosmology, our world-system goes through cosmic cycles. Periodically, a physical world-system and the lower heavens associated with it come to an end. At this time, beings from these lower levels are generally reborn in a higher "form" heaven. Then, after a long period, one of these dies and is reborn at a lower level, as a Great Brahmā. After some time, he becomes lonely and longs for the presence of others. Soon his wish is fulfilled, simply because other gods die and happen to be reborn, due to their karma, as his ministers and retinue. Not remembering his previous life, Great Brahmā, therefore, thinks that "These other beings are my creation."

His ministers and retinue agree with this erroneous conclusion, and when some of them eventually die and are reborn as humans, they develop the power to remember their previous life, and consequently teach that Great Brahmā is the eternal creator of all beings (even though his life span is only one eon, the same as that of a physical world-system).

Another ironic Buddhist story in a text called the *Kevaddha Sutta* illustrates a Great Brahmā's limitations. A monk with a philosophical question about what is wholly beyond materiality meditates so as to be able to contact gods and ask them his question. None of the gods, from the lowest heaven up to that of the retinue of Brahmā, can help him, but he is told that Great Brahmā will surely be able to do so. Yet, when asked the question, Great Brahmā only replies with his proud assertion of his creatorship. After responding three times in this way, he takes the monk on one side and says that he could not disillusion his retinue by publicly admitting that he did not know the answer; the monk had best go to the Buddha, who would surely know it. A Great Brahmā is thus seen as inferior to the Buddha in wisdom.

Critiques of God-centric views

The Buddha criticized *any* view that undermined the principle of personal responsibility, including the idea that *all* one's experiences, pleasant, unpleasant, or neutral, were due to one's past karma, the creation of a supreme being (God), or randomly arising without any cause or condition.

The Buddha did not accept that any deity created the world or its beings. He saw no need for a creator of the universe, as he saw no ultimate beginning to it. He taught that the gods of the heavenly realms are themselves trapped within the round of rebirths like all other unliberated beings, and that the physical world develops by natural laws, like all other conditioned phenomena.

Moreover, the problem of suffering is also relevant. In God-centered religions, there is the problem of why an all-good, all-powerful, all-knowing God would allow there to be suffering, especially human suffering. Of course some human suffering is the result of human actions, and theistic religions often argue that God has allowed humans to have free will. But many forms of suffering are due to the nature of the changing physical world in which we live; and this is seen as all divinely created.

The lower devas and interaction with them
While the gods of the formless and pure form levels are generally beyond contact with humans (although the Buddha and some gifted disciples were seen as conversing with some of them), those within the six heavens of the realm of sense-desire (*kāma*) are somewhat closer to the nature of humans and more open to interacting with them. They include Sakka/Śakra (Pali/Sanskrit), a disciple of the Buddha who sometimes intervened to assist him, and Metteyya/Maitreya (Pali/Sanskrit), the Friendly One, who will in time be reborn as a human who becomes the next buddha.

Sense-desire gods are seen as open to offering humans assistance in small ways, so shrines to some of them are sometimes included at Buddhist temples. If people share some of their good karma with them, they may offer help in return.

Heavenly buddhas and bodhisattvas

The Mahayana movement came to include ideas of heavenly beings who were advanced on the long bodhisattva path to perfect buddhahood, and still existing perfect buddhas spread throughout the universe. Such advanced bodhisattvas include Avalokiteśvara, rich in the quality of compassion, of which the Dalai Lamas are seen as repeated incarnations and who is known in China as Guanyin. Another key one is Mañjuśrī, rich in wisdom. They may be appealed to for help in times of need, or for help in progress on the path, and, in this respect, are akin to the deities of other religions. Among the heavenly buddhas, Amitābha (known as Amida in Japan), or Infinite Light, is most popular, and is seen as having an ideal "Pure Land" where the conditions for attaining enlightenment are ideal. In the Japanese Nichiren school, the historical Buddha Śākyamuni is seen as still existing at a heavenly level, and his power can be drawn on through chanting *Myo-ho-renge-kyo*, which reveres the eternal Dharma expressed in the *Lotus Sutra*.

About the author

Peter Harvey is Professor of Buddhist Studies (retired), University of Sunderland, UK, and co-founder of the UK Association for Buddhist Studies. He researches on Buddhist ethics, meditation, and early Buddhist thought.

Suggestions for further reading

In this book

See Chapters 1 (is Buddhism a religion?), 13 (bodhisattva), 18 (karma), 23 (nirvana), 25 (saints), 39 (contemporary divisions), 42 (Pure Land Buddhism), and 48 (celestial beings in Tibetan Buddhism).

Elsewhere

Gethin, Rupert. *The Foundations of Buddhism*. Oxford: Oxford University Press, 1998: pages 112–132.

Harvey, Peter. 2019. *Buddhism and Monotheism*. A Cambridge Elements booklet. Cambridge University Press.
https://www.cambridge.org/core/elements/buddhism-and-monotheism/267698FC06C6DA08332035B35C4A6EE8

Nyanaponika Thera. *Buddhism and the God-idea: Selected Texts*: Kandy, Sri Lanka: Buddhist Publication Society, 2008.
https://www.bps.lk/olib/wh/wh047_Nyanaponika_Buddhism-and-the-God-Idea.pdf

Williams, Paul. *Mahāyāna Buddhism: The Doctrinal Foundations* (2nd edition). London and New York: Routledge and Kegan Paul, 2009: pages 209–266.

The *sutta*s mentioned in the answer can be accessed from:
https://www.accesstoinsight.org

Part Two
The Buddha

# 9
# What do we know about the historical Buddha?

Dhivan Thomas Jones

The question is more difficult than it appears, and I propose to answer it by analyzing three of its component terms—*know*, *historical*, and *buddha*—before attempting an answer to the *what*. It would seem that traditional Buddhists of Asian lands were not concerned with this kind of question. For them, as indeed for many modern Western Buddhists, the term "buddha" did not primarily refer to a particular historical personage but rather to the discoverer of the way to awakening, the founder and teacher of what has become known as Buddhism, a guide and exemplar, the first of the Three Jewels or precious things (the Triple Gem), to which Buddhists go for refuge. In short, for Buddhists, the Buddha is an object of faith and devotion.

The term "buddha" in this sense refers to a person with a traditional life story. Having, many previous lives ago, made a vow to attain buddhahood as the ascetic Sumedha, in the presence of the Buddha Dīpaṅkara, "our" Buddha descended from the Tuṣita heaven for his last existence. He entered his mother's womb and took birth as a human being. He grew up as a prince, enjoying a fine life in the palace, getting married and having a child. Having encountered aging, illness, death, and then a renunciate, someone who had left home and family for religious purposes, the Bodhisattva (Buddha-to-be) went forth, learning meditation, then practicing asceticism. Having discovered the Middle Way, he sat beneath the Bodhi tree on the banks of the river Nerañjarā and gained awakening. Arising as the Buddha, he taught the Dharma for forty-five years, and founded a Sangha (community) of male and female monastics, and lay followers, which endures to this day. Old and frail, he died and attained what Buddhists call *parinirvāṇa* (final awakening) at Kuṣinārā, surrounded by disciples, was cremated, and his remains were given to various supporters, and later interred in stupas (relic mounds or chambers).

This life story took centuries to reach its full form and is evidently legendary in character, the various events of the Buddha's life symbolizing aspects of his awakening and teaching. Let us now turn to asking what *historical* value the story may have. When historically minded European scholars of the nineteenth century began to study Buddhism, some argued that a historical character could be discerned through the theater of the Buddha legend. The character known as the "historical Buddha" consisted for them, crudely speaking, of those plausibly historical elements of the traditional life story: for instance, that the Buddha was a warrior of the Śākya clan, born in Lumbinī in present-day Nepal, who left home to join the *śramaṇa*s (renunciant ascetics—explained later) of ancient India, gained awakening, taught the Dharma, and died as an old man.

Such a "historical Buddha," however, is more or less an artefact of the Western Buddhist scholarly imagination. Let us turn to what we *know* about such a figure. The only historical evidence for the Buddha is what is contained in early Buddhist literature. There is, alas, no archaeological or inscriptional evidence whatever from that distant period of Indian history, and even the dates of the Buddha's life are uncertain, with a current scholarly consensus favoring 480–400 BCE, with a large margin of error. But early Buddhist literature was never supposed to be historical; the early Buddhists passed on, first orally and then in writing, what they understood to be the Buddha's teaching. The details of the Buddha's life and personality in that literature serve the purpose of illustrating and exemplifying the teaching.

Hence we can answer the *what* of our question. For some scholars, the *what* is nothing. Since there is simply no historical evidence for the Buddha, we know nothing of the historical Buddha. He is more like King Arthur or Agamemnon, characters whom we may suppose are based on historical figures, though those figures are now completely obscured by myth. Other scholars don't accept this. They argue that it is less likely that later Buddhists could make up the teaching of the Buddha than that there was an originating person behind it. Assuming such a figure, known as the Buddha, existed, it is possible to infer from early Buddhist literature quite a lot about him. Most importantly, he was a *śramana*, an ascetic, part of a philosophical-spiritual movement of renunciate wanderers, from whom Mahāvīra, the teacher of Jainism, was also drawn. The Buddha developed his thinking and teaching in an atmosphere of argument and debate. We may infer that he was a meditator, who enjoyed periods of retreat, as well as establishing an institutional structure for the Sangha.

It turns out, therefore, that what we know about the historical Buddha depends on what exactly we mean by our terms. If we mean "do we have any positive historical evidence that tells us something about the existence and character of the person known as the Buddha?" the answer is "no." But we could say something similar about Socrates or Jesus. But if we mean "can we make some informed inferences about the Buddha, reasoning abductively from the stories and teachings preserved in early Buddhist literature to the best explanation about the originating character behind them?" then the answer is "yes." So the answer to our question is that, through careful study, it is possible to come to some reasonable inferences, if not certain knowledge, about the life and character of the person known as the Buddha.

About the author

Dhivan Thomas Jones is a Lecturer in Philosophy and Religious Studies at the University of Chester. His research is mainly in the area of early Buddhist philosophy.

Suggestions for further reading

In this book

See also Chapters 2 (faith), 3 (ritual), 6 (images), 10 (buddhahood), 15 (can we know what the historical Buddha taught?), and 53 (influence of other religions).

Elsewhere

Drewes, David. "The Idea of the Historical Buddha." *Journal of the International Association of Buddhist Studies* 40 (2017): 1–25. Drewes argues that we do not know anything about the historical Buddha.

Strong, John S. *The Buddha: A Short Biography*. Oxford: Oneworld Publications, 2001. A study of the Buddha's traditional life story and its sources.

von Hinüber, Oscar. "The Buddha as a Historical Person." *Journal of the International Association of Buddhist Studies* 42 (2019): 231–264. Von Hinüber responds to Drewes, sketching out what we know from history.

Wynne, Alexander. "Did the Buddha Exist?" *Journal of the Oxford Centre of Buddhist Studies* 16 (2019): 98–148. Wynne also responds to Drewes, and to skepticism in Buddhist Studies.

10
How is the nature of buddhahood to be understood?

Christopher V. Jones

Asking about the nature of "buddhahood" is no small matter. Just as traditions of Abrahamic theology have not necessarily agreed regarding the nature of God, so too "Buddhology"—confessional or academic interest in buddhas and their nature—cannot provide one definitive account of what it is to be a buddha. The question invites an overview of how the Buddha (or buddhas) have been understood across roughly two-and-a-half thousand years of history. This begins in the middle of the first millennium BCE, with the earliest community of North Indian ascetics who understood their leader, Siddhārtha Gautama, to have achieved an "awakening" (Sanskrit: *bodhi*) to how rebirth/transmigration occurs and, with effort, might be ended.

Since the nineteenth century, European scholarship has often represented the Buddha visible in early Buddhist literature as someone like a philosopher, who only came to be divinized and worshipped by Buddhist communities generations after his death. However, the position among Buddhists, past and present, is much more complicated. A text in the Pali Canon (the *Doṇaloka Sutta*) reports the Buddha explaining that he is apart from all other kinds of sentient beings; the Buddha has ended those things that bring about life as a human or deity, and he is instead quite simply "awoken" (*buddha*). A buddha has in some fashion escaped the death, rebirth, and further death *ad infinitum* to which deities, humans, and other sentient beings are all subject.

It is also important to stress that not all Buddhist traditions understand the intended goal of their practice to be what they understand by "buddhahood." From an early stage in its history, Buddhism made an important distinction between someone who has achieved an end to rebirth, becoming an arhat, and the Buddha, who instructed them toward this, whose achievement was not simply nirvana but a complete understanding of how liberation from rebirth can be achieved, and at a time when the Dharma was otherwise not known. What is sometimes called mainstream Buddhism from India, today represented only by the Theravada tradition, understands that the function of a buddha is to reintroduce the Dharma into the world, and that he is able to do this due to innumerable previous lifetimes of perseverance as a being who strives for awakening, a bodhisattva. It is due to his actions performed over these lifetimes that, in his last birth, the Buddha has a body adorned with what were considered to be auspicious physical characteristics, such as the protuberance on top of his head (*uṣṇīṣa*), elongated earlobes, and a radiant complexion.

Importantly, the person born Siddhārtha Gautama is understood to be only the most recent buddha in the world, in a sequence of buddhas that stretches back through time without beginning, each of whom has at great intervals reintroduced the Dharma at a time when the world was ignorant of it. The Buddha of our age, whose title is sometimes Śākyamuni ("sage of the Śākyas," the Himalayan community among whom he is meant to have been born), is the latest buddha in various lists that have been produced in India and elsewhere: of seven buddhas, of twenty-eight, or of a great many more. Śākyamuni's activities continued up to his final moments and his climactic departure from the world which came with his death (often called his *parinirvāṇa*—final or highest nirvana). His status after this, the details of which divide Buddhist traditions, is an abiding peace apart from the process of birth and death. Yet still the Buddha's influence was not supposed to be over;

his bodily relics—which survived the cremation of his body—are believed to endure, now distributed at relic mounds (stupas) across Asia, and are commonly understood to be continuing the Buddha's work by serving as fitting objects of reverence. To make offerings to a fragment of the Buddha's body, it is believed, is just as efficacious as if one were to make offerings to a living buddha. To be a buddha is to aid those who suffer, even after death.

Everything recounted so far is uncontroversial from what scholars call a mainstream Buddhist perspective, proper to all forms of Indian Buddhism that developed before the dawn of the Common Era, and still alive in the Theravada tradition today. But buddhahood becomes a more complex matter after the advent of Mahayana Buddhism. In Mahayana Buddhism, the Buddha is not simply lauded as the revealer of Dharma, but his achievement—"the unsurpassed, complete awakening" not of an arhat, but only a buddha—is made a goal to which at least some people should themselves aspire. A conceptual gap widened between the arhat, who achieves nirvana thanks to the Dharma, and a buddha who is embodied *in* the Dharma and who worked to achieve liberation not only for his own sake, but for the sake of aiding all other sentient beings to escape rebirth also.

Mahayana Buddhists set out to become bodhisattvas, much as Śākyamuni was understood to have been. In addition, Mahayana Buddhism introduced the existence of other buddhas who, unlike Śākyamuni, are still alive and teaching, but are resident in parallel worlds (often called "Pure Lands") that a bodhisattva can in theory access in a future life. Today these buddhas remain objects of devotion especially across East Asia, the most important of whom must be the Buddha Amitābha (Amida in Japan), resident in the Pure Land of Sukhāvatī, "the land of bliss." To complement the notion of there being many (indeed, "innumerable") buddhas, some Mahayana texts explain that behind all of these buddhas—each of whom, in their true nature, must be identical to one another—there is a primordial buddha, sometimes identified as Vairocana ("he who is radiant"), who in some traditions has been venerated as the archetype of all buddhas teaching across all worlds. Then again, there is the notion in some traditions of the Mahayana that our buddha, Śākyamuni, did not in fact depart from the world, and that every aspect of his life—his birth, renunciation, awakening, teaching, and death—were all displays or apparitions by the Buddha, produced from beyond the world as we see it, in order for him to teach in accord with our limitations and expectations. The notion of a transcendent buddha, who must have been awakened long before he only *displayed* his awakening in the world, is prominent in works like the *Lotus Sutra*, which continues to play a major role in East Asian Buddhism today.

More sophisticated buddhological models developed to help make sense of the diverse ways in which the Buddha appears to teach across Mahayana literature. Often the Buddha retains his form familiar from earlier Buddhist sources, but sometimes he teaches while resident in one or other heavenly realm, in a glorious body fit for the company of gods; sometimes he is said to be present wherever the Dharma endures, enigmatically "embodied in the Dharma" wherever it is uttered or written down. These ideas came to be known as the "three bodies" doctrine—that the Buddha exists in these three modes. Other expressions of Mahayana teaching, for example in Tantric Buddhism, complicate the picture further, and understand that buddhahood is attributed not only to buddhas, as well as (in all but name) to advanced, god-like bodhisattvas who have yet to take recognizable form as a buddha, but also to Buddhist deities who are the Dharma embodied in vibrant, regal, or sometimes ferocious forms, with whom a practitioner can interact through esoteric ritual procedures.

Still elsewhere in Mahayana Buddhism, there exist other understandings of buddhahood. For example, in the Zen traditions of Japan (what in China was called Chan) awakening is something realizable in this very life, even if only for brief moments of sudden, clear awareness, and is not so much occupied with the notion of a cosmic process of the Dharma being realized and revealed by a succession of awakened beings. Yet all of these different understandings of buddhahood have roots in the ancient Indian model discussed above, and retain the notion that what is most valuable for the world, even if it is not something that just anyone can realize, is the appearance of an individual who manages to "wake up" to the truth of the human condition, and who is committed to teaching the world how best to respond to it.

About the author
Christopher V. Jones is a Bye-Fellow of Selwyn College, and affiliated lecturer and research associate at the Faculty of Divinity, University of Cambridge. A primary focus of his research is the history of Mahayana Buddhist thought in the early centuries of the Common Era, preserved in Sanskrit, Chinese, and Tibetan literature.

Suggestions for further reading

In this book
Chapters 2 (faith), 4 (relics), 6 (images), 7 (narrative), 8 (is Buddhism atheistic, non-theistic, or theistic?), 9 (what we know of the historical Buddha), 13 (Bodhisattva), 14 (devotion to the Buddha), and 48 (celestial beings in Tibetan Buddhism).

Elsewhere
Gethin, Rupert. *The Foundations of Buddhism*. Oxford: OUP, 1998: pages 27–34.

Strong, John. *Buddhisms: An Introduction*. London: Oneworld, 2015: pages 39–111, 235–256.

Williams, Paul. *Mahāyāna Buddhism: The Doctrinal Foundations* (second edition). London: Routledge, 2009: pages 172–186.

Williams, Paul, with Anthony Tribe and Alexander Wynne. *Buddhist Thought: A Complete Introduction to the Indian Tradition* (second edition). Abingdon and New York: Routledge, 2012: pages 124–142.

11
How does one "read" a Buddha-image?

Ronit Wang

Images of the Buddha are some of the most recognizable features in Buddhism. Found in temples, monasteries, shrines, homes, altars, and museums, the form of these images differs from country to country and among different schools of Buddhism. They also incorporate styles and characteristics that are often specific to a particular time or place.

How then do we respond to a Buddha-image? While it is impossible to ignore the artistry of Buddha-images, and the craftsmanship involved in their creation, it is vital to look beyond the physical form of the figure, approaching it not as art but rather as an instrument through which the qualities and attributes of the Buddha himself are embodied.

Let us illustrate this idea through the story of the Buddha-image that was commissioned by king Pasenadi of Kosala, according to one medieval Ceylonese Buddhist text, the *Kosalabimbavaṇṇanā*. One day, the king arrived to visit the Buddha and was very disappointed to discover that the Buddha was away from his usual dwelling place. In the Buddha's absence, the king presented an offering to his seat. Later on, upon the Buddha's return, the king asked for his permission to create a statue that could be venerated at times when the Buddha was away. The Buddha agreed and the king instructed the best craftsmen to build an image of the Buddha using the most precious sandalwood. Once completed, the king positioned the image on an altar and invited the Buddha to view the creation. Upon the Buddha's arrival, the actual image felt humbled and descended from its shrine to pay respect. The Buddha, however, stopped it and asked it to remain in its place, telling the statue that the religion of the Buddha would endure for five thousand years. It would, therefore, be the image's duty, long after Buddha's entrance to nirvana, to remain in the Master's place, serving all others for this period of time.

In spite of this story's legendary character (images of the Buddha did not appear until several hundred years after the Buddha's death), it helps us understand the image's purpose as an embodiment of the living presence of the Buddha, endowed with qualities of the Buddha himself. Therefore, the Buddha-image consists of a twofold presence: figurative, symbolizing the Buddha, and commemorative, consecrating the Buddha in his physical absence. This dual force, communicated to the devotee, creates a powerful relationship between image and viewer.

In this way, the qualities contained within the image mirror those of the Buddha, prompting recollection of his teachings among practitioners, who may then venerate it, through prostrations, offerings, incense-burning, and chanting. Veneration of a Buddha-image is considered meritorious insofar as it contributes to the production of positive karma. Furthermore, the Buddha-image may then be used as an object of meditation, for the Buddha reminds one that the ultimate goal (awakening) is achievable from the human state.

The erection of a Buddha-image itself is a source of great merit for its creators. A statue is merely a material object until it is officially endowed with the Buddha's attributes. This is done by a meticulous process, which adheres to a comprehensive set of rules, varying among different traditions, and incorporating manuals, sacred sounds, and elaborate rituals—for example, an eye-opening ceremony which is believed to transform a mere likeness into a holy presence. The potency of images that carry the qualities of the Buddha is also reflected in the fact that many are considered to have supernatural powers, perhaps enabling wishes to come true

Touching-the-earth posture, Suvisuddharama Buddhist Temple, Colombo, Sri Lanka
Elizabeth Harris, 2014

for those who venerate them; while still others may have a marvelous history of extensive travels and withstanding physical damage or decay through time.

Beyond encompassing the qualities of the Buddha, images may also act as a means of depicting multiple facets of the Buddha's life story. Hand gestures, which are called *mudrā*s, might depict specific scenes from this life. For example, in one prevalent *mudrā*, the Buddha's right hand is seen touching the ground, recalling the moment when the Buddha as bodhisattva calls the earth to witness to his right to sit under the Bodhi tree on the night of his enlightenment. Similarly, the position of the image, whether it is seated, standing, walking, or reclining, represents notable moments from the Buddha's life as well. In this way a reclining image depicts the last moments of Buddha's earthly life, before his entrance to *parinirvāṇa* (final or highest nirvana). In addition, the Buddha-image includes visual attributes that are associated with the Buddha. For instance, his robes communicate the Buddha's renunciation and austerity.

The way in which we today experience images as art can be problematic in such cases as these, because Buddha-images were always seen by devotees to possess the potential to transform the world around them. Therefore, a Buddha-image should always be read first in terms of its religious significance, as an embodiment of the living presence of the Buddha: a source of reverence and guidance that facilitates the continuation of Buddhism in the absence of the physical Buddha

About the Author
Ronit Wang is a PhD candidate at the School of Oriental and African Studies, University of London. Focusing on contemporary Thai Buddhism, her research looks at Buddhist cosmological parks in Thailand.

Suggestions for further reading

In this book
See Chapters 2 (faith), 3 (ritual) 4 (relics), 6 (images), and 50 (Buddhist art).

Elsewhere
Crosby, Kate. "Devotion to the Buddha in Theravada and its Role in Meditation." In *The Intimate Other: Love Divine in Indic Religions,* edited by A. King and J. Brockington, 244–277. New Delhi: Orient Longman, 2005.

DeCaroli, Robert. *Image Problems: The Origin and Development of the Buddha Image in Early South Asia*. Seattle: University of Washington Press, 2015.

Lachman, Charles. "Buddhism: Image as Icon, Image as Art." In *The Oxford Handbook of Religion and the Arts*, edited by Frank B. Brown, 367–378. Oxford: Oxford University Press, 2014.

Swearer, Donald K. *Becoming the Buddha: The Ritual of Image Consecration in Thailand*. Princeton, NJ: Princeton University Press, 2004.

12
Who is the fat Buddha figure?

Paulina Kolata

Surprising as it may be, the fat Buddha is not a more rotund version of Gautama Buddha himself, although he has earned his nickname because of this misconception, and hence his name is often capitalized. The "fat Buddha" figure, also known as the "laughing Buddha," represents a semi-historical, popular, non-canonical figure, derived from Chinese folklore, who became incorporated into the Chan (Zen in Japan) Buddhist tradition. Known as Budai in China, Hōtei in Japan, and Podae in Korea, the "fat Buddha" appeared in Chinese iconography during the Song dynasty (960–1279) and was allegedly modeled on Qici (–916), an eccentric Chinese Buddhist monk from the Chan tradition who lived around the tenth century during the Five Dynasties and Ten Kingdoms period (907–60) in the Wuyue kingdom.

Little is known of the fat Buddha's origin, but he has been nonetheless celebrated as a folkloric wandering vagabond and a "mendicant priest" in the Chan tradition. He became a famous Buddhist figure known for granting wealth and prosperity, whose gold and jade statues can now often be encountered displayed in people's homes and businesses, as well as in front of the entrance hall of temples across China, Japan, Korea, Taiwan, Thailand, Vietnam, and in the European and North American contexts.

Budai's name, meaning "cloth bag," derives from the cloth bundle that he carried on the end of his staff which, according to

Budai surrounded by arhats, Felai Feng, Hangzhou, China
Christian Luczanits, 2019

the legends, contained sweets for children or rice plants for the poor. As such, his sack became a symbol of benevolence and prosperity. As a wandering monk, he was often inclined to sleep rough, while his mystical powers warded off the bitter colds of snow and left his body unaffected. Patting Budai on his round potbelly was also meant to grant good luck.

He became a popular ink painting theme: an early seventeenth-century painting by Kanō Kōi (–1636) on display in Tokyo Metropolitan Museum depicts Budai (Hōtei) as a very portly figure usually associated with an unrefined and carefree manner of speech. His depiction in this fashion—jovial, bald, with his robe hanging open exposing his stout round body—has distinguished him from other Buddhist figures and he became widely recognized as the "laughing Buddha" or "happy Buddha." As such, his tubbiness symbolizes happiness, good luck, and abundance.

Owing to his generous and giving nature, he became identified as a manifestation of the Bodhisattva Maitreya, the future Buddha. Hōtei also became an important figure within folklore traditions.

In Japan, he became one of Seven Lucky Gods or Seven Gods of Fortune, who have their origins in ancient gods of fortune derived from Hinduism, Chinese Taoism and Buddhism, and Japanese folklore. Along with other "Lucky Gods," Hōtei is believed to grant good luck and was often represented in *netsuke*, miniature sculptures designed to serve a practical function as a button-like toggle and which evolved into objects of great craft and artistic merit. He continues to be celebrated as a Buddhist and folk figure through art and popular practices such as pilgrimage, representing both contentment and abundance.

About the author
Dr. Paulina Kolata is a Postdoctoral Fellow at Lund University, Sweden, and an Early Career Research Fellow at the University of Manchester, UK. Her work focuses primarily on contemporary Japanese Buddhism, depopulation, economy, death, social networks, belonging, and materiality in Buddhism.

Suggestions for further reading

In this book
See also Chapters 11 (reading a Buddha-image), 13 (bodhisattva), 25 (saints), and 41 (Zen).

Elsewhere
Hyers, Conrad. *Laughing Buddha: Zen and the Comic Spirit*. Wolfeboro, NH: Longwood Academic, 1989.

Levine, Gregory, and Yukio Lippit. *Awakenings: Zen Figure Painting in Medieval Japan*. New York: Japan Society, 2007.

13
What is a bodhisattva?

Jiancheng Shi

In Sanskrit, *bodhi* means "awakening" and *sattva* refers to a sentient being. In a narrow sense, the term "bodhisattva" is primarily restricted to the historical Buddha, Siddhārtha Gautama, in his numerous previous lives before accomplishing buddhahood. Broadly speaking, a bodhisattva can refer to any sentient being who has vowed to pursue the path to buddhahood, which is called the bodhisattva path.

The two fundamental mental qualities that a bodhisattva cultivates are compassion and wisdom, which are described as like two wings of a bird. In many Buddhist texts, the past lives of the historical Buddha are illustrated as a prolonged process of developing these two qualities by performing benevolent acts. Either in human form or other life forms, the Buddha, when he was a bodhisattva, vowed to give bliss to sentient beings unconditionally and liberate them from sufferings. For example, in one past life, the Buddha as bodhisattva was a king who witnessed a pigeon being chased by a hawk and wanted to save its life. He promised the hungry hawk that he would ransom the pigeon with his own flesh and cut his body piece by piece on the scale to equal the weight of the pigeon. However, as more and more flesh was placed on the scale, the heavier the pigeon became. Lastly, the king jumped onto the scale to offer himself to the hawk. The hawk then changed back to his original identity as a heavenly king who intended to testify to the bodhisattva king's determination to protect lives. The tale shows that a bodhisattva undergoes numerous challenges in the quest of awakening.

Such extraordinary giving, involving mental and physical endurance, would not be possible without wisdom. The compassion of a bodhisattva does not arise from mundane emotions, but instead originates from a deep understanding of reality as impermanent, unsatisfactory, and not-self, which is what wisdom is in Buddhism. By realizing the nature of worldly phenomena as impermanent and empty of "self," a bodhisattva can be free from fatigue, hindrances, and delusion in all circumstances. In all Buddhist traditions, the attainment of buddhahood encompasses many lifetimes. In the Theravada tradition, the standard training practices for a bodhisattva are the ten perfections: (1) generosity, (2) morality, (3) renunciation, (4) insight, (5) energy, (6) patience, (7) truthfulness, (8) resolution, (9) loving-kindness, and (10) equanimity. In Mahayana Buddhism, six perfections are commonly recognized: (1) generosity, (2) morality, (3) patience or tolerance, (4) courage or diligence, (5) concentration or meditation, and (6) wisdom. Furthermore, a bodhisattva, particularly in the Mahayana tradition, needs to develop a wide range of knowledge and needed skills, such as the science of logic, medicine, fine arts and crafts, and languages. According to the distinct capacities and characteristics of each individual sentient being, a bodhisattva utilizes flexible methods and multiple techniques to inspire them to take up the path toward enlightenment.

The conception of the bodhisattva path, therefore, differs between different traditions. Theravada Buddhism stresses that there are only a handful of buddhas in every eon of time, each gaining awakening when the Dharma was unknown, and only beings on the path to become such a buddha are seen as bodhisattvas. Others who are on the path to nirvana, through hearing the teaching of a buddha, are not seen as bodhisattvas. Mahayana Buddhism, on the other hand, recognizes that all sentient beings have the potential to pursue the path to buddhahood; each of them can embark on the bodhisattva path. In Mahayana Buddhism, therefore, a myriad of buddhas can exist at the same time and

Bodhisattva Senju (1000-armed) Kannon, at pilgrimage temple no. 58, Senyū-ji, Shikoku, Japan
Yuka Itawaki, with the help of Ryofu Pussel

the bodhisattva path is the ultimate path to full enlightenment or buddhahood. Accordingly, the term "bodhisattva," in the context of Mahayana Buddhist monasteries, is sometimes used as an honorary title to address either monastic or lay Buddhist practitioners, or volunteers in recognition of their merits while following the bodhisattva ideal. A bodhisattva path toward buddhahood entails different stages, from an ordinary beginner who just makes an initial determination to seek buddhahood to a saint who is highly advanced and will soon be a buddha.

The great bodhisattvas, who are regarded as having miraculous powers to bless sentient beings and to help them work toward the end of suffering, are popularly worshipped in Mahayana Buddhism. For example, the four major bodhisattvas are commonly enshrined in Chinese Buddhist temples and each of them represents different spiritual attributes of bodhisattva-hood. For instance, Avalokiteśvara Bodhisattva represents a spirit of compassion.

Mañjuśrī Bodhisattva represents wisdom. In Buddhist art, we can see that the earliest bodhisattva images were presented in a male form between the first and third centuries CE. However, in countries such as China, Japan, and Korea, these images also adopted female forms. Avalokiteśvara, for instance, known as Kannon (Japanese) or Guanyin (Chinese), was represented in male and female forms.

So, what is a bodhisattva? It depends on how we understand the term, and which angles we take. A bodhisattva can signify a saint who will soon become the next buddha, or, in Mahayana Buddhism, any ordinary being who embarks on the path to ultimate enlightenment as a buddha. Metaphorically, a bodhisattva is also an image of compassion and wisdom, or even of just a thought that is directed toward benefiting others.

About the author
Jiancheng Shi received her PhD degree from Lancaster University, UK in 2021. Her PhD dissertation examines mindfulness in contemporary Chan monastic life.

Suggestions for further reading

In this book
See also Chapters 10 (buddhahood), 44 (bodhisattva vow), and 48 (celestial beings in Tibetan Buddhism).

Elsewhere

Analayo, Bhikkhu. *The Genesis of the Bodhisattva Ideal*. Hamburg: Hamburg University Press, 2010.

Kawamura, Leslie (editor). *The Bodhisattva Doctrine in Buddhism*. Waterloo, Ontario: Wilfrid Laurier University Press, 1981.

Ng, Zhiru. *The Making of a Savior Bodhisattva: Dizang in Medieval China*. Honolulu: University of Hawai'i Press, 2007.

14
How do Buddhists show their devotion to the Buddha?

Paulina Kolata

Be it through receiving blessings, merit-making practices, prostrating, offerings, chanting, pilgrimage, and various incarnations of meditation practice, devotional expression is part of contemporary Buddhism and Buddhism in the past, with primary focus on the Three Jewels of the Buddha, the Dharma, and his community, the Sangha. The most important symbols of Buddhist devotion include the Buddha-image, the Wheel of the Dharma, the lotus flower, and the Bodhi tree, all symbolizing the path to enlightenment. Devotion to the Buddha and other holy beings is thus a common practice across the Buddhist world, through which Buddhists aim to accumulate good karmic fruits for themselves and others, including the living and the dead.

The early Buddhist devotional practices probably resembled those of today, namely the making of offerings and the chanting of specific verses and formulas intended to recall the qualities of the Buddha. Although such practices might have been initially focused on symbols such as the Wheel of the Dharma and stupas (a place of burial or a receptacle for religious objects/relics), from the second century CE the Buddha-image gradually became a focus of Buddhist devotional and meditation practices. Equally important were practices of chanting Buddhist sutras, especially those recited

Devotion to the Buddha at the Bodhi tree, Kelaniya Temple, Sri Lanka
Elizabeth Harris, 2010

as protective chants warding off unsympathetic demons, disease, and accidents.

Although devotional practices developed distinctive forms as Buddhism traveled and developed, there are shared characteristics across geographies and cultures. While in Theravada Buddhist countries such as Sri Lanka, devotion and worship may predominantly focus on the figure of the historical Buddha and previous buddhas, as well as important objects and places connected to the historical Buddha's life such as the Bodhi tree, in Mahayana tradition we encounter much more diversity of focus, encompassing multiple buddhas and bodhisattvas, founders of Buddhist lineages, sutras, mantras, and even the dead. For instance, bodhisattvas embodying compassion such as Avalokiteśvara (Kannon in Japan and Guanyin in China) are widely venerated in Mahayana as figures who hear the cries of all sentient beings and untiringly support those who call upon them. Within both traditions, however, devotion and worship play a vital role in monastic and lay Buddhists' pursuit of spiritual aspirations.

What objects and what spaces do Buddhists use to express their devotion? Buddhist devotional practices can take place at a person's home or a Buddhist temple, and they can be focused around a specific Buddhist figure and a chosen or prescribed form of meditative practice that constitutes an "auspicious action" or a "meritorious action." These actions, in turn, lead to the generation of good karmic fruits. Such action can be performed by lay Buddhist practitioners themselves or, in some Buddhist traditions, on their behalf by a Buddhist monk or nun, whose actions are deemed more efficacious. The objects used in the process often include images of buddhas and/or Buddhist texts in various formats.

A key aspect of expressing devotion in Buddhism is the act of generosity. The practice of giving constitutes the bedrock of the tradition. It is the responsibility of lay practitioners to support the community of monks and nuns so as they can pursue their path to enlightenment. A gift offered to the monastic Sangha is a gift to the Buddha himself. One of the most common offerings given to a Buddhist temple or presented at a Buddhist altar is food in its various incarnations: from rice grains, vegetables, and fruit placed in a monk's begging bowl on the streets of Bangkok to elaborate village feasts hosting Tibetan Buddhist monks, thrown by wealthy Chinese patrons. In everyday practice, acts of generosity can thus involve donations of food, robes, incense, money, time, and effort. Such offerings are meant to arouse in the giver the religious emotion of faith and commitment to Buddhist values.

Pilgrimages to the sites associated with the events of the lives of the buddhas, local sacred locations and temples, and the routes associated with holy figures are also an important devotional practice. A person setting off on a Buddhist pilgrimage is believed to be walking in the footsteps of the Buddha himself. For instance, one of the famous Buddhist pilgrimage sites in Japan is Mount Hiei, where Tendai Buddhist monks known as "marathon monks" perform an ascetic practice of pilgrimage, involving continuously walking the route circling the mountain. Legend has it that the monks run one thousand marathons in one thousand days, while offering prayers at halls, shrines, and sacred places along the route. The monks who complete the practice are believed to have reached enlightenment in this life. Lay practitioners may choose less arduous forms of pilgrimage or alternatively offer alms to Hiei monks to inspire and aid them on their path to enlightenment.

One of the most important festivals in the Buddhist calendar is celebrated in April–June across the whole Buddhist world: in Tibetan Buddhism it is referred to as Saga Dawa and in Theravada as Vesak, celebrating the Buddha's birth, enlightenment, and death, while in Mahayana Buddhism, it celebrates the Buddha's birth (with the Buddha's awakening and death celebrated separately). In many East, Southeast and South Asian Buddhist countries, it is a public holiday. In South Korea, colorful lanterns are hung in temples, people's homes, and in the streets, while temples offer free meals and tea to all visitors. In Japan, Buddhist temples often hold a ceremony re-enacting the legend of the Buddha's birth, while people taking part pour a beverage prepared from hydrangea serrata on a small statue of the baby Buddha decorated with flowers.

Buddhist images, as well as other representations of the Buddha, are the key object of devotion. Producing, buying, and worshipping in front of such objects of devotion are meritorious, as is cleaning, repairing, and maintaining them. A Buddhist may also purchase a talisman representing a buddha or a bodhisattva, and carry it attached to their keys or dangle it from their car mirror. Others may choose to wash and dress Buddhist statues found at the side of the road in the countryside to protect them from cold. For example, in Japan, images of Bodhisattva Jizō—protector of travelers and children—can often be found dressed in children's clothes, or red hat and bib. The Covid-19 pandemic saw many Buddhist statues in Thailand, China, and Japan being equipped with face masks for protection from the virus. Nonetheless, when sitting in front of images and paintings of Buddhist figures of worship or a mandala depicting a Pure Land, a Buddhist practitioner is most likely to offer some food, light, and incense, and chant Buddhist sutras, with hands arranged in prayer and possibly adorned with a Buddhist rosary.

Buddhists chant to express devotion but also to awaken spiritual power. The texts in Buddhism are not just records of Buddhist teachings. In most Buddhist traditions, they are also believed to contain implicit powers, seen as "objects" that hold and liberate spiritual power through the sounds and meanings contained within them. Comparably to Buddhist relics, mantras and sutras are regarded as a means of harnessing the power of the buddhas.

So while it is clear that Buddhists show their devotion to the Buddha and other holy beings in a multitude of ways, the precise object of that devotion and the complexities of how and why may differ depending on geographical, historical, and cultural contexts. Seeking the Buddhas' protection, benevolence, and help for oneself and others, including on one's path to enlightenment, is at the center of Buddhist devotional practices. Generosity and meritorious action underpin the morality of Buddhist devotion. But equally important are the daily, this-worldly struggles and concerns, and diverse and emerging technologies facilitating Buddhist practice, such as Tibetan prayer wheel apps for smartphones and digital Buddhist household altars in Japan.

About the author

Dr. Paulina Kolata is a Fellow at Lund University, Sweden, and an Early Career Research Fellow at the University of Manchester, UK. Her work focuses primarily on contemporary Japanese Buddhism, depopulation, economy, death, social networks, belonging, and materiality in Buddhism.

Suggestions for further reading

In this book

See Chapters 2 (faith), 3 (ritual), 4 (relics), 5 (texts), 6 (images), 18 (karma), 26 (why Buddhists meditate), 29 (chanting), 30 (role of monasticism), 34 (lay Buddhists), 37 (relations with Brahmanism), 39 (contemporary divisions), 42 (Pure Land Buddhism), 44 (bodhisattva vow), 50 (Buddhist art), and 51 (mandala).

Elsewhere

Gethin, Rupert. *The Foundations of Buddhism*. Oxford: Oxford University Press, 1998: pages 165–169.

Jerryson, Michael. *The Oxford Handbook of Contemporary Buddhism*. Oxford: Oxford University Press, 2017.

Lewis, Todd. *Buddhists: Understanding Buddhism through the Lives of Practitioners*. Chichester and Oxford: Wiley-Blackwell, 2014.

Lopez, Donald S. *Buddhism in Practice*. Princeton, NJ: Princeton University Press, 1995.

Part Three
What the Buddha taught (1)

15
Can we know what the historical Buddha taught?

Rupert Gethin

To ask this question is to ask how the teachings of the Buddha presented in ancient Buddhist texts relate to what the historical Buddha taught. It is clear that the collections of texts regarded by Buddhists today as "the word of the Buddha" are very diverse and date from various periods. If we assume that the oldest texts—those closest in time to the historical Buddha (c. fifth century BCE)—are the texts most likely to contain what the historical Buddha taught, then we must ask whether we can reliably identify a set of texts relatively close in time to the historical Buddha. The answer to this question is, in broad terms, yes, we can do this, by paying attention to ancient disputes about the authenticity of the texts, and by considering their contents.

There are three principal canonical collections of Buddhist texts: (1) the Pali Canon preserved by the Theravada tradition; (2) the Chinese "Great Store of Scriptures," a vast library of Indian Buddhist texts translated into Chinese; and (3) the Tibetan "Translated Words of the Buddha," a collection of Indian Buddhist texts translated into Tibetan. Fragments of the canonical collections of other ancient Indian schools of Buddhism (principally the Sarvāstivāda and Dharmaguptaka) survive in Sanskrit and the ancient Indian language of Gāndhārī.

It is apparent that the authenticity of two classes of Buddhist texts was disputed relatively early in the history of Buddhism: the

Abhidharma and the Mahayana sutras (discourses of the Great Vehicle). In contrast, there was broad agreement about the authenticity of the set of texts to do with the discipline and training of Buddhist monks and nuns (the *Vinaya Piṭaka*) and the set of discourses of the Buddha (Sanskrit: *Sūtra Piṭaka*; Pali: *Sutta Piṭaka*). When we examine the different collections of Buddhist texts, we find a number of versions of the *Vinaya*, of the discourses, and of the Abhidharma. In the case of the *Vinaya* and the discourses, while there are differences in detail between the versions, there is significant and substantial agreement. In the case of the Abhidharma, the differences are more substantial. Moreover, the Abhidharma texts contain significant and divergent doctrinal developments when compared with the discourses. As for the Mahayana discourses, they are missing entirely from the Pali Canon, and also contain significant doctrinal developments. This allows us to conclude that the oldest Buddhist teachings are found in the *Vinaya* and Sutra collections, excluding the Abhidharma texts, the Mahayana sutras and Tantras (exclusive to the Chinese and Tibetan Canons), which all belong to later strata of Buddhist literature, further removed in time from the historical Buddha.

Six different versions of the *Vinaya* survive, each belonging to different ancient Buddhist monastic lineages: Mahāsāṃghika, Sarvāstivāda, Mūlasarvāstivāda, Mahīśāsaka, Dharmaguptaka, and Theravada. While the precise number of rules varies in the different versions, they contain a common core of rules that are substantially the same. This allows us to identify a set of rules and a monastic constitution that is relatively early in date and the core of which at least goes back to the time of the Buddha.

The discourse (sutra/*sutta*) collections survive in three versions: Theravada (complete in Pali), (Mūla-)Sarvāstivāda (in Sanskrit fragments, and partial Chinese and Tibetan translation), Dharmaguptaka (in Gāndhārī fragments, and partial Chinese translation). When we examine these different versions, while again there are differences in detail, there is substantial agreement on the main teachings: the doctrines of not-self, dependent origination, and the practice of meditation. Can we know that these texts contain what the Buddha taught? Some scholars argue that this is not possible, because these texts cannot be reliably dated earlier than the fourth century CE (when Buddhist writers we can date quote them, and when they begin to be translated into Chinese). The problem with this approach is it denies Buddhist doctrine any history: it is quite obvious, for example, that Buddhist texts we can date to the third or fourth centuries CE contain doctrinal developments not found in the Abhidharma texts; it is quite obvious that the Abhidharma texts contain doctrinal developments not found in the discourse collections. The discourse collections must, therefore, have become fixed earlier than the third century CE. The problem is how much earlier. There is no scholarly consensus on this question. The position scholars take is based on the weight given to various pieces of evidence, each inconclusive by itself. For example, the oldest Buddhist manuscripts (those found in what is now Afghanistan and Pakistan) date from the first or second century BCE. This means that the type of content they contain (which includes fragments of the discourse collections and Mahayana sutras) must be at least as old. Some of the content of early Buddhist texts is illustrated in carved friezes on Buddhist monuments dating from the first or second century BCE. The doctrinal developments found in the Abhidharma texts and Mahayana sutras must have taken some time. In an inscription from the third century BCE, King Aśoka names specific Buddhist texts that can be related to texts found in the extant discourse collections. All this means that it is not unreasonable to suggest that the texts we find in the extant discourse collections can be dated to the third century BCE. Such a date is still as much as two centuries after the death of the Buddha (c. 400 BCE). Can we push the date of these texts further back? Some scholars think so. But here issues of interpretation of the content of the texts come in, as well as the significance of the fact that, like other Indian literature of this period, the earliest Buddhist texts were composed and transmitted orally for several centuries. Some scholars suggest that, on close reading, the teachings contained in the extant discourse collections (of the Theravada, Sarvāstivāda, and Dharmaguptaka schools), claiming to be the word of the Buddha, turn out to be in places inconsistent and even muddled. These scholars go on to suggest that by applying the methods of textual criticism we can begin to stratify these texts chronologically and so get closer to what the historical Buddha taught. But there is no clear scholarly consensus on these questions.

In sum, the collections of discourses (sutras/*sutta*s)—preserved in full in the Pali Nikāyas and incompletely in Sanskrit and Gāndhārī fragments and in Chinese and Tibetan translations—contain the Buddhist teachings closest in time to the historical Buddha. They can be reasonably dated to at least the second if not the third century BCE. They thus tell us what the Buddhist tradition of that period understood the Buddha to have taught. How accurately that reflects what the historical Buddha taught remains disputed by scholars. Some scholars are more willing than others to attempt to distinguish older from later strata in these texts and thereby identify more precisely what the historical Buddha taught.

About the author
Rupert Gethin is Professor of Buddhist Studies at the University of Bristol. His main research interests are Pali Buddhist literature and Indian Buddhist systematic thought (Abhidharma).

Suggestions for further reading

In this book
See Chapters 5 (texts), 9 (What can we know of the historical Buddha?), and 38 (early splits).

Elsewhere
Gethin, Rupert. *The Foundations of Buddhism*. Oxford: Oxford University Press, 1998: Chapter 2.

Gethin, Rupert. "Gethin on Gombrich, 'What the Buddha Thought.'" H-Net Reviews, 2012. https://networks.h-net.org/node/6060/reviews/16095/gethin-gombrich-what-buddha-thought

Gombrich, Richard. *What the Buddha Thought*. London: Equinox, 2009.

16
What part does belief in rebirth play in Buddhism?

Peter Harvey

In Buddhism, various aspects of practice can be done without reference to the idea of rebirth, such as generosity, kindness, helpfulness, chanting, and meditation. While some modern, secularized forms of Buddhism avoid reference to rebirth, seeing it as an inessential hangover from ancient Indian belief, this can itself be seen as an importation into Buddhism of certain modern, mainly Western attitudes and beliefs.

In the Buddha's day, some kind of belief in repeated lives had already been developed within Brahmanism (which later developed into Hinduism), and another version of it existed in Jainism, one of the renunciant traditions that critiqued Brahmanism. Buddhism itself originated as such a non-Brahmanical renunciant tradition, and others included materialists, who denied rebirth, skeptics, who saw knowledge of such things as impossible, and fatalists, who believed in rebirth driven forward by blind fate, rather than by individual action (karma).

The Buddha taught a form of rebirth, basing this on insights gained from a state of deep meditative calm, concentration, and mindfulness. Buddhist texts describe him as attaining this on the night of his becoming a buddha, when he attained a series of four *jhāna*s, or meditative absorptions, and then from the fourth of these, in a state of great mental stillness and mindful sensitivity, probed back into his memory and remembered many, many past lives. He then tuned in to how other people were at that time dying and being reborn in various ways, according to the quality of their intentional actions. He saw that wholesome, skillful actions—rooted in generosity and non-attachment, kindness and compassion, and calm mental clarity and understanding—led to rebirth as a human or in one of a variety of heavenly rebirths. On the other hand, he also saw bad rebirths, as some kind of animal (including land animals, birds, fishes, and insects), a frustrated ghost, or as a hell-being undergoing experiences akin to prolonged nightmares. He saw such rebirths as the product of actions rooted in greed, hatred, and delusion.

He saw that no such rebirth lasted forever, though, and that they would be followed by further rebirths, again and again and again, in a process of *saṃsāra* or "wandering on." The goal, then, was not coming back to yet another life, with all its problems, but to attain liberation from the round of rebirths, through attaining nirvana.

The idea of rebirth, then, provides the framework for the full Buddhist project. It is not just about living a better and happier life in this life, though it certainly includes this, but also about building on good characteristics developed in this rebirth, and ultimately transcending any rebirth. While it is seen as possible to personally confirm rebirth by deep meditation, as the Buddha did, most Buddhists work with the idea as a *belief*, trusting the Buddha's teaching on this.

In the Buddhist Noble Eight-factored Path, the first factor is "right view," in the sense of understanding and insight in accord with the truth. This is seen as having different levels. The highest level is direct experience of the insights that bring liberation. But the more preliminary and ordinary level is belief in karma and rebirth.

While the karma and rebirth beliefs form a coherent, rational, and motivating perspective on life for Buddhists, Buddhist texts emphasize that it is inappropriate to mistake belief in them with actual knowledge of them. In one Pali text, the *Caṅki Sutta*, the Buddha says that if one has faith in a handed-down teaching, but do not know it is true, one preserves truth by acknowledging that it is simply a belief that one holds. But one awakens to truth by finding a teacher of good mental states and behavior, investigating their teaching, and practicing in accord with their teaching, so as to eventually awaken to truth.

Moreover, in the *Kālāma Sutta* the Buddha taught that people should test out any beliefs by assessing whether they lead to beneficial or harmful behavior, irrespective of the source of the beliefs. From one's own experience, one can know that greed, hatred, and delusion (which could include false beliefs) tend to lead to actions that bring suffering to people and animals, such as through intentional killing, stealing, sensual misconduct, and lying, and that actions free of greed, hatred, and delusion do not have these effects, and bring happiness and praise from those that are wise. Moreover, a person who is kind and compassionate can be assured that: if rebirth and karma are real, he will have a good rebirth; if they are unreal, he will still have a happy life; if bad results come to one who acts in an evil way, he will be free of these; if they do not, he will be happy in being free of evildoing here and now.

Buddhism does not accept the idea of a God who created the world and its many kinds of beings. Hence there is no idea of a first rebirth. The round of rebirths is seen as without discernible beginning, going back and back through the eons, into what we would now call past universes. As things only arise from previous conditions, any rebirth must have had past rebirths before it.

This has ethical implications, for it means that any person or animal we meet, however much they may be causing us problems at present, will probably have been met with, in *some* past life or lives, and there been a close relative or friend. Thus we should not be fixated on how they are now, but be mindful that they may well have been very good to us in the past.

Moreover, any suffering we see other humans or animals as undergoing is not something we can separate ourselves from, as, according to Buddhism, we will have experienced such things in past lives, and may do so again if we do not attain liberation, and especially if we generate bad karmic results.

As regards contemporary support for the idea of past lives, there are empirical studies of young children, from various countries, who give accounts of who they used to be, and who have impressive knowledge of a traceable past person's life and experiences, even though there is no evidence that they could have got information about them by any normal route. In the Tibetan tradition, there are also advanced practitioners known as tulkus, or incarnate lamas, who are seen as rebirths of famous past lamas, or spiritual teachers. The past lama makes a prediction on where they will be reborn, then later children from that locality are assessed, to see if one of them has certain qualities and gifts, including the ability to recognize and pick out a number of possessions of the past lama from others similar to them.

About the author
Peter Harvey is Professor of Buddhist Studies (retired), University of Sunderland, UK, and co-founder of the UK Association for Buddhist Studies. He researches on Buddhist ethics, meditation, and early Buddhist thought.

Suggestions for further reading

In this book
See Chapters 2 (faith), 8 (is Buddhism atheistic, non-theistic, or theistic?), 19 (what is reborn), 21 (Four Noble Truths), 23 (nirvana), and 24 (enlightenment).

Elsewhere
Anālayo, Bhikkhu. *Rebirth in Early Buddhism and Current Research.* Somerville, MA: Wisdom Publications, 2018.

Harvey, Peter. *An Introduction to Buddhism: Teachings, History and Practices* (2nd edition). Cambridge: Cambridge University Press, 2013: pages 22–33, 29–49.

Kālāma Sutta: https://www.accesstoinsight.org/tipitaka/an/an03/an03.065.than.html

Nyanatiloka Mahathera. "Kamma and Rebirth." Part of *Fundamentals of Buddhism: Four Lectures*. Wheel booklet no. 394–96. Kandy, Sri Lanka: Buddhist Publication Society, 2005. https://www.accesstoinsight.org/lib/authors/nyanatiloka/wheel394.html

17
Does Buddhism see the mind as separate from the body?

Peter Harvey

A key Buddhist belief concerns rebirth: that a person does not fully come to an end at death, but goes on to another rebirth. So the Buddha saw the view of materialists as mistaken, characterizing them as "annihilationists." A person is more than the material body, then. The most common Buddhist analysis of a person is in terms of the five *khandha*s (Pali; Sanskrit: *skandha*s): "aggregates" or "bundles." These are:

- material form (*rūpa*): four primary elemental processes termed "earth", "water," "fire," and "wind," plus other processes dependent on these;
- pleasant, unpleasant or neutral feeling tone (*vedanā*);
- perception (Pali: *saññā*; Sanskrit: *saṃjñā*), which labels, classifies, and recognizes/misrecognizes sense-objects;
- volitional activities (Pali: *saṅkhāra*; Sanskrit: *saṃskāra*), in the form of tendencies, emotions, attitudes, and volitional responses;
- consciousness (Pali: *viññāṇa*; Sanskrit: *vijñāna*), the awareness of any object of the physical senses or mind.

Sometimes, Buddhism analyzes a person in terms of six elements: the above four mentioned under "material form," plus space and consciousness. A key feature shared by consciousness and the other mental states dependent on it is that they are *intentional*, in the philosophical sense of taking an object; while material processes do not refer beyond themselves. This feature of mental states is truly amazing. A key aspect of what they are is what they are aware of. The eye may generate electrical impulses in the optic nerve, but *seeing* is the activity of visual consciousness.

Sometimes the first four *khandha*s are grouped as *nāma-rūpa*, literally "name and form," to refer to the body and the mental states that process sense-objects, with all this seen as enlivened by consciousness. The arrival of a stream of consciousness from a previous life, according to one Pali text, is seen as an essential ingredient in the process of conception in the womb.

Elsewhere, it is said that the conception of an embryo takes place when three conditions come together: sexual intercourse, at the right time in a woman's monthly cycle, and the presence of a being awaiting to be reborn. The flow of a stream of consciousness from a previous life is seen as driven principally by craving as well as by deluded misconceptions about the sense objects that consciousness has been and is dependent on. Hence, a being is an interplay of consciousness, and other mental and physical processes.

The subtlety and complexity of this interaction mean that the Buddha did not accept either that "the life principle is the same as the mortal body" or "the life principle is different from the mortal body," as some kind of independent, disembodied self or soul. Buddhism sees mental and physical processes as dependent on each other, constantly interacting, in a dance of changing processes. For the body to move, consciousness and volition are necessary. And feelings and thoughts are mostly concerned with things that we sense around us, or remember having sensed in the past. None is seen as unchanging, permanent, eternal, or separate from everything else. All are processes that depend on other processes. For instance, the mental states developed by meditation have been shown to have physical effects within the body, such as reducing tensions, heart rate, and how we respond at an emotional level. Moreover, some types of meditation, when very deeply developed, are seen to enable the production of psychic powers over the physical, such as walking on water or flying. An interesting fact is that the texts of Buddhism show no awareness of the brain as specifically the site or seat of mental processing, though it is accepted that there is some kind of physical support for this.

Other than humans and animals, who have gross physical bodies, there are seen to be many kinds of mortal gods (*devas*) in a variety of heavenly rebirths, which are seen to have subtle bodies. However the subtlest kind of rebirth is seen as "formless," completely beyond any kind of materiality or awareness linked to input from the physical senses. Beings of this level, without any body, however subtle, are strange forms of life that last many eons. Mental processes completely separated from physical processes are seen to become very different from normal. The formless rebirths are of four kinds: those of the sphere of infinite space; those of the sphere of infinite consciousness; those of the sphere of no-thingness; and those of the sphere of neither-perception-nor-non-perception. Beings of these levels have no individual names (unlike other kinds of god), and the Buddha is never described as interacting with any of them, while he does interact with other kinds of god. Even between lives, consciousness is seen to be accompanied by a kind of subtle body.

Buddhism also emphasizes that the world of our lived experiences is something that occurs within our conscious, perceiving organism, in which the mental and the physical are interdependent. Our lived world is drawn from the range of objects our physical senses are able to detect. Then, our attention picks up what is relevant to our own desires and fears, putting a particular "spin" on it, like the different editorial perspectives of different newspapers. The end result is the "world" we wake up to in the morning, conditioned and constructed by our drives, interests, and preoccupations.

Within the Mahayana movement in Buddhism, one philosophical strand, known as the Yogacara (Conduct of Yoga) or Citta-mātra (Mind-only) school, greatly emphasized that the world we experience is shaped, flavored, and constructed by what our minds are doing, e.g., being lazy, or irritated, or relaxed, and our mental projections and fears. Its teachings are very subtle, but are open to two kinds of interpretation. The first is that all that we *experience* is mental, and that ideas of anything beyond the mental are speculative projections. The second is that the only things that *exist* are mental in nature.

Overall, while Buddhism sees mental processes as not reducible to physical ones, neither physical nor mental ones are seen as lasting *substances*, so Buddhism does not accept a mind–body substance dualism. Moreover, neither the mind nor the body is seen as one thing but a collection of interacting, interdependent processes, with neither being able to stand alone.

About the author
Peter Harvey is Professor of Buddhist Studies (retired), University of Sunderland, UK, and co-founder of the UK Association for Buddhist Studies. He researches on Buddhist ethics, meditation, and early Buddhist thought.

Suggestions for further reading

In this book
See Chapters 8 (is Buddhism atheistic, non-theistic, or theistic?), 19 (what is reborn), 20 (non-self teaching), and 28 (forms of meditation).

Elsewhere
Harvey, Peter. *The Selfless Mind: Personality, Consciousness and Nirvana in Early Buddhism*. Richmond, VA: Curzon Press, 1995: pages 78–88, 111–121.

Harvey, Peter. *An Introduction to Buddhism: Teachings, History and Practices* (2nd edition). Cambridge: Cambridge University Press, 2013: pages 55–73, 128–134.

Williams, Paul, with Anthony Tribe. *Buddhist Thought: A Complete Introduction to the Indian Tradition*. London and New York: Routledge & Kegan Paul, 2000: pages 31–34, 41–52, 112–118.

18
Do Buddhists see all that happens to one as due to karma?

Peter Harvey

The word "karma" (Pali: *kamma*: Sanskrit: *karma*) means "action," particularly the intentional, volitional impulse behind a physical or verbal action, or behind a mental action (an active line of thought). This then sets going a chain of causes culminating in a karmic fruit.

The doctrine of karma is that one's intentional actions generate karmic fruits for the future, shaping and conditioning it, so that a fair amount of what one is, and also experiences—pleasant or unpleasant—depends on past actions and their nature. What one does *matters*. Note that results of karma are not seen as "punishments" or "rewards," but as natural results of the karmic seeds that one plants by one's actions.

A crucial kind of result of karma is one's form of rebirth, whether as a human or in one of various (non-eternal) heavens (good rebirths, due to good actions) or as some kind of animal, a frustrated ghost, or in a (non-eternal) hell (bad rebirths, due to actions that are intended to harm other beings, and are rooted in greed, hatred, or delusion). Each person is seen to have a beginningless past behind them and thus a long history of actions, some still with the latent power to bring results in the present and/or future, when the conditions are right.

However, Buddhism does not say that everything that happens to one is due to one's past karma. The Buddha criticized theories which saw all experiences and associated actions as due either to past karma, the diktat of a god, or pure chance. These views, according to the Buddha, imply a form of fatalism that strips one of responsibility for one's present actions and gives one no motivation to improve what one does. So, Buddhism stresses that present action is not fixed by past action. Rather, present action can bring about liberating change in a person.

Indeed, once a person has attained stream-entry, the first stage of enlightenment, they can no longer be reborn at less than a human level. This does not mean that past bad karma no longer catches up with them, though. In one story in the Pali texts, Mahā-moggallāna a fully enlightened arhat disciple of the Buddha, was beaten to death, as the final karmic result of having killed his blind parents numerous lives ago, after previously having been reborn in a hell due to this. As a verse in the popular text the *Dhammapada* (v. 127) says: "Not in the sky, not in mid-ocean, nor on entering a mountain cave, is found a place on earth, where abiding one may escape from (the consequences of) an evil deed."

While belief in the law of karma can sometimes degenerate into a form of fatalism, the Buddha emphasized that deterministic fate and karma are very different. The idea of karma emphasizes the importance of human action and its effects: people make their own "destiny" by their actions. Karma and fatalism differ on two scores. Firstly, humans have freedom of choice; their present actions are not the karmic results of previous actions, though karmic results may influence the type of action that a person tends to think of doing, because of their karma-shaped character. Secondly, not everything that happens to a person is seen as due to karma, as I have stressed.

Past karma, for instance, is only one among several causal conditions that can lead to an illness or other unpleasant experiences. Karma is a real, specific kind of cause, not a metaphysical explain-all. All volitional actions have karmic effects but that does not mean that all we experience arises specifically from one's past karma. New experiences come from present sense-input, and new volitional actions are new karma.

Of course, having a body prone to human illnesses comes from being reborn human, and this depends on past karma. In this sense the body is "old karma." Moreover, birth in a family in which certain illnesses are hereditary will mean that karma leads to one undergoing such illnesses. In modern terms, one gets one's genes from one's parents but one's parents from one's karma. Nongenetic illnesses can have a range of causes, however.

The aspects of life that Buddhism sees as the result of past karma include not only one's form of rebirth, social class at birth, and some aspects of one's health, but also one's character, situation, and what one notices, thus conditioning one's experienced "world." Karma brings effects from life to life, year to year, mood to mood, and even moment to moment. One's bad and good volitional actions:

- form one's character and habits, condition one's beliefs and views, preferences and desires, hang-ups and problems, or lay down positive qualities, sometimes in the form of unsuspected inner resources. Through one's actions, one grows these into oneself;
- influence one's visual appearance—a life of anger, or of calmness, in time becomes etched on one's face—and aspects of one's health;
- lead to one bringing oneself into various situations the potential of which for happiness or unhappiness is influenced by one's past actions.

We continually shape and reshape ourselves, and so just as past actions condition the present, so present actions condition the future. Thus one needs to be mindful and heedful of one's actions. Those rooted in the motives of greed or hatred, or arising from delusion, scar, constrain, dull, and weigh down the mind, creating problems; while those rooted in non-attachment (generosity, and non-clinging), loving-kindness, and mental clarity uplift the mind and bring joy, peace, and mental strength. Actions intended to harm any being have bitter fruits, while those intended to genuinely benefit them have pleasant fruits. As one's world of experience is shaped to a fair extent by one's actions and related concerns, there is for a Buddhist no place for complacency.

A particular point to be borne in mind is that karma affects what one tends to notice in the world around one—(real or apparent) pleasant or unpleasant aspects. The Abhidhamma (Pali; Sanskrit: Abhidharma) (a kind of technical philosophy of mind) of the Theravada school says that consciousness of any of the objects of the five physical senses arises as a result of past karma. What one notices is dependent on one's karma-shaped interests, concerns, and fears. Out of the mass of sense-data, one only ever gets "edited highlights" of what lies around one. Hence, Buddhism says that the world—in the sense of the lived world of our experience—lies within our body, perceptions, and mind. A relevant example is how a rich person may live as a miser, without bringing happiness to himself and his family, or being generous to others.

As an aid to planning courses of action in a karma-influenced world, many traditionalist Buddhists use divination methods such as astrology at certain points in their lives, so as to try to gauge what their karma has in store for them. As a person never knows what aspect of any situation may have been determined by karma, difficult situations are not to be passively accepted, but a person should do his or her best to improve them. Only when things happen in spite of efforts to avert them might they be put down to past karma.

The idea of the influence of karma, while not fatalistic, does encourage a person to live patiently with a situation. Thus when one comes up against unpleasant situations, whether mental or physical, especially those that one cannot alter, do what one might, it can aid patience to reflect that these may be the fruit of one's past actions, rather than react with anger, blaming, resentment, retaliation, sulking, or self-pitying dejection, especially as doing so can produce further bitter karmic fruits. One has made one's bed and one must lie on it—for as long as the situation persists, for everything is subject to change—and one should do what one can to change the world for the better.

In accepting that some of the sufferings of other people will be the fruit of their past actions, this does not at all mean that one should "blame" them for their sufferings; rather, one should have compassion for them having to experience these unfortunate results, and do what one can to help.

About the author

Peter Harvey is Professor of Buddhist Studies (retired), University of Sunderland, UK, and co-founder of the UK Association for Buddhist Studies. He researches Buddhist ethics, meditation, and early Buddhist thought.

Suggestions for further reading

In this book
See Chapters 16 (rebirth), and 24 (enlightenment).

Elsewhere
Harvey, Peter. *An Introduction to Buddhist Ethics: Foundations, Values and Issues*. Cambridge: Cambridge University Press, 2000: pages 14–31.

Harvey, Peter. *An Introduction to Buddhism: Teachings, History and Practices* (2nd edition). Cambridge: Cambridge University Press, 2013: pages 39–49.

Nyanaponika Thera. *Kamma and its Fruit*. [1996] 2004. https://www.accesstoinsight.org/lib/authors/nyanaponika/kammafruit.html

Thanissaro Bhikkhu. *Kamma: A Study Guide*. 2000. https://www.accesstoinsight.org/lib/study/kamma.html

19
What is seen as reborn, according to Buddhism?

Peter Harvey

For Buddhism, a person is not completely destroyed at death, but it is not an eternal, unchanging soul or self that carries on to another life. Rather, there is a stream of "conditions" that flows on beyond this life, becoming a key factor in the arising of a new life in the next rebirth.

A central Buddhist teaching is "conditioned arising" or "dependent origination" (Pali: *paṭicca-samuppāda*; Sanskrit: *pratītya-samutpāda*). This is about how mental and physical phenomena are not substantial, independent entities, but processes that depend on other processes for their arising and (temporary) existence. This applies both during life and from life to life. Over any three consecutive lives, there is said to be a sequence of twelve conditions, each being a key condition for the next: (1) spiritual ignorance → (2) volitional activities → (3) consciousness → (4) mind-and-body/the sentient body → (5) the six sense-bases → (6) sensory stimulation → (7) feeling → (8) craving → (9) grasping → (10) a way of being → (11) birth → (12) aging, death, sorrow, lamentation, pain, unhappiness, and distress.

Here, a new life starts at link 4, then 11. The sentient body starts to develop in the womb, from the time of conception, when there are the appropriate physical conditions, and a stream of consciousness from a previous being arrives. That stream is directed by the volitional activities of body, speech, and mind—the karma—of the previous being. The "birth" of link 11 does not refer to a child leaving the womb but the birth of an embryo in the womb. The "way of being" is how someone lives and behaves, the kind of things that they are attuned to and put energy into. So, again, it is volitional activities that lead to a new rebirth, with the emphasis here on how these are fed by what one grasps at and clings to, rather than, as with link 2, one's non-awareness of the true nature of reality.

Some texts say that the "evolving" or "conducive" consciousness is the crucial link between rebirths. At death, the momentum set up by volitional activities (and craving) impels this consciousness to spill over beyond one life and help spark off another. Conditioned arising here provides a "middle" way of understanding, which avoids the extremes of "eternalism" and "annihilationism": the survival of an eternal self, or the total annihilation of a person at death. Hence, of a person in two consecutive rebirths, it is said, "He is not (unchangingly) the same and he is not (completely) different." No unchanging "being" passes over from one life to another, but the death of a being leads to the continuation of the life process in another context, like the lighting of one lamp from another. The "later" being is a continuation of the "earlier" one, on which he or she is causally dependent. They are linked by the flux of consciousness and the accompanying seeds of karmic results, so that the character of one is a development of the character of the "other." After death, a changing personality-flux flows on—a little like a river that has gone underground and then reappeared in a different place with a different name. Given long enough, a personality-stream will become *very* different from how it is in the present life, yet how it is in that distant future life will have developed from its actions in this life.

Typically, children have no memory of their past lives, though there are examples of children who do seem to have such memories, for a while, and Buddhism holds that deep meditation is also able to recover such memories.

There are different views in Buddhism on the time span between rebirths. The Theravada view came to be that the moment of death is immediately followed by the moment of conception in a new life. The view in the Mahayana tradition is that there is an "intermediary existence" of up to seven weeks, as a time of adjustment. Even the early Theravada texts can be seen to talk of a period of adjustment, in which there is a time of "inclination"—a kind of craving-induced "what's next?"—then a period of "coming and going," seeking a new rebirth, then a "falling-away and re-arising" in a new rebirth context which one was attracted to according to one's karma-shaped tendencies. In the Tibetan tradition, it is said that one has various visions in the between-lives *bardo* period, and, if these are responded to appropriately, this can accelerate spiritual development.

About the author

Peter Harvey is Professor of Buddhist Studies (retired), University of Sunderland, UK, and co-founder of the UK Association for Buddhist Studies. He researches Buddhist ethics, meditation, and early Buddhist thought.

Suggestions for further reading

In this book
See Chapters 16 (rebirth), 17 (mind–body), 20 (non-self teaching) and 46 (emptiness).

Elsewhere
Harvey, Peter. *The Selfless Mind: Personality, Consciousness and Nirvana in Early Buddhism*. London: Curzon Press, 1995: pages 95–108.

Harvey, Peter. *An Introduction to Buddhism: Teachings, History and Practices* (2nd edition). Cambridge: Cambridge University Press, 2013: pages 65–73.

Sogyal Rinpoche. *The Tibetan Book of Living and Dying*. London: Rider, 1992.

20
To what extent does Buddhism "deny the self"? The non-self teaching.

Christopher V. Jones

Buddhism has long been associated with the claim that it "denies the self," and that this distinguishes it from all other religious traditions. The applicability of non-self teaching to contemporary ideas about human identity in the West—informed, for example, by comparisons to the findings of cognitive science—is an evolving field. In early Buddhism, the notion that things are non-self is a subtle one, very much born out of Buddhism's Indian heritage, and is easily misconstrued. To understand the original context of non-self teaching, we must locate it in Indian literature, where we first find it expressed, in which the context is the Buddha's attempts to explain experience, suffering, and also rebirth in a setting quite different from any twenty-first-century culture, Buddhist or otherwise.

The "self" in question translates the Sanskrit *ātman*. Insofar as this term works like a reflexive pronoun (similar to the English "myself"), Buddhism has no contention; non-self teaching does not challenge the discreteness of different persons; and, indeed, the desire to end suffering and achieve liberation is premised on the sense that I, in some fashion, exist as an individual. Instead, Buddhist teaching about non-self (Sanskrit: *anātman*; Pali: *anattā*) encourages the attitude that nothing about our person should be mistaken for an enduring, essential kernel of our identity, and so either sought or clung to as something intrinsically valuable. From early in its history, Buddhism identified the view that there is something permanent, unchanging, and worthy of attachment in our experience to be particularly insidious and detrimental to our happiness—a cause of continued suffering in this life, and a significant factor in our rebirth after it.

Most other ancient Indian religious or philosophical traditions that are known to us—Jainism, Brahmanism, and what come to be known as forms of Hinduism—all teach, not unreasonably, that, if our existential condition is characterized by ongoing death and rebirth, then there must be something of us, some "self," that is both the victim and to some extent perpetrator of this process. Literature like the Brahmanical Upaniṣads, some examples of which were contemporaneous to the beginnings of Buddhism, invest great importance in "finding one's self," and in different ways articulate that discovering what is proper to our identity, across this and successive lives, is an important step in liberating ourselves from rebirth. In contrast to this, Buddhism teaches that the search for a self is misguided, and that human experience—including rebirth—can be better understood, and indeed transformed, without need of the idea of there being some enigmatic, somehow valuable center to our identity.

Where Buddhist literature describes things as "not being the self," it frequently situates this teaching in an account of five types of phenomena that can be mistaken for what is either "mine" or "my self": the so-called "heaps" (Sanskrit: *skandhas*; Pali: *khandhas*) to which we become attached. One might naturally think that our physical body, sensations, consciousness, ideas, or attitudes (rough translations of these five heaps) are "us," or that, within these, there is something that endures and so is either our self or a means of locating it. But a key observation in Buddhist teaching is that all things that we experience are transient—our bodies change, our consciousness is in perpetual flux, and our thoughts are never the same twice—such that nothing in our experience of "ourselves" is worthy of attachment: neither intrinsically valuable, nor a trace of something unchanging that we properly are.

It is important to understand that, at its origins, teaching about non-self referred to a kind of introspective strategy of thought: reflection on our lives that does not take any of what we feel or think to be anything more than ephemeral moments in the flow of experience, brought about by antecedent factors that themselves beget new mental events. Beyond this strategy, Buddhist authors developed sophisticated ways of talking about identity and its continuity, without supposing such a thing as an enduring self, by which Buddhism creatively distinguished itself from other Indian systems of thought. This situates Buddhism between two broad views that it takes to be erroneous: that certain kinds of action (karma) cause something about me, i.e. my self, to be reborn after death (so-called "eternalism"), and, on the other hand, the view that no actions have existential consequences, such that bodily death must be the end of my existence (so-called "annihilation-ism"). Buddhism acknowledges the efficacy of actions and so the sorry process of rebirth, in which further consequences to our actions play out, but denies that there is an unchanging self in all this process that moves from one life to the next. Nothing in rebirth is apart from the mechanics of causation and conditioning, which exhaustively explain how moments of our experience come about; there is nothing worthy of calling "the self" hidden within it.

Although teaching about non-self might seem counter-intuitive or unnerving—and, indeed, it made Buddhism a target for philosophical objectors in India and elsewhere—it has at its heart the liberating notion that one's future existence is determined by one's own actions. Ending suffering is not a matter of finding what one truly is, so much as transforming one's self—that is, one's person: a bundle of matter, thoughts, and attitudes—from a state of attachment to things or ideas, and ignorance about what we truly are, to something different. Most expressions of Buddhist teaching, including literature proper to the Theravada and Mahayana traditions, are premised on the idea that liberation is a matter of developing one's character, and particularly the mind, to a state in which afflictions (ignorance, desire, hatred, and so on) do not influence our thoughts or deeds, and that this constitutes nirvana—an experience that is apart from rebirth and, at last, satisfying.

It is also the case that some types of Buddhism, especially forms of Mahayana Buddhism, came to teach differently, and introduce, with varying degrees of caution, the idea that there is something about us—for example, a very basic, unobservable nature or condition of the mind—that endures across lives and is a basis for our identity. Particularly contentious are some expressions of Buddha-nature teaching, in which we sometimes find the claim that our latent potential to achieve the status of a buddha can be called the self. Such ways of expressing the Dharma remain influential across forms of Tibetan and East Asian Buddhism, although these and other traditions remain committed to the idea that Buddhist practice requires the discernment that everyday moments of our experience are nothing more than they appear to be; they neither are nor belong to us, but are the stuff of an ultimately unsatisfying kind of existence that one can, through wisdom and diligence, leave behind.

About the author
Christopher V. Jones is a Bye-Fellow of Selwyn College, and affiliated lecturer and research associate at the Faculty of Divinity, University of Cambridge. A primary focus of his research is the history of Mahayana Buddhist thought in the early centuries of the Common Era, preserved in Sanskrit, Chinese, and Tibetan literature.

Suggestions for further reading

In this book
See Chapters 16 (rebirth), 17 (mind–body), 19 (what is reborn), and 45 (Buddha-nature)

Elsewhere

Collins, Stephen. *Selfless Persons: Imagery and Thought in Theravāda Buddhism*. Cambridge: Cambridge University Press, 1982.

Harvey, Peter. *The Selfless Mind: Personality, Consciousness and Nirvana in Early Buddhism*. London: Curzon Press, 1995.

21
What are the "Four Noble Truths" about?

Arjuna C. B. Ranatunga

The Four Noble Truths form the crux of the Buddha's teachings. They are the focus of his first (formal) sermon, given shortly after his enlightenment, and they recur as a subject throughout his discourses, as recorded in the texts of Buddhism. When they were first taught, a light was said to appear in the world. "The Wheel of the *Dhamma*" was set in motion; a movement was begun.

Essentially, they encompass the subject of suffering (or the unsatisfactoriness of life) and the release from it. Expanded upon, however, they form the basis of what came to be popularly known as the Buddha's 84,000 teachings. One important text reveals that to see one of the four truths is to see them all. So they all actually interpenetrate and coalesce. In this sense, looking at them is like looking at different facets of a cut diamond. We can look at them from different sides, but they are ultimately the same gem.

The four sides or truths are usually presented as: suffering; the cause of suffering; the end of suffering; and the path leading to the end of suffering.

The first truth

The first truth is the truth—or reality—of *dukkha* (Pali; Sanskrit: *duḥkha*). The term is difficult to translate, as it has a wide breadth of meaning. It includes "suffering," as well as the pain, anguish, and deep unsatisfactoriness of life. It includes things like relationship breakups, putting up with things we don't like, growing old or sick, or not getting what we want. The Buddha summarized it by saying that *dukkha* is life with grasping, clinging, attachment. We suffer because we graspingly identify ourselves with things that are impermanent and subject to change, unaware of their being inherently inconstant. Rebirth comes into this, too, since it is seen as part of *dukkha*: to be born is to undergo all of the aforementioned forms of suffering.

The second truth

The second truth stresses that the cause of suffering is, at root, ignorance and "craving." We crave for things to be other than they are, like seeing "the grass to be greener on the other side," while unaware that it is not. It is a kind of discontent, a thirst, an itch. It can cause us, if unchecked, to have an endless flow of desires, attachments, and aversions, which can extend even into future lives. The resulting process of repeated birth and death is called *saṃsāra* in Buddhism. It is further fueled by the three defiling "poisons" of greed, hatred, and delusion (from which stem countless other defilements).

The third truth

The third truth concerns the end of suffering. It proclaims that, when ignorance and craving are eradicated, mental suffering or *dukkha* can no longer exist. This latter principle of cause and effect lies at the very heart of Buddhism. The resulting state of being released from *dukkha* is known as nirvana (Pali: *nibbāna*). It is the ultimate happiness in Buddhist thought, the liberation of the mind, and liberation from rebirth. It is a form of purity and right release, the extinction of craving, ignorance, and all defilements. It is supramundane in nature.

The fourth truth

The fourth truth is the path. It is known as the Noble Eightfold Path, because its development ennobles a person. It encourages a progressive and simultaneous development, in ethical conduct, and meditative calm and insight. It is a "middle path" which avoids the extremes of attachment to sensual indulgence on the one hand, and to self-mortification on the other—neither being too hard on ourselves nor too soft. The Buddha once said that the Noble Path is developed through friendship, companionship, and comradery with admirable people, and that this process of socialization was the whole of the holy life because it enabled people to follow the path.

The eight elements within the Path are: right understanding, right thought, right speech, right action, right livelihood, right effort, right mindfulness, and right meditative concentration. These factors need to be worked on individually as well as together, to convert each factor from its wrong form to its right one.

Right understanding or view consists of recognizing that one's actions have karmic consequences, the existence of a hereafter, our duties to our parents, and the existence of knowledgeable teachers and contemplatives. At a higher level, it is insight into the noble truths. Right thought or resolve involves directing one's thoughts toward non-clinging, kindness, and compassion. Right speech involves not lying, not speaking harshly, not speaking divisively, nor gossiping frivolously. Right action involves not killing living creatures, not taking what's not given (stealing), and not misconducting oneself sexually. Right livelihood involves earning one's living in an honest and upright way, not being overly greedy, nor harming others (human or animal) in one's pursuit of making ends meet. Right effort involves mental cultivation, replacing negative and unwholesome states of mind with positive and wholesome ones during the day and in meditation. Right mindfulness is anchored ethically, and involves developing mindfulness or awareness of: the body's nature, postures and movements, and breathing; feeling tones; mind states; and significant realities such as components of body and mind, mental hindrances, awakening factors, and the

Four Noble Truths. Right concentration is singleness or unification of mind, in the *jhāna*s: deep states of meditative absorption and calm.

There are thus aspects of both wisdom and conduct within these Four Noble Truths. They combine an accurate diagnosis of our fallible human condition, with a principle providing release from this condition (the principle of ethical and psychological cause and effect), as well as prescribing a path toward this release. Together they lead to the fulfillment of one's obligations, as a Buddhist, and to the embodiment of the Enlightened Life.

About the author
Arjuna Ranatunga studied Medicine at Cambridge University and studied Buddhism at Peradeniya University in Sri Lanka, as well as at Sunderland University in the UK. He is the administrator of several online Buddhist groups.

Suggestions for further reading

In this book
See also Chapters 15 (can we know what the historical Buddha taught?), 19 (what is reborn), 23 (nirvana), 24 (enlightenment), and 55 (vows/precepts).

Elsewhere
Harvey, Peter (translator). *The Dhammacakkappavatana Sutta.* 2007. https://www.accesstoinsight.org/tipitaka/sn/sn56/sn56.011.harv.html

Bhikkhu, Thanissaro (translator). *The Gavampati Sutta.* 2020. https://www.dhammatalks.org/suttas/SN/SN56_30.html

Bhikkhu, Thanissaro (translator). *The Mahā Cattārisaka Sutta.* 2008. https://www.accesstoinsight.org/tipitaka/mn/mn.117.than.html

22
What is non-attachment in Buddhism?

Dhivan Thomas Jones

There is an old joke: "Why can't Buddhists vacuum under the sofa?" Answer: "Because they have no attachments." The joke works because non-attachment is regarded as important in Buddhism, despite the term not translating any one term or idea in the tradition. However, the term "non-attachment" can be easily misunderstood to mean emotional independence or indifference, with the idea that Buddhists no longer experience the difficulties of relationships. This misunderstanding partly stems from our modern, positive sense of "attachment" which comes from the work of psychologist John Bowlby. According to Bowlby's attachment theory, human beings come into the world ready to love and become attached to their parents; disruptions in relationships during a child's development can impact their ability to form deep and lasting attachments in later life. The idea of non-attachment in Buddhism, in the light of this, can suggest a kind of coping strategy for people who for whatever reason find relationships difficult.

Several things work against this interpretation of non-attachment, however. Firstly, Buddhist teachings include the development of friendliness (Pali: *mettā*; Sanskrit: *maitrī*), love for all living beings. Secondly, the Buddha emphasized the importance of "spiritual friendship," and the Buddhist tradition is full of deep and lasting love and respect between teachers and students, as well as between friends and family members. Thirdly, the Buddhist ideal of awakening involves a compassionate desire to help others, and not a shrinking away from relationship. So, whatever non-attachment means in Buddhism, it is not a refusal of deep and lasting relationship. This needs to be borne in mind as I turn to three ways in which non-attachment is presented in Buddhism.

The first, relatively straightforward, meaning of non-attachment in Buddhism is practical and even ethical. It concerns the value of renunciation. The Buddha was a renunciate, an ascetic (Pali: *samaṇa*; Sanskrit: *śramana*), who instituted the practice for his followers of undertaking a formal "going forth" from home into the wandering, homeless, monastic life. Many Buddhists have lived out versions of this renunciate lifestyle through the history of Buddhism. While the monastic lifestyle implies non-attachment to home, security, money, personal possessions, and so on, it also involves an inner attitude of renunciation, which is the opposite of a commitment to a life devoted to sensual pleasures (*kāma*). This attitude of renunciation forms an element of the Noble Eightfold Path, the second part of which is "right intention," defined as the mental attitude or intention of renunciation, non-ill-will, and harmlessness. Renunciation of sensual pleasures is not just a lifestyle choice: it is an existential choice about where to look for meaning and purpose in life. The word *kāma*, or "sensual pleasure," does not refer primarily to the pleasures of sex or chocolate, but rather to the values associated with ordinary household life, with wealth, children, and status. The renunciation of sensual pleasures implies non-attachment to ordinary worldly values. This is non-attachment as an ethical orientation toward a renunciate lifestyle, which values the peace of meditation over the pleasures of the world.

Second, while non-attachment as renunciation is a practical decision and practice, non-attachment in personal relationships is more like a strategy or way of life. Verse 212 in the popular Buddhist collection of verses the *Dhammapada* might seem to sum up the Buddhist attitude to personal relationships:

> Grief is born from love.
> Fear is born from love.
> For one released from love,
> there is no grief—whence fear?

Since love gives rise to grief and fear, one should steer clear of love. The same is said of affection, delight, desire, and craving (*Dhammapada* verses 213–216). There are stories in early Buddhist discourses which show the Buddha giving solace to recently-bereaved parents and grandparents with the advice that "grief, sorrow, pain, misery and despair are born of love, brought forth by love." The Buddha's advice is to avoid love, by which he means the human tendency to base a sense of well-being on specific relationships. This kind of non-attachment seems rather heartless, but another story helps explain it. When the Buddha's friend and disciple Sāriputta died, the Buddha's attendant Ānanda, also a friend of Sāriputta, became disoriented with grief and loss. But the Buddha helped Ānanda by asking whether Sāriputta's death had taken away from him all those good qualities that his friend represented. The answer is, of course, "no." The Buddha reminded Ānanda that we know that all conditioned things pass away, that people are born and die, and there is little we can do about this. But we can pay attention, not to feelings of grief and loss, but to what we appreciate and admire in those we love. This kind of non-attachment to people can be liberating.

There is a third and deeper meaning of non-attachment in Buddhism, of being a result or fruit of insight into the nature of our existence as humans. According to Buddhist doctrine, the way that the mind works involves clinging (*upādāna*). This tendency toward grasping, holding on or appropriation (making one's own) of experience happens based on a fundamental craving or desire (Pali: *taṇhā*; Sanskrit: *tṛṣṇā*) in our nature, and, according to Buddhism, it results in continued existence in this life and in future lives. The whole of what Buddhists call *saṃsāra*, or the cycle of birth and death, is rooted in the tangle of desire and attachment that continuously plays out in human life, and this is the root cause of pain or unsatisfactoriness (Pali: *dukkha*; Sanskrit: *duḥkha*).

The Buddhist path involves gradually unraveling this tangle and reducing the craving that fuels it. This culminates in a deep letting-go of the sense of "I," "me," and "mine," which goes along with clinging. This kind of non-attachment involves a disenchantment with and dispassion toward worldly life and values, as a corollary of an understanding of the nature of our existence as humans. This understanding implies the end of unnecessary unsatisfactoriness, so that non-attachment, as the result or fruit of Buddhist practice, is a blissful release.

About the author
Dhivan Thomas Jones is a Lecturer in Philosophy and Religious Studies at the University of Chester, UK. His research is mainly in the area of early Buddhist philosophy.

Suggestions for further reading

In this book
Chapters 20 (non-self teaching), 21 (Four Noble Truths), 23 (nirvana), 24 (enlightenment), and 63 (non-attachment and compassion).

Elsewhere
Murcott, Susan. *First Buddhist Women: Poems and Stories of Awakening*. Berkeley, Parallax Press, 2006. A study of the *Therīgāthā*.

Norman, K. R. (translator). *Poems of Early Buddhist Monks (Theragāthā)*. Oxford: Pali Text Society, 1997. Verses ascribed to early monks, recording their renunciation, non-attachment, and release.

Rhys Davids, C. A. F., and K. R. Norman (translators). *Poems of Early Buddhist Nuns (Therīgāthā)*. Oxford: Pali Text Society, 1989. Verses ascribed to early nuns, whose stories illustrate non-attachment.

23
What is nirvana?

Arjuna C. B. Ranatunga

Nirvana (Pali: *nibbāna*) is the "good goal" of which the Buddha spoke; and to work toward this provides ultimate meaning to the life of a Buddhist. It is attained by those who, through purification in ethics, meditation, and liberating wisdom, have become "noble disciples." These have seen it as a timeless reality beyond any form or suffering (Pali: *dukkha*) and any type of rebirth; and the highest noble disciple, the arhat, has fully experienced it and gone beyond rebirths.

Nirvana refers to the blowing-out or extinction of craving. During the life of the arhat, it is their experience of the extinction of the "fires" of greed/attachment, hatred, and delusion. It is the definitive end of the spiritual ignorance, craving, and grasping that bring suffering during life and cause those who are not enlightened to be reborn in some form. Arhats experience nirvana as the culmination of the Noble Eightfold Path.

When an arhat dies, without any rebirth, nirvana is the extinction of all the conditioned mental and physical processes that he or she was previously composed of as an individual. The state of an arhat beyond death is beyond description, although some passages in the early texts suggest that it is a radiant, radically transformed state of consciousness.

The Buddha affirmed nirvana as a definite, existing reality in a text called the *Udāna*, within the *Khuddaka Nikāya*:

> There exists, monks, that sphere where there is neither earth, water, fire nor wind [= the four basic elements of the material world]; nor the spheres of infinite space, infinite consciousness, no-thingness, or neither-perception-nor-non-perception [= the four most subtle, formless, rebirths]; neither this world, nor a world beyond, nor both, nor sun-and-moon; there, monks, I say there is no coming, nor going, nor maintenance, nor falling away, nor arising [all aspects of the cycle of rebirths]; it is really unsupported, lacking in continued temporal existence, and objectless. This truly is the end of the painful (*dukkha*). (*Udāna* 80)
>
> Monks, there exists the not born, not come into being, not made, and not constructed. Had there not been the not born, not come into being, not made, not constructed, there would not be made known, here, an escape from that which is born, come into being, made, and constructed. It is because there is the not born, not come into being, not made, and not constructed that there is made known escape from the born, come into being, made, and constructed. (*Udāna* 81)

Being beyond time and limitation, nirvana is beyond the many kinds of heavenly rebirths that the Buddha taught as existing; for even the most refined, long-lasting rebirth eventually ends in death and further rebirths. There are a range of synonyms for nirvana. In one Pali text, the following are given:

> Monks, I shall teach you the unconditioned and the path leading to the unconditioned. . . . the uninclined and the path leading to the uninclined . . . the without intoxicating inclination . . . truth/reality . . . the beyond . . . the subtle . . . the very-hard-to-see . . . the undecaying . . . the lasting . . . the undisintegrating . . . the non-manifestive . . . the unproliferated . . . the peaceful . . . the deathless . . . the sublime . . . the auspicious . . . the secure . . . the destruction of craving . . . the marvelous . . . the amazing . . . the unailing . . . the unailing state . . . nirvana . . . the unafflicted . . . non-attachment . . . purity . . . freedom . . . the unclinging . . . the island (amidst the flood) . . . the shelter . . . the place of safety . . . the refuge . . . the destination. (*Saṃyutta Nikāya* IV. 362–373)

Experientially, during life, and beyond death, nirvana is a kind of "stopping" of any kind of "world": that is, of conditioned, limited realms, with all their baggage, stresses, problems, and ephemeral delights, and also of any bad actions. When not experiencing this, a living arhat has great calm, equanimity, and imperturbability, and is open to experiencing joy at the beauty of wild nature, such as mossy rocks. It is known as the highest bliss, as seen in verse 204 of the *Dhammapada*.

Ordinary people, through ethical discipline, meditative calm, and contemplative insight into the impermanent nature of the things we cling to, can build up the qualities that enable them to become a noble person, who gains insight that sees beyond the conditioned world to the unconditioned nirvana. Then, at arhatship, this is fully experienced.

For the Mahayana, though, the advanced bodhisattvas choose to stay within the round of rebirths even when they reach a level at which they could leave it and enter nirvana. They then use their time to further help others, and build up the qualities needed for perfect buddhahood, which is seen as the definitive kind of nirvana.

About the author

Arjuna Ranatunga studied Medicine at Cambridge University and studied Buddhism at Peradeniya University in Sri Lanka, as well as at Sunderland University in the UK. He is the administrator of several online Buddhist groups.

Suggestions for further reading

In this book
See Chapters 5 (texts), 10 (buddhahood), 13 (bodhisattva), 21 (Four Noble Truths), 24 (enlightenment), 25 (saints), 44 (bodhisattva vow), and 45 (Buddha-nature).

Elsewhere
Collins, Steven. *Nirvana: Concept, Imagery, Narrative.* Cambridge: Cambridge University Press, 2010.

Gethin, Rupert. *The Foundations of Buddhism.* Oxford: Oxford University Press, 1998: pages 72–79.

Harvey, Peter. *An Introduction to Buddhism: Teachings, History and Practices* (2nd edition). Cambridge: Cambridge University Press, 2013: pages 73–81.

Pasanno, Ajahn, and Ajahn Amaro. *The Island: An Anthology of the Buddha's Teachings on Nibbāna.* Redwood, CA: Abhayagiri Monastic Foundation, 2009. https://forestsangha.org/teachings/books/the-island-teachings-on-nibbana?language=English

24
What is it to be "enlightened" or "awakened"?

Peter Harvey

The term *bodhi* means "enlightenment" or "awakening." At *bodhi*, according to one Pali text, there arises "vision, knowledge, wisdom, true knowledge, and light." "*Bodhi*" is related to the verb meaning "understand," so it is an awakening from ignorance. As an "awakening," *bodhi* does not mean the awakening *of* something, i.e., a beginning of something, but a final awakening *from* delusion, etc. and *to* deep insight into the nature of reality.

To be enlightened, in a Buddhist sense, is to be completely free of any attachment, hatred, or delusion; to have experienced the complete destruction of greed, craving, grasping, and clinging, whether in *attachment* to certain things or *aversion* to them, and the destruction of spiritual ignorance in the sense of an ingrained blindness to, and misperception of, the nature of reality. For early Buddhism and the Theravada school, this is ignorance of the fundamental realities known as the Four Noble Truths.

The kind of person who has attained such enlightenment is called an arhat (Sanskrit; Pali: *arahat*). He or she has ended the last five of a set of ten spiritual "fetters," having previously ended the first five:

1. "Self-identity view": taking any aspect of body or mind as a permanent, essential Self or as owned by Self;
2. vacillation in commitment to the Buddha, Dharma, and Sangha and to the worth of ethical discipline;
3. grasping at rules and observances;
4. sensual desire;
5. ill-will;
6. attachment to subtle forms seen in deep meditations and the rebirth worlds corresponding to these;
7. attachment to the even deeper formless meditation states and worlds;
8. the "I am" conceit: self-centeredness, self-importance, perhaps now in the form of lingering spiritual pride, in taking "I/me" as superior to others, inferior to them, or even in a complacent or competitive sense as equal;
9. restlessness;
10. spiritual ignorance.

Arhats are free of the conditions for any further rebirth, even in heavenly realms linked to deep meditation. They have the joy and relief of freedom, liberation from any mental suffering in this life, and from any more rebirths and the various kinds of suffering that these entail.

Arhats are often also described as having destroyed the four deeply ingrained mental faults, which Buddhists call "intoxicating inclinations," "taints," "outflows," or "cankers," toward: sensual pleasures, continued existence in some way of being, fixed views, and spiritual ignorance—all of which inclinations are conditioned *by* spiritual ignorance.

Of the first five fetters, the first three are ended when someone becomes a "stream-enterer:" one who has definitively entered the "stream" that is the Noble Eight-factored Path, which, according to the Pali texts, will lead to arhatship within seven lives at most.

None of these lives will be at less than a human level, i.e., as an animal, frustrated ghost, or in a hell.

The fetters of desire for sense-pleasures and ill-will, anger, are greatly weakened for the person who reaches the stage after the stream-enterer, the "once-returner." These two fetters are then completely ended when a person becomes a "non-returner" to rebirths below the higher heavens, the next stage.

Spiritually transformed people from those on the brink of stream-entry upward are known as "noble ones." Among these, the more advanced ones are rarer, and more likely to be monks or nuns than lay people.

For Theravada Buddhists, all arhats have fully attained enlightenment, as they have ended all defilements. Beyond this, some, like the Buddha, also have meditation-based special knowledges or psychic powers. The Buddha was an arhat himself, but his knowledges are seen to have gone far beyond that of other arhats. He said that what he taught, compared what he knew, was like a handful of leaves compared to the leaves in a forest. In time, especially in the Mahayana traditions, he came to be seen as omniscient. All traditions see him as a *sammā-sambuddha* (Pali; Sanskrit: *samyak-sambuddha*), a "perfectly and completely enlightened one," who discovered enlightenment and the path to it himself, and taught these to others. Such rare beings were also found in some past ages and eons, and will also arise in future ones.

All schools of Buddhism accept that the universe is huge, and has many inhabited worlds as well as our own. All say that perfect buddhas are rare on earth, but the Mahayana talks of many perfect buddhas spread through the universe, some of which have generated Pure Lands, where the conditions for attaining enlightenment are ideal. The Mahayana urges all to aspire to become perfect buddhas, by treading the long path of the bodhisattva, the "being for enlightenment/buddhahood" over many, many lives, so as not to aspire for the quicker exit from the round of rebirths attained by the arhat. At the advanced levels of this path, bodhisattvas are seen to become heavenly savior beings, close to perfect buddhas in their powers. They and such buddhas of other worlds are also seen to incarnate on earth—for example, as the Dalai Lamas—to help and teach devotees. In the Mahayana, delusion-transcending wisdom is variously described as seeing: how all phenomena are empty of a separate nature or existence, due to being deeply inter-conditioned; how all we experience is shaped by the mind, perhaps indeed being only mental in nature; how we all have an inner Buddha-nature, which also infuses everything; and how every item in the universe reflects and in a sense includes everything else. A key idea is that when we truly understand the nature of the conditioned world, we see it is non-separate from, indistinguishable from, nirvana.

About the author
Peter Harvey is Professor of Buddhist Studies (retired), University of Sunderland, UK, and co-founder of the UK Association for Buddhist Studies. He researches Buddhist ethics, meditation, and early Buddhist thought.

Suggestions for further reading

In this book
See Chapters 10 (buddhahood), 20 (non-self teaching) 21 (Four Noble Truths), 23 (nirvana), 25 (saints), 28 (kinds of meditation), and 45 (Buddha-nature)

Elsewhere
Gethin, Rupert. *The Foundations of Buddhism*. Oxford: Oxford University Press, 1998: pages 33–34, 74–84, 226–234.

Harvey, Peter. *An Introduction to Buddhism: Teachings, History and Practices* (2nd edition). Cambridge: Cambridge University Press, 2013: pages 29, 73–87, 114–193.

Williams, Paul. *Mahāyāna Buddhism: The Doctrinal Foundations* (2nd edition). London and New York: Routledge & Kegan Paul, 2009: pages 63–148, 214–218.

25
What kinds of "saints" does Buddhism have?

Arjuna C. B. Ranatunga

According to every school of Buddhism, people can be divided into different categories and, between schools, there is some overlap. Generally speaking, there are ordinary people, noble disciples, bodhisattvas, and buddhas. People who are following the Buddhist path can move upwards through these categories, to some extent.

Ordinary people
The technical term for an "ordinary person" means "one of the many folk." People in this category are fairly worldly-minded, and have not yet attained any of the noble states described below. They generally see no harm in sensual pleasure and lament when touched by woe. They lack insight into the three characteristics of existence (impermanence, unsatisfactoriness, and non-self) or the Four Noble Truths. Some include priests and contemplatives who go to the other extreme, and self-mortify, thus missing the moderation and balance of the middle path. All of this is considered as being conducive to suffering.

Some Buddhists will still be in this category, but the more committed, with strong faith in the Buddha, the Dharma, and the Sangha, ethical and mental discipline, and strong and maturing insight into the three characteristics of existence, are beyond this level.

Noble disciples

According to the Pali texts of Theravada Buddhism, there are four main types of noble disciple: those who have attained four irreversible spiritual breakthroughs. If one also includes those definitively on the path to these, then there are eight noble disciples.

The first of the four main noble disciples is the stream-enterer, who has attained some direct insight into the truth of the Buddha's teachings. They have entered the stream that leads to nirvana (Pali: *nibbāna*) within seven lives at most, none at less than a human level.

The second main type of noble disciple is the once-returner, one who has considerably reduced sensual desire and ill-will. These two fetters constrain, imprison, and bind the mind by their very nature. So the mind of a once-returner is more liberated than that of a stream-enterer. Consequently, their future rebirths will include only one more in the sensual sphere, i.e., at levels below the higher heavens.

The third main type of noble disciple is the non-returner, who has completely eliminated ill-will and sensual desire, and thus will not be born again as a being in the sensual sphere.

The fourth main type is the arhat: the perfected disciple, or "worthy one," in Buddhist terms, an enlightened saint. They have eliminated through wisdom and meditative development all ten of the defiling and mentally limiting fetters, including attachment to subtle realms, restlessness, conceit, and ignorance. They have laid down the burden, are bearers of their final body, and will not be reborn. They have attained nirvana.

Bodhisattvas

Early Buddhism recognized that every buddha prepares for buddhahood by being a bodhisattva (a being oriented toward enlightenment) but then it was also believed that every eon of time only had a handful of buddhas. Mahayana Buddhism expanded on this idea by positing that everyone could follow the bodhisattva path and become a buddha, in this or another part of the universe.

This form of Buddhism recognizes numerous celestial bodhisattvas that can help beings on their way to enlightenment.

Bodhisattvas are seen as highly developed, powerful, and compassionate beings. They go through an incalculably long process of evolution through many lives to perfect themselves to the point where they can become a buddha, while compassionately helping others. They are said to go through stages or levels of purification, known as *bhūmi*s. Traditionally, there are ten in Mahayana Buddhism. Those bodhisattvas who have attained the highest stages (8–10) become celestial savior beings.

Buddhas

Buddhas are said in early Buddhism to be of three types, corresponding to three types of enlightenment. The highest of these is a *sammā sambuddha* (Pali: Sanskrit: *samyak sambuddha*), a perfectly self-awakened one; often, the term "buddhas" refers specifically to this kind of perfect buddha. A *sammā sambuddha* (like Gautama Buddha) is one who becomes enlightened at a time when the Dharma is lost to the world, and who goes on to teach, establishing a Buddhist dispensation or culture. In Theravada Buddhism each eon of time only has a handful of *sammā sambuddha*s. Secondly, there are arhats, who awaken to the full experience of nirvana, by following the teachings of a *sammā sambuddha* but lack the extensive extra knowledges of a perfect buddha. They are sometimes referred to as *sāvaka buddha*s (hearer buddhas). The third type of buddha is known as a silent or private buddha (*pacceka buddha*), as they attain enlightenment unaided in their final birth but are unable to teach the way effectively to others. They also, though, become enlightened when the teaching of a buddha is not known.

Mahayana Buddhism argued that there should be only one final goal, that of perfect buddhahood, which is made possible because, within the universe at large, an eon of time can have as many buddhas as there are grains of sand on the banks of the River

Ganges. In some of its forms, it also upholds that each sentient being has Buddha-nature within them and is a potential buddha. For the Mahayana, perfect buddhas are in kinds of super-heavens, though they may also choose to incarnate in our world.

To conclude, all schools of Buddhism revere saints of some sort, namely those who have purified themselves and developed their minds, to the extent that they can understand others, feel compassion toward them, and help lead them out of suffering. These saints are known as the noble (*ariya*) Sangha—the community of enlightened and partially enlightened beings. The leader and inspiration for all these saints is a fully enlightened *sammā sambuddha*. Their goal is to emulate such a buddha's example, to varying extents. In doing this, they focus first on their own ethical and spiritual development, and then they help others to cross the ocean of birth and rebirth, in order to arrive at the safe ground of nirvana.

About the author
Arjuna Ranatunga studied Medicine at Cambridge University and studied Buddhism at Peradeniya University in Sri Lanka, as well as at Sunderland University in the UK. He is the administrator of several online Buddhist groups.

Suggestions for further reading

In this book
See Chapters 8 (is Buddhism atheistic, non-theistic, or theistic?), 10 (buddhahood), 13 (bodhisattva), 23 (nirvana), 24 (enlightenment), 44 (bodhisattva vow), 45 (Buddha-nature), 48 (celestial beings in Tibetan Buddhism), and 55 (vows/precepts).

Elsewhere
Harvey, Peter. *An Introduction to Buddhism: Teachings, History and Practices* (2nd edition). Cambridge: Cambridge University Press, 2013: pages 76–87, 151–193.

Prebish, Charles S., and Damien Keown. *Introducing Buddhism*. London and New York: Routledge, 2006: pages 54–55, 98–105.

Rahula, Walpola. "Bodhisattva Ideal in Buddhism." In *Gems of Buddhist Wisdom*, 461–471. Malaysia: Buddhist Missionary Society, 1996.

Part Four
What the Buddha taught (2)
Meditation

26
Why do Buddhists meditate?

Sarah Shaw

It is a rare pleasure to do something because we consciously like and choose to do it. The Buddhist texts say that the Buddha, when he was a child, was left for the first time on his own, under a rose-apple tree. It was a happy day: his father, the king, was leading the ceremonial plowing. So the boy decided to experiment, he said later, and stumbled across something we now call meditation. Legends say he was exploring his breath. He noticed that as he watched its rise and fall, he could train it, and after a while he spontaneously entered a state of great joy and unification. He was still applying his mind and he was still exploring. Doing this with interest allowed his mind to settle. Great joy and happiness arose. He entered what Buddhists call *jhāna*, a state free from hankerings for the senses, ill-will or annoyance, and trouble—which had wisdom, too. His mind and body experienced great unification. Then, on the night of his awakening, he developed these meditations, and they became a central part of his path to liberation: right effort, right mindfulness, and concentration.

The main thing about the state he experienced as a child is that it produced a great happiness. Later in life, when he practiced self-mortifications and other meditations in his pursuit of awakening, he realized this was key to finding the path to wisdom. The mind needed to be refreshed, unified, and, importantly, interested, if wisdom was going to be helpful. So the state he remembered as a child became the basis of all four of the *jhānas* he later described. The second drops the applying of the mind and exploring, because joy becomes so powerful; there is an internal silence which needs no thought. The third drops joy, resting in happiness with an increase of alertness and mindful alertness. The fourth *jhāna* drops even happiness, finding a balance characterized by equanimity, the purification of feeling so that it is untroubled by happiness or sorrow, pleasure or pain. From here, the Buddha taught, it is possible to develop meditation further: to explore the very foundations of the mind's constructings, in formless meditation, or to develop the mind's power, so that it is possible to know the minds of others or to remember past lives. All of these later practices need a basis in the fourth *jhāna*, where there is equanimity and balance, so that the practitioner is not swayed by partiality.

So why do them? The Buddha said that some, and sometimes all, of these practices were important for the path, to reach awakening. If the mind can become still, and rest in a meditation like loving-kindness, which pervades all directions with a wish for the happiness of all beings, it will not hanker after sensory gratification. It will know a peace that can then take the practitioner to insight, and the final goal. Not all practitioners need to cultivate one or more of these states. But most do. Most importantly, most Buddhists who try them out want to practice them. Meditations of this kind are restorative, bringing the mind to health and vitality, as well as offering a way ahead based on peace and confidence.

Variations on meditation practices are found in all the Buddhist traditions, which vary greatly in their approaches. The Zen practice of *shikantaza* (just sitting), for instance, does not emphasize *jhāna*. Instead, all events in the mind and body are noted as awareness grows and deepens in "just sitting." Meditation is matched with insight into rise and fall: how events in mind and body come into being and pass away. Meditation is often accompanied by other activities. In a Soto Zen temple, morning *sesshins* (meditation practice) include paying respects to the shrine and to the cushion, acknowledging the presence of other meditators, sitting together in *shikantaza*, walking together in silence around the temple, and offering and unpacking the ceremonial rice meal. All of these support the meditation. The alertness of the meditation then nourishes the walking, chanting, and paying of respects.

Meditation is, in the end, there as something people want to do. It makes people feel better, setting them on a path that is sometimes not comfortable. Meditation can reveal aspects about oneself and the mind that are not necessarily what we want to find. But it brings, too, a way of understanding them, coming to know them and helping one feel at ease with them. It also transforms their potential into something else: hatred and irritation can become, through mindfulness, great joy and love. Desire for sense objects become peace and contentment, when not fed by stimuli from outside. Meditation brings peace and fulfillment, as it clears the mind and body of hindrances and problems.

Sometimes people think they have to empty the mind to meditate. Anyone who has tried this knows that this is not possible! Rather, our minds are like bees, to use an ancient image. They need to go somewhere, have something to explore and something to keep them occupied. Buddhist calm meditation encourages the practitioner to become engaged and interested in a simple, unifying meditation object, like the breath, rather than trying to empty the mind of all thoughts. Gradually, over time, an object like the breath becomes more interesting than the "flowers" elsewhere: the breath feels rich and engaging, the pollen more satisfying. Wisdom is easier to integrate when found in peace. The mind's natural disposition to be curious, explore, and criticize finds an object where these aspects are changed, and come to settle in one place. Wisdom arises instead of criticism; peace instead of restlessness and doubt. Insights need this sustenance if they are to be balanced and helpful to us.

Why would anyone want to practice meditation? The best answer comes from the life stories of the Buddha and his awakened followers. It is sometimes said that wisdom is more important than meditation in Buddhism. But wisdom, the Buddha said, needs meditation, just as meditation needs wisdom (*Dhammapada* verse 282). And if we look at the stories of the Buddha and his followers *after* their awakening, we find they all still like to practice meditation. It was not just a necessary chore on the way to enlightenment. They clearly enjoyed it, and found it was where their minds felt most at home. Perhaps that is the reason why most other Buddhists meditate too and find it so helpful for daily life.

About the Author
Sarah Shaw is the Khyentse Foundation Reader in Buddhist Studies at the University of South Wales, UK, a fellow of the Oxford Centre for Buddhist Studies, and a member of the Faculty of Oriental Studies, University of Oxford, UK. She researches Buddhist meditation, ritual, narrative, and chant.

Suggestions for further reading

In this book
Chapters 21 (Four Noble Truths), 27 (mindfulness), 28 (kinds of meditation) and 41 (Zen).

Elsewhere
Gethin, Rupert. *Foundations of Buddhism*. Oxford: Oxford University Press, 1998: pages 174–201.

Roebuck, Valerie. *The Dhammapada*. London: Penguin, 2010.

Shaw, Sarah. *Spirit of Buddhist Meditation*. London: Routledge, 2009.

Thera, Nyanaponika, and Hellmuth Hecker. *Great Disciples of the Buddha*. Boston, MA: Wisdom Publications, 1997.

27
What is "mindfulness" in Buddhism? And does it differ from modern secular "mindfulness"?

Tse-fu Kuan

The quasi-term "mindfulness" is an English translation of *sati* in Pali or *smṛti* in Sanskrit. This Indic word originally meant "memory," but the Buddha assigned the word new meanings consonant with his own system of thought. "Mindfulness" has become the most popular English translation or even the only possible translation of *sati*. What does "mindfulness" mean in the context of early Buddhism? How does it differ from modern secular "mindfulness"? These are the questions I attempt to address.

Somewhat inadequately rendered into English as "mindfulness," the Buddhist term *sati/smṛti* covers a much wider range of mental faculties than "mindfulness" as Western psychology usually describes it. Let us first look at this term in early Buddhist literature, which includes the *suttas*/sutras (discourses) that were transmitted by early Buddhist schools. Among these schools, only the Theravada survives until today, and so their corpus of *suttas* in Pali is the only complete and extant collection of early Buddhist discourses, and I take this as my primary source, highlighting five aspects of it before comparing these with secular mindfulness.

Mindfulness in early Buddhism: five aspects

Basic definition of mindfulness: memory and recognition
One Pali text describes "mindfulness" as "A noble disciple has mindfulness, possesses supreme 'memory and discrimination,' remembers and recollects what was done and said long ago" (*Sutta* 48:10 of the *Saṃyutta Nikāya*). Mindfulness here involves not only memory or recollection, but also discrimination, which entails the ability to recognize various objects and experiences.

Simple awareness
This aspect of mindfulness involves noticing what is happening in the present moment, whether in daily activities or meditation. One of the most popular texts on this, the *Satipaṭṭhāna Sutta* ("Discourse on the Establishments of Mindfulness") states:

> Breathing in long, he knows: "I breathe in long"; breathing out long, he knows: "I breathe out long." Breathing in short, he knows: "I breathe in short" . . .
>
> When walking (standing, sitting, lying down, or however his body is disposed), he knows: "I am walking (standing, etc.)" . . .
>
> When feeling a pleasant feeling, he knows: "I feel a pleasant feeling"; when feeling a painful feeling, he knows: "I feel a painful feeling" . . .

So this kind of "mindfulness" consists of non-judgmental observation and recognition. The mind is simply aware of an object in the present moment without evaluating the object, the subject (i.e., the observer or the mind) or the interaction between the two.

Protective awareness
With mindfulness, one is further aware of how the mind reacts to objects. In this instance, mindfulness is related to the restraint of the senses and requires judgment. One Pali text gives a simile about a city with six gates and the gatekeeper keeps out strangers and admits acquaintances. Here "city" stands for the individual.

"Six gates" stand for the six senses, namely the eye, ear, nose, tongue, tactile organ, and mental organ. "Gatekeeper" represents mindfulness. This aspect of mindfulness is protective. The six senses are guarded by mindfulness so that evil unwholesome states do not flow into the mind through the sense-doors.

Protective awareness is also conducive to physical well-being. One text records that King Pasenadi (a contemporary of the Buddha) was overweight. He followed the Buddha's instruction on mindfulness so that he was aware of moderation in the food he ate. Just as a gatekeeper controls the inflow of people, mindfulness helped Pasenadi control his intake of food and become slim.

Introspective awareness
Mindfulness can have an introspective function, which serves as a remedial measure when "protective awareness" fails to act. If evil unwholesome states arise in one's mind, one may activate mindfulness in order to recognize them and get rid of them in time. One text uses a simile to describe this function of mindfulness: "Suppose a man were wounded by an arrow smeared with poison . . . A surgeon would cut around the opening of the wound, then he would probe for the arrow with a probe, then he would pull out the arrow and would expel the poisonous humor." Here, "wound" is a designation for the six senses. "Poisonous humor" and "arrow" represent ignorance and craving, respectively. "Probe" stands for mindfulness (*Sunakkhatta Sutta* of the *Majjhima Nikāya*). Again, mindfulness operates in the context of the six senses, but here it acts as an antidote to the unwholesome states that have invaded an individual rather than a preventive or a guard against them.

Constructive conceptualization
This function of mindfulness does not happen at the same time as perceiving things through our senses. It consists in forming constructive conceptions based on memories. Mindfulness of the Triple Gem, Buddha, Dharma, and Sangha, is one example of this. Here, mindfulness involves "recollection." A Buddhist constantly calls to mind these three "jewels" and recollects their noble and

beneficial qualities. Another example, mindfulness of death, according to the texts, could go like this. When day has passed and night has commenced, practitioners remind themselves that there are many chances of death and that they may die at any time, so that they must prepare right now for their afterlife or liberation. They thus exercise mindfulness to identify if they have any evil unwholesome states, which would be a hindrance to them if they die tonight, and abandon those states. Accordingly, mindfulness of death serves as a means of motivating introspective awareness and protective awareness.

The well-known *Mettā Sutta* ("Discourse on Loving-kindness") describes the cultivation of loving-kindness (*mettā*) as a practice of mindfulness. It compares the practitioner to a mother of only one son and all beings to her only son. This practice entails imagination. Practitioners first imagine themselves as a mother with just one son and how much she cares about him. Through this "constructive imagination," they develop boundless loving-kindness toward all beings in the same way as the mother loves her only son.

So mindfulness helps Buddhists move toward positive states of mind, which conduce to the calm and insight that are necessary in the Buddhist path to liberation.

Comparison between Buddhist mindfulness and secular "mindfulness"

Modern secular "mindfulness," which has been derived from Buddhism, is concerned about worldly welfare, including physical and mental health. Mindfulness in Buddhism can also promote well-being in the present life. For example, mindfulness helped Pasenadi control his weight! But, ultimately, Buddhist mindfulness is aimed at the supreme goal, nirvana, which transcends the world; it can lead one to liberation from the cycle of rebirths, whereas secular "mindfulness" cannot.

Contemporary psychology has adopted mindfulness as a measure to enhance health by preventing or reducing emotional distress and cognitive vulnerability to such distress. Scholars have developed such programs as "mindfulness-based cognitive therapy" (MBCT) and "mindfulness-based stress reduction" (MBSR). The secular mindfulness that many scholars have advocated is non-judgmental, present-centered awareness in which each thought, feeling, or sensation that arises in the attentional field is acknowledged and accepted as it is, without reacting to it. Such mindfulness represents just one of the diverse aspects of Buddhist mindfulness: that is, "simple awareness" discussed above.

By contrast, as I've shown, there are more dimensions to Buddhist mindfulness than this. Besides simple awareness, Buddhist mindfulness also encompasses protective awareness, introspective awareness, and constructive conceptualization, all of which have evaluative or judgmental elements. It steers the processes of the mind in such a way that one's cognition is rendered wholesome in a Buddhist sense. The evaluative aspects with ethical significance are central to mindfulness in Buddhism. This marks the major divergence from modern secular "mindfulness." As an excellent scholar of Buddhism, Bhikkhu Anālayo, says: "Mindfulness has become a commercialized product and as such has been taught, for example, to improve the combat skills of soldiers, a development that is rather problematic from a Buddhist ethical perspective."

About the author
Tse-fu Kuan is Associate Professor at Yuan Ze University, Taiwan. He works on early Buddhist literature in Pali and Chinese.

Suggestions for further reading

In this book
See Chapters 5 (texts), 26 (why Buddhists meditate), 28 (kinds of meditation), 60 (engaged Buddhism), 62 (compassion), and 71 (methods of science).

Elsewhere

Anālayo, Bhikkhu. "The Myth of McMindfulness." *Mindfulness* 11 (2020): 472–479.

Bodhi, Bhikkhu. "What Does Mindfulness Really Mean? A Canonical Perspective." *Contemporary Buddhism* 12(1) (2011): 19–39.

Gethin, Rupert. "On Some Definitions of Mindfulness." *Contemporary Buddhism* 12(1) (2011): 263–279.

Kuan, Tse-fu. *Mindfulness in Early Buddhism: New Approaches through Psychology and Textual Analysis of Pali, Chinese and Sanskrit Sources.* London: Routledge, 2008.

Online translation of the *Satipaṭṭhāna Sutta*: https://www.accesstoinsight.org/tipitaka/mn/mn.010.nysa.html

28
What kinds of meditation are there in Buddhism?

Dhivan Thomas Jones

Meditation is a distinctively Buddhist activity, at least in the popular imagination. The image of the Buddha sitting beneath the Bodhi tree, cross-legged, deep in meditation, represents the defining moment of the Buddha's life, as he gained awakening (*bodhi*) in the third watch of the night. The Buddha went on to teach a range of meditative methods, with different aims and for different kinds of people. The Buddhist traditions have added further methods, so that Buddhist meditation now includes a huge repertoire of practices, with their own associated preparatory stages, practical instructions, and associated theories. Meditation in Buddhism is too diverse to be systematized, but this diversity is deceptive. Borrowing words from the Buddha, the many kinds of meditation in Buddhism have one taste: the taste of liberation. I will summarize the range under six headings, which are also some of the various words in Buddhism for what we call "meditation," including the word *bhāvanā* or "development," the most important term for the cultivation of positive states.

Firstly, *mindfulness* (Pali *sati*; Sanskrit *smṛti*) is the cultivation of deliberate awareness or recollection, and is the indispensable basis for mental transformation. Mindfulness is a faculty to be developed through constant practice, while sitting, walking, standing, or lying down; in short, in all postures and all activities. Mindfulness implies being present to what is happening, turning toward the content of experience, rather than drifting with the tendency to distraction and escape. Mindfulness also implies clear knowing from moment to moment, and a constant carefulness regarding thoughts, speech, and actions. The *Satipaṭṭhāna Sutta* ("Discourse on the Establishments of Mindfulness") in the Pali texts presents a range of meditative exercises for seeing the true nature of the body, feelings, the mind, and Buddhist teachings, which can be undertaken based on mindfulness. This discourse has profoundly influenced Buddhist meditation methods, especially in Theravada lands and in the modern West.

The second kind of meditation is *absorption* (Pali: *jhāna*; Sanskrit: *dhyāna*). This method is pre-Buddhist, having its origins in the ancient yoga tradition of India, with features in common with shamanism worldwide. The Buddha learned methods of absorption from meditation teachers of his day, and later worked them into his own teaching. The meditator, alone, in a comfortable seated posture, takes attention to a simple aspect of sensual experience, whether this be a colored disc, a mantra, a tactile sensation, or the breath. By constantly returning to this single point of awareness, his or her awareness undergoes a profound shift into an interior absorption that is blissful and self-sufficient. Such meditative experience transforms the meditator's sense of what is really worthwhile. Early Buddhist texts describe meditative absorption in a formula with eight stages and attractive similes. While dedicated absorption meditation is mostly for monastic specialists, the quality of peacefulness or calm (*samatha*) that arises from a degree of absorption is a valuable discovery for all meditators.

Third, there is *insight* (Pali: *vipassanā*; Sanskrit: *vipaśyanā*). The development of insight, together with calm, is another way in which the Buddha is recorded as teaching meditation. Insight concerns seeing deeply into the three characteristics of conditioned existence: namely, unsatisfactoriness, impermanence, and non-self. Such seeing may be the result of formalized meditative reflection. In the *Ānāpānasati Sutta* ("Discourse on Mindfulness of Breathing"), the Buddha describes a method of meditation in sixteen stages, starting from awareness of the breathing process, proceeding through a deliberate calming of body, feelings, and mind, and culminating in reflection on the impermanent nature of the breath. Contemporary insight meditation methods from the Burmese Theravada tradition include investigating bodily sensations for their impermanent nature. Insight meditation dissolves rigid emotions and fixed views, allowing the meditator to experience knowing and seeing what is actually the case. Insight may also be the informal result of other formal meditation practices—Buddhist meditation is ultimately an art, a creative process, and its techniques and methods are not ends in themselves.

A fourth kind of meditation concerns the development of unbounded or immeasurable emotions: friendliness or kindness (Pali: *mettā*; Sanskrit: *maitrī*), compassion (*karuṇā*), sympathetic joy (*muditā*), and equanimity (Pali: *upekkhā*; Sanskrit: *upekṣā*). These beautiful, expansive emotional states are also called "divine abidings" (*brahmā-vihāra*). While the Buddha is said to have taught how the meditator may develop these states by an imaginative radiation to all beings in all directions, later Buddhist traditions devised more formal methods. The Theravadan commentator Buddhaghosa describes a five-stage development of friendliness, working through love toward oneself, a friend, a neutral person, and an enemy, and culminating in the radiation stage. In contrast, contemporary Tibetan Buddhists in the Mahayana tradition practice *tonglen*, "giving and taking," imaginatively breathing in the suffering of living beings, and breathing out kindness and compassion.

A fifth kind of meditation is the imaginative encounter with archetypal buddhas and bodhisattvas, and the development of a vividly imagined relationship with them. Such meditation has its roots in the Indian religious movement called Tantra, which, in its Buddhist form, has been especially preserved in Tibetan Buddhism. Meditation in this tradition consists in the formal imagining of a specific buddha or bodhisattva figure. Following a ritual initiation and commitment, and under the guidance of a guru (teacher), a meditator practices a detailed visualization and auditory repetition of that figure's seed syllable or mantra. The meditator experiences him- or herself in relation to their chosen buddha, who not only gives teachings and blessings, but brings about a transformation of the meditator's mind.

In contrast to the complex, formal practices of Vajrayana or Tantric Buddhism is a sixth kind of meditation, practiced in the Zen tradition, of just sitting (Japanese: *shikantaza*) or seated meditation (*zazen*). Although the word "Zen" is the same as the Chinese word "Chan," which derives from Sanskrit *dhyāna*, the Zen practice of just sitting derives much of its inspiration from the Chinese tradition of Daoism, with its immanent goal of an effortless harmony with nature. The Zen meditator may practice formal methods of meditative concentration, or reflection on a koan, but the culmination is a spontaneous, deep, present abiding in the nature of reality, beyond words or teachings. This true *zazen* has a parallel in the Tibetan Buddhist tradition of *dzogchen* (great perfection), which is likewise an effortless dwelling in the primordial purity of phenomena.

The different kinds of meditation in Buddhism suit different kinds of practitioner at different stages of the path. It is said that those prone to mental states of greed should practice mindfulness of the unattractive (such as the human body's less attractive workings), while those prone to hate should develop friendliness (*mettā*). Those prone to confusion should practice mindfulness of breathing. While mindfulness and *mettā* are suitable at all stages, a meditator's mind may only after some considerable time become ready for transformative insight practice, for the visualization of a buddha, or for dwelling effortlessly in the true nature of things.

The foregoing may suggest that meditation in Buddhism is primarily a means to the realization of the goal of awakening. But this is misleading, since meditation when fully developed is the goal. The word *samādhi*, meaning "concentration," "integration," and "unification," exemplifies this kind of meditation. As the eighth part of the Noble Eightfold Path, right *samādhi* is the culmination of the preceding parts of the path. It is usually defined in terms of absorption, but more broadly it means the quality of mind that is the result of meditative practice, and is the doorway to liberation. In mainstream Buddhism, the "wishless," "signless," and "emptiness" *samādhi*s are such doorways, resulting from insight reflection on the unsatisfactory, impermanent, and non-self character of conditioned existence. In Mahayana literature, countless profound *samādhi*s characterize the infinite meditative achievements of bodhisattvas. For Buddhists of all traditions, the meditative experience of *samādhi* is the realization of the innate purity and brilliance of the mind.

About the author
Dhivan Thomas Jones is a Lecturer in Philosophy and Religious Studies at the University of Chester, UK. His research is mainly in the area of early Buddhist philosophy.

Suggestions for further reading

In this book
See Chapters 26 (why Buddhists meditate), 27 (mindfulness), 29 (chanting), 41 (Zen), 60 (engaged Buddhism), and 62 (compassion).

Elsewhere
Bhikkhu Anālayo. *Mindfulness of Breathing: A Practice Guide and Translations*. Cambridge, UK: Windhorse Publications, 2019. An in-depth study of the *Ānāpānasati Sutta*.

Kamalashila. *Buddhist Meditation: Tranquillity, Imagination and Insight*. Cambridge, UK: Windhorse Publications, 2012. A practical guide to the range of Buddhist meditation methods.

Ray, Reginald. *Secrets of the Vajra World: The Tantric Buddhism of Tibet*. Boulder, CO: Shambhala, 2002. An introduction to the worldview and meditation methods of Tibetan Tantra.

Shaw, Sarah. *The Spirit of Buddhist Meditation*. New Haven, CT: Yale University Press, 2014. An overview of Buddhist meditation in early and traditional Indian Buddhist texts.

29
What is the role of chanting in Buddhism?

Xiaoqi Tang

Buddhist chanting often accompanies Buddhists when they are making offerings, praising the Three Jewels (the Buddha, the Dharma, and the Sangha), preventing unwholesomeness and developing wholesomeness, and liberating ghosts, among other things. As recorded in Buddhist scriptures, there are five benefits of chanting: not getting tired, not forgetting, not becoming slack, not losing voice, and being easy to understand. And there are five purities of the Buddhist chanting sound: it is upright, elegant, harmonious, clear, and profound. As the *Lotus Sutra* says, if people:

> employ persons to make music, striking drums, or blowing horns or conch shells, playing pipes, flutes, zithers, harps, balloon guitars, cymbals, and gongs, and if these many kinds of wonderful notes are intended wholly as an offering; or if one with a joyful mind, sings a song in praise of the Buddha's virtue, even if it is just one small note, then all who do these things have attained the Buddha way.

So, chanting enables Buddhists to understand and follow the Buddhist path. It can help people come close to the virtues of the Buddha, as well as improving their health and reducing their nervousness.

Chanting is one of the most fundamental features of Buddhist practice, both in monasteries and among lay people. Chants include passages from the sutras or whole sutras, incantation,

Chanting of the *Perfection of Wisdom Sutra*, Pema Yoedling Dratsang, Gelephu, Bhutan
Cathy Cantwell. 2013

praise, verse, and so on. It can be done at a personal or a public, ceremonial level. Chanting is used in various Buddhist rituals, including daily practice (morning chanting, evening chanting, chanting before eating), Buddhist ceremonies (e.g., the birthday of the Buddha or a bodhisattva, various Dharma assemblies, repentance ceremonies, etc.), and when monks gather to recite their monastic discipline. Theravada, Mahayana, and Tantric Buddhism all have their traditions of chanting. Taking refuge in the Three Jewels, paying homage to the buddha(s) and reciting holy texts are common practices for all these three families, and chanting can accompany each. However, chanting the five precepts (voluntarily undertaken moral guidelines) is most common in Theravada, repetitive chanting of the name of a buddha or bodhisattva is characteristic of Mahayana, and mantra chanting is a feature of Tantric Buddhism. Theravada Buddhists chant in Pali, Mahayana Buddhists chant mainly in Chinese, Cantonese, or Japanese, and tantric practitioners chant in Tibetan. Since chanting is so widely practiced, what role does it play in Buddhism? This question can be discussed from several aspects.

First, chanting is a kind of meditation practice. Chanting settles the mind to enter meditation in order to develop mindfulness, calmness, and concentration. Chanting requires practitioners to focus on the chanting content and listen carefully to their own sound. For group chanting, people not only need to listen to their own sound but also to others and chant in harmony. In this way, their ability in concentration and mindfulness can be developed. According to Mahayana scriptures, two bodhisattvas, Avalokiteśvara and Mahāsthāmaprāpta, achieved enlightenment by listening to their own voice. In China and Japan, repetitive chanting of the name of Amitābha Buddha (Amida in Japan) is believed to lead to rebirth in the Pure Land for followers of the Pure Land school.

Second, by chanting in front of the Buddha and making offerings of pure sound to the Buddha, people cultivate respect, loving-kindness, and wholesomeness. Meanwhile, chanting and listening to chanting helps to reinforce the Buddha's teaching in people's minds, which guards their minds from unwholesome tendencies related to greed, hatred, and delusion, so that they better understand the path to peace and happiness.

Third, chanting functions to preserve and spread Buddhist teaching. Throughout the history of Buddhism, musical vocalization has been used to increase the mind's capacity to store and remember religious doctrines so that they can be communicated to others. In the early years of Buddhism, the Buddha's teachings were orally transmitted, so people memorized and spread them by chanting, and the chants were structured to enable this memorization. Buddhist chanting not only enables people to memorize Buddhist teaching but has also attracted wide interest for its unique musical style. In Chinese Buddhism, for instance, in 230 CE, Prince Caozhi visited Fish Mountain and heard some beautiful Chinese Buddhist chanting. Impressed by the melody, he recorded the music score and handed it down, such that it is now recognized as part of China's national cultural heritage.

Fourth, Buddhist chanting has been proved to reduce negative emotions, therefore acting as a therapy with positive benefits. In the traditional Chinese characters, "music (*yue* 樂)," "medicine (*yao* 藥)," and "therapy (*liao* 療)" have the same origin. Music has a natural connection with medicine and therapy. Music can relax the body, promote blood circulation, and maintain physical health. Like medicine, music has the ability to regulate the body. Indeed, music therapy is one of the methods of secular psychotherapy. As a special genre of music, Buddhist chanting also has the function of psychotherapy. In Japan, Yozo Taniyama and eight other scholars did an experiment which suggested that listening to sutra chanting reduces bereavement stress, even for those not closely familiar with the sutra itself. In 2017, the University of Hong Kong published research which proved that repetitive chanting of "Amitābha Buddha," as in Pure Land Buddhism, changes the human brain's response to negative pictures. It means that those who practice receptive religious chanting do not suffer mentally from negative things such as fear-provoking or stress-provoking events/pictures. Therefore, chanting works effectively as psychotherapy, whether for reduction of one's own negative feelings, such as the fear of death, or for the alleviation of sadness, anger, and other negative emotions.

In conclusion, chanting as a meditation practice plays an important role in Buddhism and to a large extent fulfills the function of Buddhist study and practice to reduce and even eliminate sufferings. It preserves the Dharma, develops mindfulness, cultivates loving-kindness, and helps in the performance of Buddhist rituals. It is also a style of musical art, psychotherapy, and complementary medicine. However, how to make the best use of Buddhist chanting as a means of psychotherapy and auxiliary medical treatment is worthy of further study.

About the author
Xiaoqi Tang is a PhD student of Religious Studies at Lancaster University, UK. Her research interests are Buddhist women, Buddhist chaplains, and the professionalization of Chinese Buddhist monastics.

Further reading

In this book

See Chapters 26 (why Buddhists meditate), 28 (kinds of meditation), 39 (contemporary divisions), and 42 (Pure Land Buddhism).

Elsewhere

Chen, Pi-Yen. *Fanbai: Chinese Buddhist Monastic Chants*. Middleton, WI: A-R Editions, 2010.

Indaratana, Elgiriye. *Vandanā: The Album of Pāli Devotional Chanting and Hymns*. Penang: Inward Path Publisher, 2002.

Taniyama, Yozo, Carl Becker, Hara Takahashi, Sadako Tokumaru, Iwayumi Suzuki, Kazuki Okui, Josef Gohori, Yosuke Imai, and Takafumi Morita. "Listening to Sutra-Chanting Reduces Bereavement Stress in Japan." *Journal of Health Care Chaplaincy* 27(2) (2021); 105–117.

Part Five
Monasticism and lay people in Buddhism

30
What is the role of monasticism in Buddhism?

Ann Heirman

Shortly after attaining enlightenment, the Buddha visited five ascetics with whom he had previously observed extreme ascetic practices, such as food deprivation. However, during this meeting, he advocated the so-called Middle Way—a method that lay somewhere between extreme asceticism and indulgence. The five former ascetics adopted this practice and were subsequently known as "almsmen" (Sanskrit: *bhikṣu*; Pali: *bhikkhu*), because they wandered from community to community, surviving on gifts from lay people. In effect, they were the first Buddhist monks. This community (Sangha) of wandering monks grew rapidly and soon started to accept offers of permanent buildings for use during the rainy season. Indeed, over time, ever more monks (and nuns) became resident monastics throughout the year, with the donations on which they continued to rely also delivered to the monasteries. Since then, many monastics have combined life in a monastery with alms rounds in the lay community, although the latter custom has never been widely practiced in East Asia.

At first, it was possible to become a monk simply by accepting a direct invitation from the Buddha. This is reflected in the ritual sentence "Welcome, monk." Thereafter, as the monastic community continued to grow, new members were recruited without the presence of the Buddha. Later still, a formal division was established between "going forth" (that is, entering a state of homelessness) as a novice and full ordination (Pali and Sanskrit: *upasaṃpadā*) as a monk. Teenagers could become novices, whereas the minimum age for full ordination was set at twenty. Each new monk had to observe a long list of rules of conduct, some of which are still in use today.

There was significant expansion of the monastic community both during the Buddha's lifetime and thereafter, as monks disseminated his teachings throughout the Indian subcontinent, including Sri Lanka. The community also reached Central Asia and, by the first century CE, China. From these bases, it spread even further—to present-day Vietnam, Korea, Japan, Myanmar, Thailand, Laos, and Cambodia. There was another significant Buddhist community in Indonesia, but this started to decline with the growing influence of Islam in the region from the sixteenth century onwards. Thereafter, only a handful of isolated communities continued to practice Buddhism within the archipelago.

The monastic community has always been in the vanguard of the propagation of Buddhism and Buddhist practices across the Asian continent. From the very beginning, monks—and, to a lesser extent, nuns—broadcast the Buddha's teachings and stimulated interest in Buddhism by their mere presence in wider society (although, of course, their influence has varied considerably depending on both time and place). Through these efforts, the monastic community became a so-called "field of merit," which means that every gift to the Sangha was believed to generate good karma to the donor. Throughout Asia, donors have thus pledged vast sums of money for the construction and maintenance of monasteries in the hope of gaining karmic benefits for themselves and their families or simply because they supported the Buddha's message. The vast majority of these donors have been lay people, but a number of monastics have made significant contributions, too. In this way, donors have been a crucial factor in the dissemination of Buddhism across the Asian continent.

Consequently, since the time of the Buddha himself, there has been a rich, mutually beneficial relationship between the Buddhist monastic community and lay society. Monasteries have been established in each and every region where Buddhism has gained a foothold, with many of them becoming important religious centers within their specific contexts. More recently, however, and especially since Buddhism's arrival in the West in the twentieth century, there has been a subtle but undeniable shift in the relative importance of monastics and lay practitioners. Although a number of individual monks and nuns have certainly enjoyed considerable prestige in both North America and Europe, lay Buddhists have also started to achieve unprecedented levels of influence in these regions. As a result, many of the West's principal Buddhist centers have few if any direct links with a monastery. Moreover, a similar pattern is becoming increasingly evident in the traditional Buddhist regions.

Monasteries and their roles

Monasteries have played a variety of roles throughout history, depending on time and context. Many offer guidance through lectures or forums to both their own members and lay disciples. Monks continue to preach the Buddha's message in village contexts, but it is also increasingly transmitted in Buddhist centers, on television, and even via social media. For centuries, these lessons have been founded on the monks' study of their monasteries' extensive collections of manuscripts and books. In the process of assembling these libraries, some monasteries became major centers of knowledge and indeed technological innovation. For instance, in China, Buddhist monks not only played a crucial role in the invention of woodblock printing but also developed sophisticated building techniques. They also made full use of murals—such as in China's famous Dunhuang caves—and book illustrations to aid the dissemination of Buddhism throughout the country's largely illiterate society. Monastic schools for children have also played an important part in Buddhist cultures.

In addition to their educational activities, Asia's monks and nuns have a long history of participating in a variety of social events, such as saying prayers at funerals or blessing new homes or business ventures. Such practices vary widely from region to region, but they are all indicative of Buddhist monastics' close involvement with secular society and everyday life, except for those who choose to be "forest monks" and concentrate on meditation. This is especially evident in Southeast Asia, where many young boys spend at least some time in a monastery before leaving to resume their secular lives. Meanwhile, in Nepal and Japan, some monks' engagement with wider society goes even further as they are permitted to marry and raise families. These are exceptional cases, because celibacy remains the norm for most Buddhist monastics, but that has not prevented their active participation in the world outside the monastery walls. For instance, for several hundred years, a series of Buddhist monks—the Dalai Lamas—have been the effective Head of State in Tibet. Meanwhile, in South and Southeast Asia, monks have participated in electoral and protest politics as both individuals and well-organized groups. Previously, a number of large monasteries were powerful players in agriculture and trade. Their influence in these sectors has declined over the past two centuries as their focus has shifted even more firmly to religious, social, and cultural activities, although some of them still possess vast landholdings.

While Buddhist monastics have always ventured into secular society, there is an equally long tradition of lay people visiting monasteries. As a result, several of these institutions have become important cultural centers, with few restrictions placed on public access to their libraries, meditation halls, and gardens. Some of the most famous monasteries have even become tourist attractions, while others, especially in Thailand and Taiwan, have founded schools or universities.

In summary, Buddhist monasticism has played a highly influential role in the study, dissemination, and impact of Buddhism. Indeed, monastics may be seen as both the guardians and the transmitters of Buddhist culture, particularly in Asia. Consequently, it is safe to say that Buddhist history—and, by extension, Asian history—would have developed very differently in their absence.

About the author
Ann Heirman is Professor of Chinese Language and Culture and head of the Centre for Buddhist Studies at Ghent University in Belgium. Her research interests focus on Chinese Buddhist monasticism and the development of disciplinary rules.

Suggestions for further reading

In this book
See also Chapters 31 (ordination), 32 (monastic rules), 33 (nuns), 34 (lay Buddhists), 36 (preaching), 43 (Dalai Lama), and 61 (Buddhism and politics).

Elsewhere
Bechert, Heinz, and Richard Gombrich (editors). *The World of Buddhism*. London: Thames & Hudson, 1984: pages 77–89, 94–98, 133–146, 161–170.

Benn, James, Lori Meeks, and James Robson (editors). *Buddhist Monasticism in East Asia: Places of Practice*. London: Routledge, 2009.

Harvey, Peter. *An Introduction to Buddhism: Teachings, History and Practices* (2nd edition). Cambridge: Cambridge University Press, 2013: Chapter 10.

Kieschnick, John. *The Impact of Buddhism on Chinese Material Culture*. Princeton, NJ: Princeton University Press, 2003.

31
How does one become ordained?

Ann Heirman

The first community of Buddhist monks may be traced to the Buddha's visit to five ascetics following his attainment of enlightenment. In essence, then, these disciples became monks simply by accepting the Buddha's invitation to follow his teaching. Thereafter, more adherents were admitted into the nascent monastic community (Sangha) with the Buddha's greeting of "Welcome, monk," whereupon they immediately gained the status of full members. Later, though, as the community continued to expand, the monks themselves started to invite new members to join, even when the Buddha was not present. In these circumstances, the candidate had to recite the formula of triple refuge: "I take refuge in the Buddha, in the doctrine, and in the community." With this declaration, the candidate not only left their homes and families but simultaneously received full ordination. Later still, a formal difference was established between novice ordination and full ordination. It was only during the latter ceremony that a candidate would become a monk (or nun) and accept all the rights and duties of a full member of the monastic community.

Early Buddhist disciplinary texts (*vinaya*s) discuss the age at which a young boy may be deemed fit to enter the monastic community as a novice (Sanskrit: *śrāmaṇera*; Pali: *sāmaṇera*). Some of these texts specify a minimum age of twelve, others fifteen, but all agree that a boy may be admitted when he is sufficiently strong to chase away crows. That said, no novice should be younger than seven, regardless of his strength. Each novice must observe ten fundamental rules (with small variations among the various traditions): (1) he must not kill; (2) he must not steal; (3) he must not behave in an unchaste manner; (4) he must not lie; (5) he must not drink alcohol; (6) he must not wear flowers or perfume; (7) he must not sing, dance, make music, or attend performances; (8) he must not use a high or large bed; (9) he must not eat after noon; (10) he must not handle gold, silver, or other valuable items. Having observed all of these proscriptions throughout his novitiate, the novice could become a full member of the monastic community—a monk (Sanskrit: *bhikṣu*; Pali: *bhikkhu*)—from the age of twenty. In addition to respecting a long list of rules of conduct, each monk is expected to undertake several duties within the monastic community. Today, three ordination traditions survive, as described in the next answer.

Traditionally, all female candidates had to complete an additional step between their novitiate and full ordination as nuns (Sanskrit: *bhikṣuṇī*; Pali: *bhikkhunī*): they were obliged to spend two years as probationers, during which time they received special training while paying particular attention to a number of extra rules. Today, however, full ordination for women is only possible in East Asia and in some of Sri Lanka's monastic communities. In East Asian regions, the probationary period is often waived and a novice may proceed directly to full *bhikṣuṇī* status.

In countries where Mahayana Buddhism is prevalent, so-called bodhisattva ordination has been added to the other ceremonies. In medieval China, for instance, the bodhisattva rules and a bodhisattva vow were incorporated within formal ordination ceremonies. However, since then, this part of the ceremony has always followed full monastic ordination based on the guidelines outlined in the traditional *vinaya* texts.

Regional variations

There are a number of significant differences in ordination practice across the Buddhist world. For instance, East Asian Mahayana Buddhists introduced so-called "Triple Platform Ordination" in the seventeenth century. As the name suggests, this ritual, which is held in one place over a short period of time, begins with novitiate ordination, followed by full ordination, and finally bodhisattva ordination.

In medieval Japan, many Buddhist schools abolished the traditional ordination ceremonies and focused exclusively on bodhisattva ordination. This, and the fact that a number of schools started to tolerate marriage, resulted in marked contrasts between Japanese Buddhism and monastic life elsewhere in Asia. Moreover, these differences were reinforced in the nineteenth century, when the state officially lifted the ban on clerical marriage. Since then, many of the country's "priests" or "clerics"—the most common English terms for Japanese monastics—have married and raised families, while also looking after their own private temples. By contrast, to this day, very few Japanese nuns marry.

Nepalese Buddhists generally have a similarly relaxed attitude toward celibacy. Their ordination may be considered temporary, as they are released from their monastic vows not long after the ceremony. Indeed, after many centuries of Hindu influence, there are only a few Buddhist monks left in Nepal, although this small group—mostly drawn from the Newari community—are attempting to keep the tradition alive and continue to maintain the country's monasteries. Apart from Newari Buddhism, Nepal also has a lively Tibetan Buddhist community, mostly among people of Tibetan origin. In addition, a revival of Theravada ordinations began in the twentieth century, under the influence of South and Southeast Asian Buddhism.

In many parts of Southeast Asia, it has become common practice for young boys to take novitiate vows as a kind of rite of passage. Some of them subsequently undergo full ordination and become monks, but the vast majority return to secular life a few years later. In addition, this region has developed a pragmatic form of temporary full ordination. In Thailand, for instance, many young men enter monasteries specifically because of the high-quality religious and secular education they provide, and no stigma is attached to completing that education and rejoining secular society. Indeed, this system has strengthened the links between Thai monastics and the country's lay community.

In summary, it is clear that there are a number of significant differences in ordination practice across the Buddhist world. That said, at the very least, most regions continue to observe the traditional ordination stages of novice followed by full ordination.

About the author
Ann Heirman is Professor of Chinese Language and Culture and head of the Centre for Buddhist Studies at Ghent University in Belgium. Her research interests include Chinese Buddhist monasticism and the development of disciplinary rules.

Suggestions for further reading

In this book
See also Chapters 13 (bodhisattva) 30 (role of monasticism), 32 (monastic rules), 33 (nuns), 39 (contemporary divisions), 44 (bodhisattva vow), and 58 (marriage and family life).

Elsewhere
Harvey, Peter. *An Introduction to Buddhism: Teachings, History and Practices* (2nd edition). Cambridge: Cambridge University Press, 2013: Chapters 4 and 10.

Jaffe, Richard. *Neither Monk nor Layman: Clerical Marriage in Modern Japanese Buddhism*. Princeton, NJ: Princeton University Press, 2001.

32
What rules do monastics follow?

Alice Collett

The monastic code of Buddhism is called the *Vinaya*. These rules govern all aspects of a monastic life, and both individual and communal behavior. For the individual monk and nun, the rules range from those concerned with the most serious types of immoral, dangerous, or illegal behavior, such as murder and other sorts of violence, to simple and minor matters of decorum or etiquette, such as how to behave courteously when visiting the home of lay followers. While there is some historical basis to the traditional account of how the *Vinaya* came to be—namely, that it was recited following the death of the Buddha—it is likely that the *Vinaya* developed over a longer period, and changed during the process of oral transmission. Following the death of the Buddha, the community began to split and divide into different groups. Various reasons are given as to why this happened, one being that there was a disagreement over which *vinaya* rules should be followed to the letter, and which—if any—could be adapted to fit with a changing social world.

Different schools of Buddhism developed their own set of *vinaya* rules. On the whole, the *vinaya*s of each school are very similar to one another, although there are as well notable differences. There are several extant *vinaya*s, in different languages. The three that continue to be in use are:

- **Pali *Vinaya*** —used in countries such as Sri Lanka, Thailand, Cambodia, and Burma (Myanmar) which follow the Theravada tradition;
- **Dharmaguptaka *Vinaya*** —used in East Asian countries that follow the Mahayana tradition;
- **Mūlasarvāstivāda *Vinaya*** —used in Tibet and Central Asia, where tantric forms of Buddhism are usually practiced.

There are also parts or full versions of other *vinaya*s still extant, most of which are now only available in Tibetan or Chinese translation. There are, however, also sections and divisions of some still found in Sanskrit, such as, for instance, a complete text of the nuns' section belonging to one particular school.

There are a different number of rules in the different *vinaya*s. The rules are divided into individual rules and those governing communal life. The rules that govern individual behaviors of monks and nuns are again divided into sections—with one set for monks and another for nuns. In all extant cases, there are more rules for nuns than monks, sometimes over a hundred more. The numbers for the three *vinaya*s still in use are:

- Pali *Vinaya*: 227 for monks and 311 for nuns;
- Dharmaguptaka *Vinaya*: 250 for monks and 348 for nuns;
- Mūlasarvāstivāda *Vinaya*: 253 for monks and 364 for nuns.

Vinaya rules governing individual behavior are known as the *prātimokṣa* (Sanskrit; Pali: *pāṭimokkha*). These are chanted by the community on a regular basis. The canonical texts of the *Vinaya* include both the rules and what are known as the origin stories; these are narratives that apparently recount the events that led the Buddha to formulate each of the rules. For example, there is a rule that nuns should not hoard bowls. This rule was made, according to the origin story, because a group of six nuns did, on one occasion, do just this—hoard a stack of bowls. This was reported to the Buddha and he made the rule accordingly. Although Buddhist tradition understands these origin stories to be historical, evidence suggests that some, at least, were composed at a later date and do not originally come from the Buddha. Also, some do not relate very closely to the rule that is made. For instance, in the Sanskrit and Chinese versions of the nuns' section of one school, a story is told about a nun whose sister becomes unwell, and so the nun goes to see her. The sister dies before the nun arrives. Then the sister's husband tries to insist that the nun stays to look after him and the children. She becomes afraid of him, worrying that he will attack her, but she manages to escape by pretending to agree. The rule related to this story is that nuns should not travel alone. In other *vinaya*s, the origin story related to this rule is much more fitting.

That there are more rules for nuns than monks have brought about objections and questions about sexism. Certainly, some negativity toward women exists within Buddhist communities, and has done historically, but it can also be argued that certain of the rules were put in place to protect the nuns. For example, on the rule above, against nuns traveling alone, another of the origin stories on this relates that one day two nuns were traveling together and came to a river. The boatman who could ferry them across said that he could not take them both together, but needed to take them one at a time. He sexually assaulted each one when she was in his boat alone with him, and so the rule was made to prevent this. In addition, there are eight separate rules that all nuns must adhere to, which cast nuns as inferior to monks, but it has been recognized that these rules could not have been established at the time of the Buddha, as they mention the novice period for monastics that was not in place in the Buddha's day.

The set of individual rules are divided into sections. The following is a list of the types of rules there are, the penalties incurred on breach of them, and examples of what is included in each section.

Rules entailing expulsion from the order
These are the most serious of the rules. If these rules are broken, the monk or nun in question who failed to adhere to the rule must

leave the community, and is no longer a monk or nun. There are usually four for monks and eight for nuns. The nuns have the four the monks have, then an additional four. The monks' four are: no sexual activity, no stealing, no killing, and no lying about religious attainments. The additional set for the nuns includes two more on sexual offenses, one on collusion, and one on associating with a monk who has been expelled.

Rules entailing a formal meeting

These are the next most serious; if these rules are breached, it will not necessarily result in expulsion from the order. In these cases, a formal meeting of elder monastics is convened to assess and decide the fate of the transgressor. These rules are concerned with other types of behavior related to sex, such as not making lewd remarks, and behavior that might cause a division within the monastic community. There are thirteen of these for monks, and between seventeen and twenty for nuns, depending on tradition.

Undetermined rules

These are for monks only, and are concerned with monks being accused of inappropriate behavior by female lay followers; there are only two of these. There is no specific outcome for a monk found guilty of these offenses.

Rules entailing forfeiture and confession

These rules are concerned with robes, money, bowls, medicine, and items that have been obtained via inappropriate means and should be returned. There are thirty for monks and thirty or thirty-three for nuns.

Rules entailing confession
This is the largest category, with close to a hundred rules for monks and sometimes over two hundred for nuns. They concern a variety of issues, such as behavior in relation to eating and drinking, travel regulations, moral questions, and general conduct.

Rules entailing acknowledgment
There are four for monks and between eight and eleven for nuns. They are concerned with gifts of food.

Rules of training
These are minor rules for which transgression might result in only some admonishment. They are large in number but varied with regards to their content, and concern what might appear to be trivial matters. These rules govern etiquette and decorum such as, for instance, not arranging one's robe so that the lower edge sits too high or too low above the ground, and not eating one's food in an ungracious manner.

Rules for resolving disputes
This final category gives advice on how issues with offenses might be settled.

About the author
Alice Collett is Director of The South Asia History Project, University of Wolverhampton, UK. Her research focuses on the religious history of ancient India, especially the history of women.

Further reading

In this book
See Chapters 5 (texts), 30 (role of monasticism), 31 (ordination) 33 (nuns), 35 (gender equality), and 38 (early divisions in Buddhism).

Elsewhere
Griffith Foulk, T. "Daily Life in the Assembly". In *Buddhism in Practice*, edited by Donald S. Lopez Jr., 455–472. Princeton, NJ: Princeton University Press, 1994.

Heirman, Ann. "Vinaya Rules for Monks and Nuns." In *Oxford Research Encyclopedia of Religion*. New York: Oxford University Press, 2019.

33
What is the position of nuns in Buddhism?

Ann Heirman

All of the early Buddhist texts that discuss the position of women in the monastic community concede that the Buddha hesitated to admit them as fully ordained nuns (Sanskrit: *bhikṣuṇī*; Pali: *bhikkhunī*), including when his stepmother, Mahāprajāpatī (Sanskrit; Pali: Mahāpajāpatī), asked for admittance. The Buddha granted her request only after one of his most famous disciples—Ānanda—intervened on her behalf. Specifically, Ānanda raised three issues with the Buddha: earlier buddhas' acceptance of women; the Buddha's personal debt to his stepmother, who had raised him; and women's ability to attain enlightenment. The Buddha acknowledged that women could, indeed, attain enlightenment, and therefore placed them at an equal level to men in terms of their ability to gain liberation from rebirth.

Institutionally, however, men continued to enjoy a higher status than women. This was immediately obvious when, according to tradition, the Buddha formulated eight special rules for nuns to obey. All of these strictures are highly technical, and they serve to maintain women's subordinate position. A nun, for instance, must always bow to a monk (Sanskrit: *bhikṣu*; Pali: *bhikkhu*) and give him priority, regardless of her own seniority. Moreover, after her ordination in a nuns' order, a *bhikṣuṇī* must also be ordained by a monks' order, meaning that control over monastic admissions remained firmly in male hands. Recent historical research has suggested that these eight rules actually date from after the Buddha's lifetime, when the monastic order was already firmly established. Either way, however, for monastics, the direct link between female ordination and the Buddha himself is of primary importance.

According to early disciplinary texts (*vinaya*s), all ordination ceremonies must be conducted in the presence of a certain number of fully ordained participants: ten, under normal circumstances, or five in remote regions or in the event of some other difficulty. This stipulation became problematic due to social and political unrest in South and Southeast Asia between the eleventh and thirteenth centuries, with female ordinations eventually ceasing, as the region's nuns proved incapable of sustaining the monastic order there. Meanwhile, full ordinations for women were never introduced in Tibet, primarily because of its inaccessibility. As a result, it is only in East Asia that women are routinely fully ordained into the Buddhist monastic order (an exception to this is Sri Lanka).

Female monastics' subordinate status persists to this day, which is reflected in the fact that their institutions tend to be much poorer than the male equivalents. Equally damaging is the widely accepted notion that, although a woman may ultimately attain enlightenment, she cannot do so in her present life and body. Rather, to reach such a status, she must first be reborn as a man. This concept, which is based on the assumption that sexual desire is both an obstacle to achieving enlightenment and a source of gossip, features prominently in historical discourses and often resurfaces in present-day theological debates.

The end of the twentieth century saw the launch of a movement that aims to establish (or re-establish) the full ordination of Buddhist nuns in Tibet, South Asia, and Southeast Asia. In these regions, however, up to now only some members of the Sri Lankan monastic community have expressed support for the campaign, which was largely inspired by the work of Western female monastics with the help of fully ordained nuns in Taiwan. Although in this way higher ordination for women has been brought back to Sri Lanka, the ordinations are still not officially recognized by the state.

Nuns (*thiláshin*), Sakyadhita Nunnery, Sagaing, Myanmar
Elizabeth Harris, 2018

In addition, this campaign has prompted ongoing debates about the impact of Western-style feminism and the globalization of Buddhist traditions on collaboration among the various Buddhist schools and on how to interpret the *vinaya* rules in order to ensure that female ordinations are legally recognized in Buddhist circles.

In the context of religious women in Southeast Asia, it is important to pay due attention to those women, often also called "nuns," who have decided to follow alternative paths, either because full ordination was not available to them or because of personal choice. In Thailand, for instance, some religious women, called *maechi*, are not fully ordained, but still take a vow of celibacy and observe several other strict precepts. The *maechi* occupy a marginal position in the Thai Buddhist institutional hierarchy, and as such they receive few social benefits. Nevertheless, a number of them have been highly revered for their Buddhist knowledge and rigorous practice. Similarly, in neighboring Myanmar, several women's groups, including the so-called *thiláshin* (those who uphold morality), operate outside of the traditional *bhikṣuṇī* ordination system. However, their lives are very similar to those of fully ordained nuns as they revolve around scriptural study and strict observation of Buddhist practice. Moreover, they are expected to support the male Sangha.

In Sri Lanka, the "ten precept mothers" (*dasa sil mātā*) also devote themselves to study and practice, but they have developed their own institutions which are independent of both the community of monks and the newly established community of fully ordained nuns. These and countless other forms of renunciation testify to the increasing number of options that are available to Buddhist women in Asia. Their significance and impact vary from place to place, but their presence never goes unnoticed.

Notwithstanding their typically subordinate status, throughout history and in every Buddhist region, charismatic female teachers have emerged and female monastics have played significant social roles. Indeed, this is increasingly true today, with nuns playing leading roles in numerous social activities in Taiwan, for instance. Finally, it should be remembered that female lay Buddhist devotees have had a significant impact throughout the religion's history, and they continue to be actively engaged in countless institutions, societies, and movements, many of which help to give Buddhism a distinctly feminine face.

About the author

Ann Heirman is Professor of Chinese Language and Culture and head of the Centre for Buddhist Studies at Ghent University in Belgium. Her research interests include Chinese Buddhist monasticism and the development of disciplinary rules.

Suggestions for further reading

In this book
See also Chapters 30 (role of monasticism), 31 (ordination), 32 (monastic rules), 35 (gender equality), and 58 (marriage and family life).

Elsewhere
DeVido, Elise Anne. *Taiwan's Buddhist Nuns*. New York: State University of New York Press, 2010.

Kawanami, Hiroko. *Renunciation and Empowerment of Buddhist Nuns in Myanmar–Burma: Building a Community of Female Faithful*. Leiden: Brill, 2013.

Mohr, Thea, and Jampa Tsedroen (editors). *Dignity and Discipline: Reviving Full Ordination for Buddhist Nuns*. Boston, MA: Wisdom Publications, 2010.

Seeger, Martin. *Gender and the Path to Awakening: Hidden Histories of Nuns in Modern Thai Buddhism*. Chiang Mai: Silkworm Books, 2018.

34
What is the role of lay Buddhists?

Alice Collett

Traditionally in Buddhism, the laity, those who are not ordained as monks or nuns, have two roles or duties. Firstly, they should follow the five ethical precepts, sometimes known as lay precepts. These are described in the answer on ethical vows/precepts and focus on not harming others and oneself. The second main duty of the laity is to offer support to monastics. This is known as *dāna*, which means "giving." In some modern Theravada countries, a third duty for laity is added, which is to practice meditation. When a man or woman decides to become a monk or nun, they traditionally give up all family ties and social responsibilities, and any paid employment. As they do not work, they need to find material and financial support by other means. The laity's traditional role is to offer this: to provide food, medicine, robes—all the things a monastic might need to sustain themselves and live simply. Where monks and nuns carry out a daily alms-round, the idea is that the lay householder—often the wife, who manages the household—would put in the monastic's bowl any leftover food she had. Traditionally, she should not go out of her way to prepare fresh food for the monastics, as part of monastic renunciation is that they live off what would otherwise be discarded. Also, monastics should eat whatever is put in their bowl, and not have desire for anything other than what they are offered.

When Buddhism become established in China, this type of "begging" was not considered appropriate, and many monasteries in East Asia were built in remote locations that made a daily alms-round impractical. Different practices evolved, a new standard being that a kitchen was built as part of a monastery complex and the laity came to the kitchen to cook for the monastics, then served them at a formalized mealtime each day. This way of offering *dāna* has now become standard in many modern Buddhist countries around the world. The Japanese, however, did take up the alms-round again, which is called *takuhatsu* in Japan. So, while the idea of the laity providing material support for the monastic community remained a central facet of lay life, the exact parameters of how this was enacted changed as Buddhism was adopted in various countries, for both practical and social reasons.

Providing material support to monastics and adhering to the lay precepts comprise the traditional role of the laity in Buddhism, but there have always been exceptions to this. This is one side

Lay Buddhist pilgrims preparing Auspicious Flags for Tibetan New Year at the sacred sight of Rewalsar, Himachal Pradesh, India
Cathy Cantwell. 1982

of the reciprocal relationship; the laity provide material support for monastics and monastics offer religious services in return, including teaching. But what happens if a lay person becomes, for example, more able at meditation than the monks and nuns, or progresses more quickly on the path than the monastics around them, going against the traditional model? In such cases, this dynamic is partly reversed, as the lay person is in a position to offer instruction. And it is not prohibited for this to happen, nor is it considered outside of the possible roles a lay person may have. There are several instances of this in early Indian Buddhist texts. For example, in one narrative, the lay woman Visākhā proves herself to be more able than the monks at meditation and so offers them instruction. The best-known example of a layman being in a more advanced state than the monastics around him is in a Mahayana text called the *Vimalakīrti Nirdeśa* ("The Teachings of Vimalakīrti"). In this text, which is intended as a criticism of formalized, institutional monasticism, the layman Vimalakīrti proves himself time and again to be more able than the monks. This happens so frequently that the monks are reluctant to go and visit him, as they know they will be admonished in some way or another, and any incompetencies made manifest. And this is what happens. Monk after monk reticently goes to visit Vimalakīrti and begins a conversation with him. Each episode culminates with the layman Vimalakīrti chiding the monk. At one point, a large crowd arrives at Vimalakīrti's house, and one monk wonders where they will all sit. Vimalakīrti says to him, "Did you come here for the sake of a chair? Or for the sake of the Dharma?"

Throughout the history of Buddhism, although the monastic-lay dichotomy remains at the heart of the tradition, variations and adaptations to it have arisen. The Tzu Chi movement in modern Taiwan, founded and led by the nun Cheng Yen, is largely a lay movement within which members are engaged in employment—for example, making handicrafts to sell—and the movement is funded in this way. In the Triratna Buddhist Community, founded in the United Kingdom but now an international movement, those who are ordained do not renounce in the traditional way, so can still marry and do need to work to earn a living. In this case, the monastic–lay split is less in evidence. While there is disagreement within and between Buddhist traditions about what may or may not constitute genuine ordination, the variety of roles for laity are not usually problematic, especially as they generally continue to center around the prescribed roles of supporting the monastic community and ethical practice.

About the author
Alice Collett is Director of The South Asia History Project, University of Wolverhampton, UK. Her research focuses on the religious history of ancient India, especially the history of women.

Further reading

In this book
See Chapters 3 (ritual), 14 (devotion to the Buddha), 26 (why Buddhists meditate), 30 (monasticism), 32 (monastic rules), 35 (gender equality), 36 (preaching), and 58 (marriage and family life).

Elsewhere
Banks Findly, Ellison. *Dāna: Giving and Getting in Pali Buddhism*. Delhi: Motilal Banarsidass Publishers, 2003.

Chakravarti, Uma. *Social Dimensions of Early Buddhism*. New Delhi: Munshiram Manoharlal Publishers, 1996.

Lewis, Todd (editor). *Buddhists: Understanding Buddhism through the Lives of Practitioners*. West Sussex: Wiley Blackwell, 2014.

35
Does Buddhism support gender equality?

Alice Collett

Historically, many Buddhist traditions around the world have treated women as inferior to men. There is, however, nothing in basic Buddhist ethical principles or foundational Buddhist doctrine that supports such a view. Quite the opposite, in fact. The basic answer to the question, therefore, is that Buddhism supports gender equality in principle, but Buddhist traditions have not always done so in practice. The reason for this is likely ingestion of social norms and cultural values from traditional societies, which considered women to be inferior to men, as these are the types of societies within which Buddhism first arose and existed for centuries.

Buddhism began in ancient India, as a movement that could be considered a reaction against the prevalent religious tradition of that day—what we call Brahmanism. Within this tradition, women were not allowed access to the sacred texts as they were considered too impure. The earliest texts of Buddhism state that the Buddhist community, the Sangha, is fourfold, in that it includes monks, nuns, lay men, and lay women. This was in contrast to early Hindu tradition, in that Buddhist women could have access to the teachings, and practice on an equal footing to men. In the early texts, there are also plentiful stories of female disciples, both nuns and lay women, some of whom were exemplary teachers and practitioners. And while it is the case that we do find negative views and attitudes expressed about women in the early texts of the tradition, this is not all we find.

Focusing on what is negative in the texts and traditions of Buddhism in relation to women, four primary components can be identified. These are: (1) that women are inferior to men; (2) that it is bad karma to be born a woman; (3) that women need to be reborn as men in the next life to make progress on the path; and (4) that women cannot be buddhas. Some of these are easy to challenge, even from a Buddhist perspective. For instance, the idea that to be reborn as a woman is bad karma does not accord with the doctrine. Karma means "action" and the karma doctrine instills that actions have consequences; if one does good actions it has good consequences, and vice versa. If it is always bad karma to be reborn as a woman, this presupposes that life as any woman is always and invariably worse than life as any man. So high-status Indian queens of antiquity, who lived lives of relative luxury, who were waited on hand and foot, and who wielded significant power, in this context, would have to be understood as having lives that entailed greater misery than the life of a low-caste or outcast individual living on the fringes of society. At the time of writing this book, in the United Kingdom, we continue to have a monarchy, and a current reigning queen; so, again, in this modern case, one would need to argue that the life of Queen Elizabeth II is worse than the life of a homeless man, begging for food on the streets of London. While it may be the case that, generally speaking, women do and have historically had lives that entail greater suffering than men, karma is a principle and does not operate from the basis of generalizations.

Although many traditions throughout Buddhist history have treated women as inferior, and this has had adverse consequences, there is also a lesser-known history, which is the history of outstanding women, who have overcome unyielding obstacles to become devoted disciples, esteemed teachers, and inspirational leaders. Such women have made valuable contributions to the history, shape, and spread of Buddhism. They have founded traditions based on innovative teachings and practices (Tibet), been the first ordained Buddhist practitioners in a country (Japan), established, funded, and built nunneries (Myanmar, Korea, Taiwan), been some of the first Western translators of Buddhist texts (United Kingdom), and been the first Buddhist teachers within a country (Hawai'i, Australia).

One such woman is the Tibetan Machig Labdrön, who lived in the twelfth century. In Machig's life account, it is related that in a previous incarnation she was male, demonstrating that it is not always necessary for a woman to be reborn as a man to make progress, as in this case the opposite was true. The biographies of Machig and other exemplary women in the history of Tibetan Buddhism depict a strength and confidence in character. In Tibetan Buddhism, unlike other traditions, it is acknowledged that there are female buddhas, and it may be that these two factors are related.

Another woman worthy of note is the Taiwanese nun Cheng Yen, founder and leader of the Tzu Chi movement. Cheng Yen is an influential and esteemed figure in modern Taiwan, who has achieved something significant, in gender terms. Cheng Yen teaches her followers that compassionate action is the heart of Buddhist practice, and that rather than entreat bodhisattvas to come to one's aid, imitation of their compassion is more important. In teaching this, Cheng Yen has made what are usually considered low-status "feminine" characteristics, such as nurturing and care, into central components of the Buddhist path which should be highly valued and aspired to by all, even men.

These are just two women out of many I could mention, who demonstrate, by example, that women are not inferior to men in Buddhism. And due to the existence of such women, both now and through history, it is not accurate to assert that Buddhism is negative about women, because to do so negates both the existence and contributions of these women in the history of Buddhism. It is more accurate to say that, while there are parts of Buddhist texts that are negative about women, and that many Buddhist traditions have treated women badly, there is also a long history of accomplished women in Buddhism, who have achieved great things.

About the author

Alice Collett is Director of The South Asia History Project, University of Wolverhampton, UK. Her research focuses on the religious history of ancient India, especially the history of women.

Suggestions for further reading

In this book
See Chapters 18 (karma), 19 (what is reborn), 33 (nuns), and 60 (engaged Buddhism).

Elsewhere
Collett, Alice. *I Hear Her Words: An Introduction to Women in Buddhism.* Cambridge, UK: Windhorse Publications, 2021.

Herrmann Pfandt, Adelheid. "On a Previous Birth Story of Ma gcig Lab sgron ma." *The Tibet Journal* 23(3) (2000): 19–31.

Hueng, C. Julia. *Charisma and Compassion: Chen Yen and the Buddhist Tzu Chi Movement.* Cambridge, MA: Harvard University Press, 2009.

Shaw, Miranda. *Passionate Enlightenment: Women in Tantric Buddhism.* Princeton, NJ: Princeton University Press, 1994.

36
What is the role of preaching in Buddhism?

Mahinda Deegalle

Preaching was an ancient method of teaching within Buddhism. The Buddha himself used and displayed abundant skill in preaching his message effectively. Yet, after two and a half millennia, preaching remains vital in Buddhism, making Buddhism one of the most significant Asian contributions to human civilization, holding the attention of large gatherings, influencing their thought and practice, and taking a prominent place in ritual and festivals. For example, in contemporary Sri Lanka, the delivery of Buddhist sermons has moved into the modern, digital age. Sermons are now on regular broadcast twenty-four hours a day, seven days a week in Buddhist channels such as *Buddhist TV* and the internet. Modern technology has advanced the cause of Buddhism by enabling Buddhist preachers to reach far and wide beyond traditional temples, crossing national and international boundaries.

Preaching continues to have great spiritual and moral significance as well as immense potential for many Buddhists. Over centuries, sermons and preaching practices have dominated the Theravada and Mahayana Buddhist communities' ritual life. Delivering sermons has always been an expected, and much anticipated and revered, religious and social role of any Buddhist monastic. By far, it was the most important ritual context within which Buddhist monastics interacted with the laity to enhance their well-being. The more a Buddhist monastic became good at preaching, the more that monastic member became sought after in Buddhist communities, to the extent of acquiring celebrity status. Even today, most popular in Buddhist societies are Buddhist preachers.

Preaching's primary aim is the communication and celebration of the Buddha's teachings. According to the Buddha, a message of the Buddha delivered as a sermon must be "good" in the beginning, middle, and end. Thus, the communication of the Buddha's teaching requires a well-regulated moral and social etiquette from all participants. In Buddhist sermon contexts, an invitation from the audience is an absolutely essential prerequisite. In general, Buddhist preachers do not preach in places where there is no public or private invitation. This traditional restriction imposed on sermonizing makes the Buddhist preacher stand out among other religious preachers. The Buddhist preacher is required to function modestly with appropriate noble conduct. Aggressive, condescending, and overly enthusiastic missionary zeal in preaching is completely discouraged. Therefore, conversion-oriented preaching is wholly absent and discouraged in Buddhist preaching traditions. Indeed, in some Buddhist contexts, religious tension has arisen because of the lack of this ethic within some other religious traditions.

Buddhist preaching sessions are formal occasions. Sessions of sharing *Dhamma* (Pali; Sanskrit: Dharma) are held on a day appointed and agreed on by both the lay and monastic parties. The primary goal of preaching is not necessarily to spread the Buddha's words or increase the number of Buddhists but rather to help lay people lead righteous and wholesome lives, following the *Dhamma*. In many Buddhist societies, delivering sermons and listening to preaching is seen as a meritorious activity that generates good karmic fruits.

Over centuries, Buddhist preaching gradually became a more popular tradition with new methods developing as Buddhism spread outside India. Its popularity was largely due to the message that the rituals communicated. In particular, preachers' popularity depended very much on how skillful each preacher was in using the wealth of local materials and vernacular languages to convey the message more effectively in a convincing manner. Experienced Buddhist preachers often instruct other preachers to select teaching that is appropriate to the occasion. The preacher designs, selects, appropriates, innovates, and applies the Buddha's teachings to become suitable to a particular audience, time, space, and needs. The theme that the preacher chooses for the sermon may be attributed to the Buddha, but the full elaboration is the preacher's creation. Buddhist preachers have always been innovators of traditions. Their styles of preaching have adapted and modified in the process to fit the context and audience. Within the basic guidelines I've mentioned, Buddhist preachers have ample opportunity to innovate and create their sermons. Buddhist preachers often become free-floating speakers. The expectation is that they communicate their experience of the Buddha's words through their own words. When Buddhist preachers deliver sermons, it is noteworthy that it is not the Buddha that directly speaks from their mouths. Sacred texts form an essential part of the sermon. The preacher's sermon is often woven in and around themes suggested by textual verses. The selected textual verse provides the basic structure and foundation for the preacher to deliver an effective sermon.

In Theravada Buddhist preaching contexts, one does not often find lay Buddhist preachers. The Sri Lankan lay Buddhist reformer Anagārika Dharmapāla (1864–1933) was an exception. Dharmapāla may have been influenced too much by Protestant Christian preaching models. Breaking from the tradition, Dharmapāla presented himself as a lay Buddhist preacher with a mission to restore Buddhism and wandered around the country in his custom-made bus preaching to Buddhists. If lay Buddhist preaching existed in Theravada contexts, it was limited to special occasions such as full-moon days when lay Buddhists might read from the *Jātaka*s, texts that give stories of the Buddha's previous lives. Buddhists in Sri Lanka and Southeast Asia consider a loud and rhythmic reading of such a religious text as a form of preaching, where texts are rehearsed and episodes performed ceremonially. In some Mahayana contexts, for example, in the relatively new Japanese lay Buddhist movement Rissho Kosei Kai, lay preaching takes place.

About the author
Mahinda Deegalle is Professor of Religions, Philosophies and Ethics, Bath Spa University, UK. He publishes primarily on Theravada Buddhism in Sri Lanka, and his research concentrates on Buddhism, Conflict, Violence, and the Ethics of War.

Suggestions for further reading

In this book
See Chapters 3 (ritual), 5 (texts), 29 (chanting), 30 (monasticism), and 34 (lay Buddhists).

Elsewhere
Deegalle, Mahinda. *Popularizing Buddhism: Preaching as Performance in Sri Lanka*. Albany, NY: State University of New York Press, 2006. A historical study of texts and rituals that contributed to the development of Theravada preaching.

Deegalle, Mahinda. "Buddhists on Religious Conversion: A Critical Issue." In *Religious Conversion: Religion Scholars Thinking Together*, edited by S. Premawardhana, 63–82. West Sussex: Wiley Blackwell, 2015. A treatment of contested religious conversions from a Buddhist doctrinal perspective.

Deegalle, Mahinda. "Buddhist Protests over Non-Buddhist Evangelism: All Ceylon Buddhist Congress Commission Report on 'Unethical' Conversion." *International Journal of Buddhist Thought & Culture* 22 (February 2014): 65–86. A review of materials related to contested religions conversions in Sri Lanka.

Part Six
Development of Buddhism
Mahayana and Vajrayana Buddhism

37
How did Buddhism relate to the Brahmanism of the Buddha's day, and later Hinduism?

Christopher V. Jones

The relationship between Buddhism at its origins and Brahmanism is a still much-debated topic. Although nineteenth- and some early-twentieth-century discussions of Buddhism represented the Buddha as something like a reformist who learned from but corrected teachings of his day, most scholarship has now retired the simplistic hypothesis that Buddhism "emerged from Brahmanism," let alone from something that we can accurately call "Hinduism." For two thousand years, the Indian cultural landscape understood Buddhists of different denominations to be separate from Brahmanism or the many branches of philosophy or devotionalism with which Brahmanism became associated, many of which were threads in the rich tapestry of what would later, in the final centuries of the last millennium, come to be called Hinduism.

The Buddha who is remembered in early Buddhist literature interacted with what are usually conceived of as two kinds of religious institution. The first we generally call Brahmanism, which honored the complex sacrificial ritualism associated with the Vedas, a collection of rites and accompanying myths that were the cultural heritage of a portion of society who called themselves *brahman*s, today usually anglicized as brahmins. The second was a tradition of renunciation, in which ascetics (Sanskrit: *śramaṇa*s), among whom the Buddha must be counted, would quit their homes to seek, and sometimes teach about, responses to human suffering. The most successful of these traditions of renunciation is without doubt Buddhism, although Jainism—which has origins contemporaneous to, or a little earlier than Buddhism—also survives to this day and managed to outlive Buddhism in pockets of the Indian subcontinent. Both Brahmanism and these renouncers, the latter of whom generally rejected the authority of the Vedas, responded to an understanding of the human condition that we believe developed before the middle of the first millennium BCE (the late Vedic period): that somehow human action (karma) causes a sentient being to suffer through a process of transmigration/rebirth (*saṃsāra*)—a seemingly endless cycle of death, birth, and further death—from which we are compelled to seek some release. Teachings of Buddhism, as well as Jainism and late Vedic Brahmanism, can be considered as responses to this concern.

We have no reason to doubt that the Buddha was a renouncer who lived and taught in the region of Magadha (in modern-day Bihar), and that he expounded a distinctive way of understanding human action and how it brings about rebirth. In the Brahmanical worldview of his day, karma was understood in terms of ritual action. To correctly perform sacrifice, or to employ a brahmin to do this on one's behalf, was the efficient cause of achieving a good next birth, ideally in the company of one's ancestors and the gods of the Vedic pantheon. In traditions of renunciation that rejected the Vedas, including Jainism, karma was broadened to refer to any action that one performs. All activity was fuel on the fire of our continuing suffering through rebirth, and especially reprehensible was action that does violence to living things (lamentably typical in Vedic sacrifice). Early Buddhism, however, identified karma with intention, or otherwise the quality of the mind as one does some or other deed. In distinction to other traditions, Buddhism understood the mind to be both the engine of further rebirth and the site at which the Buddhist renouncer can attend to their behavior and alter their character, and so also their future. Buddhists considered Vedic ritual to be at best futile, and at worse—when characterized by selfish intent—actively detrimental to the pursuit of liberation.

Early Buddhist criticism of Brahmanism as an institution went further. In sources that describe the Buddha and his teachings he frequently interacts with individuals who call themselves brahmins by virtue of their birth. Brahmanical tradition, as we know it from its own literature, understood that one is born a brahmin, and so entitled because of heritage to learn the content of the Vedas and to perform sacrifice for the benefit of oneself, one's family, and others in the community. But in early Buddhist literature—for example, discourses preserved in the Pali Canon—the Buddha taught that someone is a brahmin not by virtue of birth but only by virtue of purity of practice, which essentially means accomplishment in Buddhist Dharma, such that a follower of the Dharma is in fact a *true* brahmin. This is the foundation for later Buddhist critique of the Brahmanical model of divisions in society, with brahmins at the top and individuals born into servitude at the bottom, which in turn played a significant part in the development of the infinitely more complex Indian system of castes. Buddhism, at an early stage of its history, denied that anyone should be considered noble by virtue of parentage or claimed heritage; true nobility, and so respect from society in general, comes from discipline and commitment to renunciation as taught in Buddhist Dharma.

Other facets of Buddhist teaching can be read as responses to Brahmanical ways of looking at the world. Particularly pertinent is Buddhist teaching about "not-self" (*anātman*), which is at least in part a response to Brahmanical (and wider Indian) interest in discovery of the self (*ātman*), or "what one properly is," which is supposed to be an important step in the achievement of liberation. Buddhism does not simply deny such a thing as a self so much as demonstrate that it is erroneous to take anything in our experience to be enduring or valuable, and so worthy of calling one's self; one must instead get to work altering one's worldview and character in the manner taught by the Buddha. This emphasis on personal development can also be contrasted to ancient Brahmanical interest in the gods, and later in the notion of a supreme deity who can liberate from rebirth whoever is devoted to them. Whereas the Vedas and later Brahmanical literature celebrate the immortality of gods including Brahmā, Agni, and others, Buddhism treats the names of the gods as something like positions of office. Right now, one sentient being occupies the role of the warrior-god Indra, but in time he will die and be reborn otherwise, and another sentient being will occupy the role of "Indra," until his incredibly long life has also run its course and he is replaced. In Buddhism, all sentient beings are necessarily mortal, and, in spite of their power or longevity, even gods are just as bound to rebirth as anyone else. Offerings to gods may help with worldly concerns, but only observance of the Dharma can move someone closer to liberation from suffering entirely.

Buddhism vied for influence in India, primarily against forms of Brahmanism and its devotional traditions (the worship of Viṣṇu and Śiva especially) for around two thousand years, but seems to have all but disappeared from India by the middle of the second millennium of the Common Era. Several centuries later, European colonialists and students of India came to label parts of the diverse religious world of India as Hinduism: a smorgasbord of rites, doctrines, and social structures that is heavily indebted, but not reducible, to Brahmanism. When Europeans in India asked questions about the Buddha, Hindu voices offered some confusing answers: most commonly that the Buddha had been one of the many "descents" (*avatāras*) into the world by the supreme deity Viṣṇu. This idea had existed in Brahmanical teaching for over a thousand years, and on the surface seems to understand the Buddha and his Dharma to be things taught by the benevolent Viṣṇu for particular audiences. But the origins of this myth are less accepting; Viṣṇu is supposed to have taken this form in order to deceive wicked-minded beings, who at a later point in time will be eliminated by the deity's next, more martial appearance, signifying the final triumph of Brahmanism over Buddhism. Hinduism remembered Buddhism as something that had been accommodated within its parameters, but this was enacted to undermine Buddhism's authority in India rather than to in any way legitimize it. Today, the Indian constitution recognizes Buddhism to be a mode of Hinduism: a fact that challenges some common presumptions about how different communities or authorities understand these terms and to what they refer. Of course, Buddhism long ago exceeded the borders of the Indian cultural sphere: it traversed Central and East Asia, the Indian Ocean, and beyond, long before anyone—Indian or otherwise—came to call forms of Indian thought and practice "Hindu." As of the last century, Buddhism once again has a not insignificant presence in India, and its teachings continue to be used to undermine discrimination by birth, which, in spite of many reforms, remains a feature of life in the subcontinent. Although the socio-historical context of Buddhism's origins remains at best opaque, what cannot be denied is that Buddhism has a long history of arguing over who has the right to consider themselves a true brahmin, or someone who is truly "noble," and that in these struggles many of Buddhism's primary interlocutors—its targets but also influences—have been texts, teachers, and traditions that were antecedents to modern Hinduism.

About the author

Christopher V. Jones is a Bye-Fellow of Selwyn College, and affiliated lecturer and research associate at the Faculty of Divinity, University of Cambridge. A primary focus of his research is the history of Mahayana Buddhist thought in the early centuries of the Common Era, preserved in Sanskrit, Chinese, and Tibetan literature.

Suggestions for further reading

In this book

See Chapters 3 (ritual), 8 (is Buddhism atheistic, non-theistic, or theistic?), 9 (what we know of the historical Buddha), 16 (rebirth), 53 (influence of other religions), and 54 (interreligious relations).

Elsewhere

Bronkhorst, Johannes. *Buddhism in the Shadow of Brahmanism*. Leiden and Boston: Brill, 2011.

Gombrich, Richard. *How Buddhism Began: The Conditioned Genesis of the Early Teachings* (2nd edition). London and New York: Routledge, 2006.

McGovern, Nathan. *The Snake and the Mongoose: The Emergence of Identity in Early Indian Religion*. New York and Oxford: Oxford University Press, 2019.

38
What splits were there in Buddhism in the early centuries?

Peter Harvey

Just after the Buddha's passing away (c. 404 BCE), a "communal recitation" (council) of 500 enlightened monks was held to agree the contents of the Buddha's teachings and the monastic discipline (*Vinaya*) he had developed. Perhaps seventy years later, another council was held to guard against laxity among some monks, and, a further sixteen year later, the first schism in the previously unified monastic community (Sangha) occurred; other such schisms followed. The causes of these were generally disagreements over monastic discipline, though the points of *vinaya* which separated the early monastic fraternities often arose from variant developments in geographically separated communities, rather than from actual disagreements. Discussion of points of doctrine also led to the development of different interpretative schools of thought, although, originally, these could not be a cause of schism. Early on, monastics with different doctrinal views could be found in the same monastic fraternity. But perhaps by the second century BCE, the fraternities came to be known for the specific doctrinal interpretations common among their members. By around 100 CE at least, schisms could occur over points of doctrine, and the distinction between a "fraternity" and a "school" faded. While members of different monastic fraternities could not take part in official Sangha business together, they often shared the same monasteries, and studied each other's doctrines. The laity was probably not very concerned about the differences between the fraternities or schools.

The cause of the first schism is not agreed. The Theravada tradition says that it was about lax practice. The Sarvāstivāda school say it was on doctrinal matters, though this is unlikely so early. It was probably about a minority of monks wanting to incorporate new developing practices in monastic deportment, dress, and behavior in public into the formal monastic code, to ensure monastic rigor where Buddhism was spreading into new areas. The reformist section did not win over the more conservative majority, so a schism ensued. The reformists called themselves the Sthaviras (Pali: Theras), the Elders. The majority called themselves the Mahāsāṃghikas, or those "Belonging to the Universal Sangha."

Among the Sthaviras, three systematic schools of thought developed during the third century BCE: the Pudgalavāda, Sarvāstivāda, and Vibhajyavāda. The fraternities originating from the Mahāsāṃghikas, who were more conservative on monastic discipline, were more *doctrinally* open, and so developed more new ideas and later took to Mahayana ideas more readily.

The Pudgalavādins, or "Personalists" saw the "person" as a kind of subtle Self, which, being an organic whole that included the processes of body and mind (Sanskrit: *dharma*s; Pali: *dhamma*s), was neither the same as nor distinct from them. Here, they differed from all other Buddhist schools, which saw the Buddha's references to "person" as merely a conventional way of referring to a particular collection of processes, which were empty of any self-essence.

The Sarvāstivādins, or "Pan-realists," became the dominant school in north India, especially in the northwest, and then in Central Asia on the route to China. A form of their monastic code in time became the one used in Tibet. They became known for their view that not only present phenomena (*dharma*s) exist, but also past and future ones, as they could be objects of knowledge. Moreover, past actions must still in a sense exist, to be able to have karmic effects in the present, and dispositions exist even when not influencing present experience. They also saw each of the various kinds of physical and mental *dharma*s that reality is composed of as having a kind of timeless essence, and tended to see them as fundamental and indivisible ultimate realities. The Sautrāntikas, though, who were affiliated with them, were critical of this last tendency.

In south India, the Sarvāstivādins did not have a strong presence, but the Vibhajyavādins, or "Distinctionists" did, as well as in Ceylon (now Sri Lanka) and also the northwest. Fraternities following their ideas included the Dharmaguptakas, whose *vinaya* is the one still used in China, and the Tāmraparṇīyas in Ceylon and the southeast. The latter were later called the Theravada, Pali for "school of the Elders": by implication the "Elders" of the first schism. The Theravada survived in south India until the seventeenth century, and then withdrew to its base in Ceylon, having also spread to Southeast Asia. All other pre-Mahayana schools of thought eventually died out in India.

The Vibhajyavādins saw only present *dharma*s as existing and saw nirvana as the sole unconditioned *dharma*, unlike the Sarvāstivādins, who also included space in this category. The Vibhajyavādins held that, as the unconditioned is beyond space and time, it cannot have any divisions within it. It is not distant from any place or time, however, so is always available to be experienced.

The Theravada canon of early Buddhist teachings, the Pali Canon is the only surviving complete canon of such texts, although parts of other ones are found in Chinese or Tibetan translations.

The monastic traditions of all surviving forms of Buddhism go back to fraternities descended from the Sthaviras of the first schism, which means that much less is known of the Mahāsāṃghika ones. One of their texts, the *Mahāvastu*, describes itself as a work of the Lokottaravāda, or "Transcendentalist" school. It sees Gautama as "transcendental" even before his buddhahood: although highly spiritually developed, he pretends to start from the beginning and make spiritual mistakes. For them, the Buddha was an omniscient being ever in meditation. He was never tired and ate out of mere conformity with the world.

The rise of the Mahayana

Because the only one of the early schools to now survive in all its aspects is the Theravada, "early Buddhism" is sometimes equated with it, in contrast to "the Mahayana," a new movement in Buddhism which started sometime between 150 BCE and 100 CE, as the culmination of various earlier developments, especially from the Mahāsāṃghika and Sarvāstivāda. It developed many sub-strands, which led to the forms of Buddhism in China and the rest of East Asia, and in Tibet.

The Mahayana aimed at perfect buddhahood for all, rather than to become enlightened as an arhat, which it saw as a lesser goal, hence in time calling itself the *Mahā-yāna*: the "Great Vehicle," or "Vehicle (Leading to) the Great." It thus championed the compassion-based, long bodhisattva path to buddhahood. It also developed a new cosmology arising from visualization practices devoutly directed at the Buddha as a glorified, transcendent being. And it developed a philosophical critique of the Sarvāstivāda idea that the basic ingredients of the mind and the world are fundamentally real, arguing instead that, because they are conditioned by other such *dharma*s, they are empty of a separate nature and existence, so that nothing is truly separate, not even nirvana. It saw many of the teachings of the early schools as provisional and partial.

The broad Mahayana movement originated gradually, unlike the Protestant Reformation, and it was not lay-led, as Japanese scholars have sometimes argued. It arose as a loose confederation of groups, each associated with one or more of a number of new sutras: texts attributed to the Buddha. These soon became preserved in writing, in a form of Sanskrit. Later Mahayanists integrated their ideas and systematized them in various competing ways, depending on which text was seen to contain the highest, fullest truth. This process continued in the lands of Tibet and East

Asia, where Buddhist schools also took on differing broad emphases of their own. The Buddhist canon in Chinese and Tibetan are huge libraries. Mahayanist monks and nuns continued to follow one or other of the monastic codes of the earlier fraternities.

About the author

Peter Harvey is Professor of Buddhist Studies (retired), University of Sunderland, UK, and co-founder of the UK Association for Buddhist Studies. He researches Buddhist ethics, meditation, and early Buddhist thought.

Suggestions for further reading

In this book

See Chapters 5 (texts), 13 (bodhisattva), 15 (can we know what the historical Buddha taught?), 20 (non-self teaching), 23 (nirvana), 32 (monastic rules), 39 (contemporary divisions), 45 (Buddha-nature), and 46 (emptiness).

Elsewhere

Berkwitz, S. C. *South Asian Buddhism: A Survey*. London and New York: Routledge, 2010: pages 51–103.

Gethin, Rupert. *The Foundations of Buddhism*. Oxford and New York: Oxford University Press, 1998: pages 202–252.

Harvey, Peter. *An Introduction to Buddhism: Teachings, History and Practices* (2nd edition). Cambridge: Cambridge University Press, 2013: pages 88–113.

Williams, Paul, with Anthony Tribe. *Buddhist Thought: A Complete Introduction to the Indian Tradition*. London and New York: Routledge & Kegan Paul, 2000: pages 83-123.

39
What are the main contemporary divisions in Buddhism: Theravada, Mahayana, and Vajrayana?

Christopher V. Jones

It is frequently said that in the world today there are three types of Buddhism: Theravada, Mahayana, and Vajrayana. This is certainly true, although it is wrong to think of these as monolithic entities, or as three "schools" or "sects" that differ from each other in simple matters of belief. Each of these labels has a complex history, and refers to families of still very diverse modes of Buddhist thought and practice across different regions and periods of Asian and, more recently, global religious history.

Theravada is a Pali term that means "the school (*vāda*) of the elders (*thera*s)." It is sometimes referred to as Southern Buddhism, and is prominent in Sri Lanka and across Southeast Asia (Myanmar, Thailand, Cambodia, Laos, and parts of Vietnam). One way of understanding Theravada Buddhism is that it is Buddhism that has at its heart the authority of the Pali Canon: a body of literature divided into three "baskets" (*piṭaka*s) of many hundreds of texts, most of which are held to remember things said by the Buddha himself. This literature preserves an account of the foundations of all forms of Buddhism, although types of Mahayana and Vajrayana

Buddhism understand many teachings and practices in the Pali Canon to be in need of further clarification or contextualization.

The use of the term Theravada to designate all forms of Pali Buddhism is relatively recent, although the Theravada as a monastic fraternity traces its heritage back to councils among the early Indian Buddhist Sangha, and then missionary activity considered to have been commissioned by the Indian emperor Aśoka (reign c. 268–232 BCE), in whose era Buddhism was first transmitted to Sri Lanka. It was there that Theravada identity as we know it today began to take shape, informed also by stories of the Buddha's ventures to Sri Lanka and its legitimization by him as a site for the preservation of the Dharma. Since the early second millennium, Theravada Buddhism has been the dominant form of Buddhism in Southeast Asia, where its authority has for many centuries been bound closely to that of one or other kingdom or state, and where all manner of customs and beliefs have been blended with basic Buddhist concerns about rebirth, and the benefits of knowing and doing meritorious action. Although Theravada Buddhism is certainly more than simply observance of things taught in Pali literature, and lived Buddhist practice in Theravadin cultures may involve only infrequent reference to the Pali Canon, the Theravada nevertheless understands itself as the preserver of the Buddha's "original" teachings, in distinction from all manner of ideas attributed to him in later centuries.

It is important that the Theravada not be thought to speak exhaustively for all Buddhist institutions that flourished in India either side of the year zero. Other divisions of the Buddhist Sangha revered variations of what is preserved in the Pali Canon, glimpses of which survive in literature preserved in other Indic languages, including Sanskrit and Gāndhārī, or translated into Chinese or Tibetan. Forms of what may be called mainstream Buddhism, of which the Theravada is our last living example, flourished across India and Central Asia well into the first millennium of the Common Era. This can be contrasted with forms of Buddhism that developed either a century or so before or after the start of the Common Era, and which are collectively known as Mahayana Buddhism.

Mahayana is a Sanskrit term that means "the great (*mahā*) vehicle (*yāna*)." Mahayana Buddhism flourished in India and Central Asia alongside mainstream Buddhism, and today is still prominent in China, Korea, Vietnam, Japan, Nepal, Tibet, Mongolia, and anywhere else in the world to which traditions from these cultures have since spread. Its forms are sometimes categorized in terms of Eastern Buddhism (e.g., China, Korea, Japan, Vietnam) and Northern Buddhism, which some equate with Vajrayana Buddhism (e.g., Tibet, Mongolia, Central Asia). The Mahayana in India was not one thing, and its manifestations across Asia today are no more unified. In its Indian homeland, the Mahayana may be best imagined as a second wave of innovation in Buddhist thinking, doing, and writing that was oriented around a shift in what Buddhists aspired to achieve, and which continued to evolve in India and abroad for over a thousand years.

Exponents of mainstream Buddhism in India (and today the Theravada tradition) make as their ultimate aim the achievement of nirvana. Early in the history of Indian Buddhism, a distinction was made between an arhat, who is led to liberation by the Buddha and his Dharma, and a buddha, whose emergence and promotion of Dharma after a period of its absence constitutes a transformation in the world. Scholars believe that around the turn of the Common Era some Buddhists in India had started to aspire to become bodhisattvas, and made becoming a buddha their goal. They took as sources of authority discourses attributed to the Buddha (sutras) that were unknown to mainstream Buddhism, and which remain unaccepted by Theravada Buddhism today.

Forms of Mahayana Buddhism imagine as the ultimate goal the status of a buddha, which requires a commitment to lead all other sentient beings closer to liberation, to help them become either arhats or fully fledged buddhas themselves (just some traditions of the Mahayana understand that *everyone* can attain the status of a buddha). But apart from this unifying aspiration, our sources for the history of Mahayana Buddhism boast a tremendous diversity of perspectives. At its heart, Mahayana practice entails the cultivation of "perfections" (Sanskrit: *pāramitā*s): virtues that include generosity, patience, and insight which should be developed to a superlative degree over lifetimes of dedication and toil. Mahayana literature played a formative role in the development of philosophies in India and across Asia: for example, in its commitment to explaining how all things that we experience are like illusions, or "empty" (Sanskrit: *śūnya*). Some traditions of the Mahayana, still very prevalent in East Asia today, affirm the existence of buddhas other than Śākyamuni, most famously the Buddha Amitābha (Amida in Japan), who are teaching in worlds that are parallel to our own, into whose company a devotee can be reborn in their next life. Otherwise, particularly influential texts like the *Lotus Sutra* teach that our last buddha, Śākyamuni, transcends what was seen of his physical body and continues to be influential in the world. Together with Śākyamuni and other buddhas, forms of Mahayana Buddhism also revere a pantheon of powerful, "godlike" bodhisattvas, some of whom are in all but name like buddhas themselves. Most important of these is perhaps Avalokiteśvara, a maximally compassionate figure who is an important focus of devotion across Tibet and East Asia.

A third division of Buddhism is the Vajrayana, the "diamond or adamantine (*vajra*) vehicle," which is used to refer to modes of Buddhism found especially in Nepal, Tibet, and Mongolia, although also with some presence in Japan and, more recently, in South Asia, Europe, and the Americas, due to the influence there of the Tibetan diaspora. Vajrayana is often equated with Tantric Buddhism, which might mean Buddhism that observes the authority of Tantras—a subset of sutra literature that appeared in the second half of the first millennium CE—or otherwise the esoteric ritual procedures promoted in those texts. However, Vajrayana Buddhism is not quite a "third kind" of Buddhism distinct from the Theravada and Mahayana traditions. Practitioners of Vajrayana Buddhism understand the goal of their practice to be the achievement of complete awakening, i.e., the final goal of a bodhisattva, and recognize the authority of discourses proper to Mahayana Buddhism. A Vajrayana Buddhist is necessarily a Mahayana Buddhist, although Vajrayana Buddhism prioritizes forms of practice beyond what we find in other Mahayana literature. Vajrayana Buddhism entails the practice of complex ritualism, or otherwise programs of personal self-improvement informed by these (forms of what might be called yoga). Tantric Buddhist discourses report the Buddha expounding ritual procedures that aim to aid or accelerate a bodhisattva's pursuit of awakening, and which were to be transmitted and practiced only by persons initiated into their use. There emerged a distinction between the bodhisattva's "way of perfections," referring to Mahayana teachings more generally, and the "way of incantations," which involves the use of empowered utterances (mantras), or elaborate diagrams by which one engages with powerful bodhisattvas and deities (mandalas), and a wider range of other ritual behaviors and instruments besides. Vajrayana practitioners make offerings to deities who are recognizable also from the Hindu traditions of India, as well as a great number of other gods and spirits who might be invoked as protectors, healers, or anthropomorphic embodiments of Buddhist Dharma.

In summary, the difference between Theravada Buddhism, our last living inheritor of "mainstream" or pre-Mahayana Buddhism from India, and the Mahayana is one of aspiration, while the difference between Mahayana and Vajrayana is primarily one of approach. But these simple distinctions do no justice to the diversity of ideas and practices proper to each of these three families of traditions, which have over the centuries transformed as they journeyed across Asia, then the world, and which continue to promote Buddhist Dharma by innumerable different expressions.

About the author

Christopher V. Jones is a Bye-Fellow of Selwyn College, and affiliated lecturer and research associate at the Faculty of Divinity, University of Cambridge. A primary focus of his research is the history of Mahayana

Buddhist thought in the early centuries of the Common Era, preserved in Sanskrit, Chinese, and Tibetan literature.

Suggestions for further reading

In this book
See Chapters 1 (is Buddhism a religion?), 5 (texts), 8 (is Buddhism atheistic, non-theistic, or theistic?), 10 (buddhahood), 13 (bodhisattva), 15 (can we know what the historical Buddha taught?), 23 (nirvana), 25 (saints), 40 (Hinayana), 47 (Tantra and sex), 53 (influence of other religious traditions), 54 (interreligious relations), 51 (mandala), and 61 (Buddhism and politics).

Elsewhere
Crosby, Kate. *Theravada Buddhism: Continuity, Diversity, and Identity.* Chichester, UK: Wiley-Blackwell, 2014.

Snellgrove, David. *Indo-Tibetan Buddhism: Indian Buddhists and their Tibetan Successors.* London: Serindia, 1987.

Strong, John. *Buddhisms: An Introduction.* London: Oneworld, 2015.

Williams, Paul. *Mahāyāna Buddhism: The Doctrinal Foundations* (2nd edition). London: Routledge, 2009.

40
What is Hinayana?

Elizabeth J. Harris

The term "Hinayana" has been used in three broad ways, one of which can be seen as a misrepresentation that has caused hurt to Theravada Buddhists. The term literally means lesser or lower (*hina*) vehicle or way (*yāna*). It was first used by Mahayana Buddhists to denote the early Buddhist schools that they were breaking away from. They used it together with the term *śrāvakayāna*, or vehicle of the hearers/listeners. It is found, for instance, in some ancient Chinese sources. In this setting, the term expressed the conviction of Mahayana Buddhists that their ways of seeing the Buddhist path and its goal were superior to the early schools of those who "heard" the Buddha's teaching and became enlightened as arhats.

The term also came to be used within some Mahayana Buddhist traditions, particularly in some Tibetan sources, to denote the basic, foundational training that was absolutely necessary within the Buddhist path. "Hinayana" here was the first stage of Buddhist practice, without which the rest could not happen. The use here was not pejorative, although Tibetan sources contrast it with bodhisattva practice within the next levels of training. As foundational training, it included developing morality and meditative practices. The term is still widely used by contemporary teachers within Tibetan schools of Buddhism, as any Google search will show. Some teachers, however, prefer to use the term *śrāvakayāna* to avoid implying that these practices are lesser or lower.

The third way in which "Hinayana" has been used is as a term for Theravada Buddhism. This is where misrepresentation has entered. The early Buddhist schools from which Mahayana Buddhism broke away were diverse. Not one of them can be equated with the Theravada Buddhism of today, although the Theravada monastic lineage developed from one of them and the Pali texts lie in continuity with them. So Theravada Buddhism as we know it today was not the target of early Mahayana. In fact, with the gradual disappearance of Buddhism from India, including all early schools, "Hinayana" became a term without an actual historical referent. Nor can it be argued that the basic, foundational practices taught, for instance, in Tibetan Buddhism are the same as those within Theravada Buddhism. Yet Theravada Buddhism has always seen the goal of practice to be the attainment of nirvana, as an arhat, as most of the early schools did, and this was key to what early Mahayana felt was wrong about these schools. The *Lotus Sutra* makes this quite clear. So, in some Mahayana contexts, particularly popular ones, Theravada Buddhism came to be called "Hinayana," because it shared characteristics with these early schools.

Needless to say, Theravada Buddhists have never used this term to refer to themselves and a great deal of hurt has been caused by this designation. What religious group would wish to be judged as following a lesser path? In 1950, for instance, the World Fellowship of Buddhists (WFB), gathered in Colombo, Sri Lanka, unanimously passed a resolution that "Hinayana" should not be used to describe Theravada.

Most scholars of Buddhism today do not use the term "Hinayana" to describe Theravada Buddhism, but the misrepresentation still continues in some contexts. The term is best understood historically, arising in the early centuries of Buddhist history in a polemical context, later used in some forms of Mahayana Buddhism to denote essential, foundational training.

About the author

Elizabeth J. Harris is an Honorary Senior Research Fellow within the Edward Cadbury Centre for the Public Understanding of Religion,

University of Birmingham, UK. Her research interests include Theravada Buddhism, religion and conflict, and interreligious studies.

Suggestions for further reading

In this book
See Chapters 38 (early splits), 39 (contemporary divisions), and 44 (bodhisattva vow).

41
What is Zen Buddhism?

Hiroko Kawanami

One of the stereotypical images we have of Zen Buddhism is that of a solitary monk meditating in a sitting posture or that of a serene zen garden comprised of carefully placed rocks and gravel raked to represent water ripples. The term "zen" originated from the pronunciation of *djan* which became *chan* in Chinese, deriving from *dhyāna* in Sanskrit or *jhāna* in Pali, meaning a state of "absorption" in the practice of Buddhist meditation. Chan is a school of Mahayana Buddhism, the roots of which lie in sixth-century China, and which spread to other countries in East Asia after the eighth century. It was introduced to Japan as Zen Buddhism in the twelfth to thirteenth centuries by two Japanese monks, Eisai and Dogen, who traveled to China to study the Buddhist scriptures and methods of practice. Eisai (1141–1215) founded the Rinzai school on his return to Japan. He was instrumental in introducing Zen Buddhism to the newly ascendant warrior class, who welcomed its practice to enhance their skills in martial arts and self-control. It was a time in Japanese history marked by political upheavals, natural disasters, and a major change of social order. Old Buddhist establishments were being eclipsed by new forms of Buddhism, which appealed to the peasant classes by advocating *tariki* (Japanese: relying on other higher power) or "faith" to be saved in a degenerate age (Japanese: *mappō*). Eisai's younger contemporary, Dogen (1200–1253) established the Soto school in Japan. In contrast to Eisai, Dogen rejected associations with political power and tried to find the pure Zen. His practice emphasized *jiriki* (Japanese: one's own power), and practitioners were encouraged to cultivate their inner strength through meditation to overcome many difficulties in life and eventually attain enlightenment.

Zen is characterized by a set of tendencies that might seem to be opposite to each other such as Buddha-nature and emptiness, and sudden and gradual enlightenment. It is said that the semi-legendary Indian monk Bodhidharma transmitted Chan Buddhism to China in the sixth century and employed the "sudden method" to awaken the Chan patriarch Huike. But it was Shenhui in the eighth century who emphasized "sudden enlightenment" as opposed to "gradual enlightenment." Chan Buddhism teaches how to activate "sudden enlightenment" by gaining insight into one's "Buddha-nature," regarded as to be pure and undefiled. It is said that, as one practices intensely, an insight arrives and the true nature of reality becomes suddenly clear to the practitioner. However, it is believed that "sudden enlightenment" cannot be sustained unless it is followed up by continuous training and the purification of consciousness.

In practice, Zen Buddhism goes beyond conceptual dualism and binary thought (thinking there is a separation between the self and the rest of the world, or between the mind and the body) by de-emphasizing one's adherence to intellectual knowledge. Therefore, its practice aims to gain a different level of realization which allows one to become free from social assumptions, cultural norms, and prejudices. The ultimate aim is to achieve satori, which is articulated as *kenshō* (seeing the true or original nature) in Japanese. The main method of mental cultivation emphasizes the practice of *zazen* or "just sitting" in the correct posture. *Shikantaza* is another form of sitting meditation, especially employed in the Soto school, in which the practitioner does not use any specific object or a style of practice but just sits and remains as much as possible in the present moment. The breath-counting meditation is called *susoku-kan*, and, together with the practice of repeating a mantra with the breath, it is the starting point for a practitioner as well as the main method for building on the power of concentration.

The Rinzai school is known for its use of koan, which are short riddles given by the Zen master which are not solvable by ordinary intellectual reasoning. It is designed to bypass the normal process of thinking and subsequently lead to satori. In a Zen monastery, every mode of conduct for a practitioner is ritually prescribed in the way one walks, sits, chants, eats, prostrates oneself to a teacher, or shows respect to a fellow practitioner. Thus, Zen is not only about the practice of sitting meditation, and various chants and rituals are conducted in temples to propitiate the Buddha, ancestors, local deities, and spirits. Participating in a funeral may be the most common reason for lay Buddhists to visit a Zen temple, but ritual for repentance or confession is also popular. An important element in Zen ritual is the performance of ritual prostrations, and many ceremonies are conducted specifically for sutra recitation and chanting. Most commonly recited in Japanese Zen temples are the *Heart Sutra*, the *Diamond Sutra*, and the *Guanyin Sutra* from the *Lotus Sutra*, although a wider number of Mahayana sutras will be known.

Zen Buddhism in the West has been popularized by the work of D. T. Suzuki (1894–1966), a Japanese Zen scholar who was influenced by the "New Buddhism" movement in late-nineteenth-century Japan, and promoted an intellectual version of Zen that appealed to a Western audience. Suzuki, who could be described as a "Buddhist modernist," laid emphasis on the personal, intuitive experience that transcended national and cultural boundaries. In other words, he propagated a direct Buddhist experience devoid of history, ritual, or communal worship, which was to become known as "Western Zen." Suzuki also explored the source of creativity in one's spontaneous intuitive experiences, and emphasized the relationship between Zen and the arts. As a result, certain aspects of Zen Buddhism came to be associated with avant-garde art, experimental music, theater, and poetry, and was adopted by counterculture artists and writers in mid-twentieth-century America, such as Allen Ginsberg, Jack Kerouac, Gary Snyder, and Philip Whalen, among those known as the Beat Generation.

Zen Buddhism allows one's outward actions to be guided by mindful intuition rather than by conscious effort, and the ultimate aim is to achieve a deep awareness of the reality in which one is situated. Physical work is incorporated in Zen monasteries as part of their daily training to help practitioners fully focus and stay immersed in the "here and now." Since the mind can get sluggish easily, a practitioner is normally given a menial task, such as raking the sand, peeling potatoes, or cleaning the toilet, so that he/she stays fully active and remains in the present moment. For some, however, the discipline and service involved in the practice become the means to an end. Gary Snyder wrote, "There is a body–mind dualism if I am sweeping the floor and thinking about Hegel. But if I am sweeping the floor and thinking about sweeping the floor, I am all one . . . Sweeping the floor becomes, then, the most important thing in the world, which it is" (Gary Snyder, *The Real Work* [1980]). Although the "self" has become the authority in the search for inner spirituality in the West today, the role of a Zen teacher, called a roshi, is still considered essential in the Buddhist tradition. This is because the cultivation of the mind is a gradual progress, and it requires careful guidance and "mind to mind" transmission by someone who is more advanced in practice and is responsible for the disciple's spiritual welfare. Hence, a Zen master becomes the most powerful influence in aiding the practitioner's mental development. Nonetheless, since every person has a different disposition and needs, finding the right teacher can be the most crucial part in practicing Zen.

About the author

Hiroko Kawanami is a Professor in the Department of Politics, Philosophy and Religion at Lancaster University, UK. She is known as a specialist in Myanmar Buddhism but has also conducted fieldwork in several Buddhist countries.

Suggestions for further reading

In this book
See Chapters 5 (texts) 24 (enlightenment), 26 (why Buddhists meditate), 28 (kinds of meditation), 39 (contemporary divisions), 42 (Pure Land Buddhism), 45 (Buddha-nature), and 46 (emptiness).

Elsewhere
Heine, S., and D. S. Wright. *The Koan: Texts and Contexts in Zen Buddhism*. Oxford: Oxford University Press, 2000.

McRae, J. R. *Seeing through Zen: Encounter, Transformation, and Genealogy in Chinese Chan Buddhism*. Berkeley: University of California Press, 2003.

Suzuki, D. T. *An Introduction to Zen Buddhism*. New York: Grove Press, 1991.

42
What is Pure Land Buddhism?

Wendy Dossett

Pure Land Buddhism is an umbrella term for a variety of schools of Mahayana Buddhism which draw on the three Pure Land Sutras. It is characterized by gratitude and devotion to the Buddha Amitābha, more commonly known by his Japanese name, Amida. There is evidence of Pure Land thought in Northern India/Central Asia in the first century of the Common Era, and it was to become dominant among a variety of traditions practiced in East Asia, and particularly in Japan.

The Western postcolonial standpoint can be an obstacle to the appreciation of Pure Land Buddhism because of its tendency to cast it as an "easier" or "lesser" form than the imagined Pali Buddhism of the Buddha's time, failing to live up both to the world-denying monastic ideal of the Theravada tradition and to the assumed rationalism which appealed as much to the Victorian orientalists as it does to "secular Buddhists" today. However, Pure Land thought draws strongly on the Mahayana notion of absolute compassion as a property of awakening, on a concern to avoid the potential ego-entrapments of spiritual pride, on the notion of awakening for all, and on the practice of remembering the Buddha as a form of mindfulness. In these respects, it aligns with core Buddhist ideas present from earliest times.

The *Larger Pure Land Sutra* (Sanskrit: *Sukhāvatīvyūha Sūtra*) relates the story of the monk Dharmakāra, once a king, who made forty-eight bodhisattva vows before the Buddha Lokeśvararāja, a buddha of a previous age, to bring all beings to awakening in a realm of purification (a Pure Land), through his eons of diligent practice. As the fruition of his vows, Dharmakāra becomes a buddha, commonly known by his Japanese name, Amida. Amida presides over his "buddhafield," the Pure Land, known as Sukhāvatī (Land or Realm of Bliss), thought to be unimaginably far away to the west, offering rebirth there for anyone who calls on him in despair of their ability to attain awakening through their own practice or virtue. The texts describe Sukhāvatī in gorgeous detail, as a world without sorrow or affliction, brightened by Amida's radiance. It has beautiful gardens and bejeweled trees, and the very breeze sings the Dharma. All of this is described in detail, for the purposes of contemplation and visualization. Those who harbor doubts are born into the buds of lotus flowers which will inevitably bloom, and those without doubts are born immediately into Amida's presence. Here, in this state, awakening is attained immediately.

Pure Land Buddhist ideas are found in Tibetan Buddhism, but, in China and Japan, Pure Land became a distinctive school. Here the notion of the Age of the Degenerate Dharma (Japanese: *mappō*) began to play a part in Pure Land thinking. One of the Chinese Patriarchs, Daochuo (562–645 CE), drew a distinction between the Path of the Sages, a path wide open at the time of the historical Buddha, but which was now closing or closed, and the Pure Land path. It had become too difficult to attain awakening via the practices and virtues of Pali Buddhism, because, in the current age, the passions, attachments, and karmic bonds were too strong. The only hope in this current age was the compassionate vow and infinite merit store of Amida, and the Pure Land path.

Pure Land Buddhism was to develop further during the medieval (Japanese: Kamakura) period in Japan, when there was a shift to the single-minded practice of chanting the name of the Buddha Amida (Japanese: *nembutsu*). Two monks of an older school, Hōnen (1133–1212) and Shinran (1173–1262), despaired of the traditional paths of asceticism and meditation and of the hypocrisy they saw in Buddhist institutions, left the great training monastery on Mount Hiei, and relied solely on the vows of Amida. Hōnen advocated the simple practice of the constant repetition of the *nembutsu*. Shinran, who considered himself but a follower of Hōnen, nonetheless developed Pure Land thought further, by eschewing repetition and emphasizing yet more strongly the "other power" (Japanese: *tariki*) nature of the teachings. He disrobed, married, ate meat, and fathered children, acts considered to represent serious backsliding. These acts were taken by tradition as a clear indication of his despair of meditation, and the ascetic and virtue practices linked to an idea of "self-power," and a demonstration of his trust in the vow of Amida. For Shinran, the notion of *mappō* was all-consuming. Not only was it impossible to attain awakening through the old teachings, but the aspiration to do so was founded entirely on spiritual pride and ego. Individuals must know themselves as they really are, foolish beings completely ensnared by ego. Thus, the only available orientation to the world is gratitude for the work that Amida has done, expressed in the spontaneous upwelling of the *nembutsu*. Shinran's extensive writings, and writings about him, show him as a self-searching and humble man, who identified with illiterate and socially marginalized groups. Both Hōnen and Shinran were exiled by the authorities for their heretical teachings, and the *nembutsu* was banned. In subsequent generations, their teachings were formalized into Jōdo Shu and Jōdo Shinshū respectively.

These teachings had far-reaching political and social implications. The Kamakura period saw the rise of "lay" Buddhism, which brought in those usually excluded from participation in Buddhism (e.g., certain professions, classes of people, lawbreakers, the illiterate, and, to an extent, women and children). Pure Land Buddhism increased this trend, challenging religious hierarchies and exclusions through its notion that awakening in the Pure Land is available to all—a teaching that resonated with the view that we all possess Buddha-nature, present in many Mahayana schools.

Unlike the other Kamakura Schools of Zen and Nichiren, Pure Land Buddhism has not had significant appeal in the anglophone world. It has a presence in locations with significant Japanese-American populations, for example California, Hawai'i, and to a lesser extent Brazil and other Latin American countries. However, "converts" without Asian heritage are small in number compared with, say, Zen. The Amida order, originating in the United Kingdom, is an interesting example of a small, modern order whose members are not, for the most part, of Asian heritage. It considers itself an inheritor of Hōnen's teachings. Among the most internationally well-known modern Chinese Pure Land traditions is that of the Amitābha Buddhist Society of Master Chin Kung, based in Taiwan, although with a presence in Australia, the U.S., and the UK.

The lack of appeal of Pure Land Buddhism in the West may perhaps be due to its failure to conform to the image of Buddhism, forged by the early orientalist scholars, as individualistic, striving, spiritual rationalism. It may also be due to the structural similarities with Christianity (a salvific figure, a utopian afterlife, salvation for all sinners), rendering it unappealing to those whose spiritual search has entailed the rejection of Christianity. Lack of interest at a popular level is mirrored in a decided lack of scholarly attention compared to the attention afforded to other forms of Mahayana Buddhism.

About the author
Dr. Wendy Dossett is Associate Professor of Religious Studies at the University of Chester, UK. Her PhD explored Japanese Pure Land Buddhism. She currently researches Buddhism and spirituality in addiction recovery.

Suggestions for further reading

In this book
See Chapters 8 (is Buddhism atheistic, non-theistic, or theistic?), 10 (buddhahood), 24 (enlightenment), 27 (mindfulness), 29 (chanting), and 41 (Zen).

Elsewhere

Dobbins, J. C. *Jōdo Shinshū: Shin Buddhism in Medieval Japan*. Honolulu: University of Hawai'i Press, 2002.

Halkias, G. *Luminous Bliss: A Religious History of Pure Land Literature in Tibet*. Honolulu: University of Hawai'i Press, 2017.

Hirota, D. (editor). *Toward a Contemporary Understanding of Pure Land Buddhism: Creating a Shin Buddhist Theology in a Religiously Plural World*. Albany: State University of New York Press, 2000.

Jones, C. B. *Chinese Pure Land Buddhism: Understanding a Tradition of Practice*. Honolulu: University of Hawai'i Press, 2019.

43
What is the role of the Dalai Lama?

Cathy Cantwell

The Dalai Lama is sometimes described in Western sources as a "god-king," or sometimes depicted as a kind of Buddhist Pope. These presentations indicate something of the Dalai Lama's significance in Tibet—his spiritually advanced status, his political centrality, and the religious institution associated with him—yet, in many ways, they are misleading.

To start with the spiritual status—for the Dalai Lama is first and foremost a lama (religious teacher) and the first Dalai Lamas were not Heads of State—the Dalai Lama is a tulku or a recognized rebirth in a connected line of lamas, considered as an advanced bodhisattva with control over his own rebirth. As such, he is considered able to choose where to take birth, and repeatedly returns from life to life to Tibet in order to benefit the beings there. There are many such series of reincarnating lamas in Tibetan Buddhism, and the tulku institution was already becoming established as a dominant mode for the transmission of institutionalized religious authority in Tibetan monasteries before the Dalai Lamas came on the scene. There is no fully integrated hierarchy of tulkus, yet within specific monastic orders tulkus may be ranked, and higher-ranking tulkus such as the Dalai Lama may be additionally considered to represent emanations of the principal pan-Buddhist bodhisattvas. Thus, the Dalai Lamas—like the Karmapa tulkus who head the Karma Kagyü order—are considered emanations of Avalokiteśvara, while the Sakya order's hierarchs are seen as emanations of Mañjuśrī. In the Tibetan context, Avalokiteśvara is seen as a buddha, in accordance with textual sources recounting Avalokiteśvara's attainment of enlightenment in the distant past, and also with sources emphasizing Avalokiteśvara as a primordial buddha emanation.

A further feature of the equation of the Dalai Lama with this buddha/bodhisattva figure is that Tibetan mythological narratives link Avalokiteśvara with the cultural heroes of the Tibetan imperial period from the seventh to ninth centuries, so that successive Tibetan emperors associated with the early establishment of Buddhism in Tibet, as well as the kings who preceded them, came to be seen as Avalokiteśvara emanations. Moreover, Avalokiteśvara is considered to be involved with the fate of the Tibetan people, and the recitation of Avalokiteśvara's mantra is one of the most ubiquitous popular religious practices throughout Tibetan-speaking regions. Thus, the spiritual status of the Dalai Lama blends Buddhist ideas about Avalokiteśvara and the bodhisattva path with Tibetan understandings of their own cultural history.

From the perspective of religious organization, Buddhism did not develop a single integrated and hierarchical monastic structure or "church," so neither the Dalai Lama nor any other eminent Buddhist figure can be seen as a "Pope." In Tibetan Buddhism, a number of separately structured monastic orders and groups of practitioners developed, each with their own lamas, some of which were tulkus and some hereditary lamas. In some cases, "mother" and "daughter" monasteries remained integrated, while in others they might over time break away from each other. After the rise of the Géluk order to political dominance in the seventeenth century, the Dalai Lama, as the highest-status Géluk tulku, came to have a politically eminent position, as well as being much venerated as a spiritual master throughout Tibet. Yet the Dalai Lama has no formal *religious* authority beyond his own school; and, within the non-Géluk schools, their principal lamas would be treated with equal or greater reverence. Even in the case of the Géluk order, the large monasteries had their own principal lamas—indeed, the

Head of Ganden Monastery near Lhasa is the structural head of the Géluk order. Furthermore, in the tantric religious tradition, an individual's own lama, whatever their formal status, becomes the focus of the disciple's devotions. However, perhaps partly because the Dalai Lama is to some extent removed from and in effect transcends the everyday religious structures, there has been greater scope for him to become a symbol of spiritual authority and stature beyond considerations of sectarian religious or regional affiliations.

The "Great Fifth" was the first Dalai Lama to hold political power at the apex of the state in Tibet, supported by the military intervention of the Mongol Gushri Khan in the mid-seventeenth century. The political system of a central government supported by monastic and aristocratic officials, with the Dalai Lama as Head of State, lasted from the mid-eighteenth to the mid-twentieth centuries. For much of the period, the Dalai Lamas did not directly wield political power, although the Thirteenth Dalai Lama did become an active ruler from the late nineteenth century, leaving a legacy of expectation in relation to the current Fourteenth Dalai Lama. In the period of crisis following the Chinese invasion of Tibet in 1950, the Tibetan government asked the Fourteenth Dalai Lama to assume political control when he was fifteen years old. Following the Dalai Lama's flight into exile in 1959, a new modern political structure was instituted in exile in the 1960s, progressively evolving a more democratic structure. Today, the government-in-exile has an elected President, with the Dalai Lama having retired from any formal political position since 2011.

In the contemporary period, the Fourteenth Dalai Lama has been important in helping to bridge sectarian and regional divides among Tibetans in a time when it has been crucial for Tibetans to forge a new Tibetan national identity. He has also carved out a rather new role in the international context, and has become a central figurehead in ecumenical developments in Asian Buddhism. Rather than remaining of significance only for Tibetans, the Dalai Lama has become a global symbol for peaceful resolutions of conflict, and he has sought to promote spiritual values in the complex multicultural environments of today's world, emphasizing elements common to different religious traditions, such as the cultivation of kindness and compassion. Above all, he has reached out beyond Buddhism, embracing international social and political discourses of contemporary concerns, such as issues of social justice and environmental politics.

The question remains what role—if any—there might be for a future Dalai Lama. The present Dalai Lama has made it clear that the institution will continue only as long as the Tibetans have a need for a Dalai Lama, and he has promised to leave clear guidelines on the recognition of the next incarnation, if it is decided to recognize a Fifteenth. He has emphasized that the government of the PRC (People's Republic of China) can have no legitimate part in such a recognition. At this stage, given the stature of the present incumbent and the reverence in which he is held, both by Tibetans and internationally, it seems overwhelmingly likely that the Tibetans will choose to continue to recognize the next Dalai Lama.

About the author

Cathy Cantwell is an Associate Faculty Member at the Oriental Institute, University of Oxford, and an Honorary Research Fellow at the School of Anthropology and Conservation, University of Kent. She has specialized in Tibetan and Himalayan tantric rituals of all periods from the tenth century CE, including text critical and historical analysis, as well as ethnographic study of contemporary rituals. She was President of the UK Association for Buddhist Studies, 2015–2021.

Suggestions for further reading

In this book
See Chapters 13 (bodhisattva), 28 (kinds of meditation), and 54 (interreligious relations).

Elsewhere

Dalai Lama XIV. *Freedom in Exile: The Autobiography of the Dalai Lama.* San Francisco: Harper San Francisco, 1991.

Schwieger, Peter. *The Dalai Lama and the Emperor of China: A Political History of the Tibetan Institution of Reincarnation.* New York: Columbia University Press, 2015.

Snellgrove, David, and Hugh Richardson. *A Cultural History of Tibet.* Bangkok: Orchid Press, 2004 [1968].

44
What is the bodhisattva vow?

Nick Swann

According to Buddhist literature, when the Buddha became awakened, he developed *siddhi*s, or "psychic powers." One of these was the power to see the effects of karma across all of his past lives. In one of these lives—as a merchant called Sumedha—he met Dīpaṅkara, the previous Buddha, and during their encounter Dīpaṅkara (using his own *siddhi*s) read Sumedha's mind and saw that he would one day also become a fully awakened buddha. This prophecy inspired Sumedha to follow Dīpaṅkara but to resolve to become a buddha rather than an arhat, cultivating the perfections of a buddha over a vast number of lives and then delaying entry to final nirvana (Sanskrit: *parinirvāṇa*) in order to teach the rediscovered Dharma to others. The stories that the Buddha told regarding his past lives are known as *Jātaka*s (birth stories) and in them the Buddha refers to himself as a "bodhisattva," one whose essence, in the sense of core motivating force, is to become awakened (*bodhi*).

The bodhisattva vow concerns (a) this commitment to cultivate the perfections of a buddha and (b) the aspiration to achieve buddhahood in order to benefit all sentient beings. This is in contrast to the kinds of awakened beings who enter final nirvana upon physical death, individually escaping *saṃsāra*'s round of birth and rebirth and leaving others behind. The bodhisattva vow is overwhelmingly associated with Mahayana and Vajrayana

(Tantric) Buddhism, but bodhisattvas are identified in contemporary Southern (Theravada) traditions too.

Along with this overarching vow, more specific guidance is found in the bodhisattva or *bodhicitta* precepts (note these are sometimes referred to as vows as well). *Bodhicitta* translates as the "awakening mind" and it is something that a bodhisattva tries to arouse. There are two kinds of *bodhicitta*; one is to do with resolving to achieve awakening, the other is about actually engaging to make the effort in one's daily life to become awakened. The eighth-century Indian monk Śāntideva compared them to wanting to go traveling and actually setting out on the road, respectively. The bodhisattva/*bodhicitta* precepts are like a training regime to help bodhisattvas detach themselves from *saṃsāra*, while simultaneously cultivating a compassionate attitude to other sentient beings and acting for others' benefit.

There are living lineages of the bodhisattva precepts in both Northern and Eastern Mahayana Buddhist traditions. In Northern traditions there are commonly eighteen root and forty-six auxiliary precepts relating to engaged *bodhicitta*. The root precepts discourage things like: abandoning the whole bodhisattva idea altogether; taking back offerings given to the Buddha, Dharma, and Sangha; and showing contempt for the Dharma by criticizing non-Mahayana Buddhist teachings (after all, the Buddha taught all vehicles). All pretty heinous stuff, but to completely breach one of these precepts bodhisattvas would need: to be fully conscious of what they were doing and not think of it as wrong; show no regret; feel happy about what they had done; and have no shame about the impact of their action on others. The forty-six auxiliary precepts are grouped in sections which more or less map to the six perfections of generosity, morality, patience, effort, meditation, and wisdom, helping the bodhisattva to develop each of these.

In Northern traditions, the bodhisattva vow can be received in an elaborate formal ceremony in its own right, or as part of a tantric initiation. In the case of the former, at one point, the preceptor giving the vow makes a prophecy that those receiving the vow will become buddhas, echoing Dīpaṅkara's prophecy about Sumedha.

In a tantric initiation, the bodhisattva vow is a relatively brief but extremely important phase of the whole process. Buddhist tantric practitioners must also be bodhisattvas to ensure that they use any of their *siddhi*s for the benefit of others and not just themselves. In fact, one of the auxiliary precepts states that, if a bodhisattva has *siddhi*s that can help another (in a Buddhist sense, such as steering someone away from a karmicly bad course of action), then they are obliged to use them.

About the author
Nick Swann is a Senior Lecturer in Buddhist Studies at University of South Wales, UK. His research interests include Buddhist Ethics, Buddhist Tantra, and Anthropology and Religion.

Suggestions for further reading

In this book
See also Chapters 10 (buddhahood), 13 (bodhisattva), 39 (contemporary divisions), and 47 (Tantra and sex).

Elsewhere
Bhikṣuni Heng-Ching Shi (translator). *The Sutra on Upāsaka Precepts*. Berkeley, CA: Numata Center for Buddhist Translation and Research, 1994.

Śāntideva. *The Bodhicaryāvatāra* (translated by Kate Crosby and Andrew Skilton). New York: Oxford University Press, 1995.

The Bodhisattva Vows. Portland, OR: Foundation for the Preservation of the Mahayana Tradition, 2017. https://fpmt.org/wp-content/uploads/education/teachings/texts/prayers-practices/bodhisattva_vows_c5.pdf

45
What is Buddha-nature?

Christopher V. Jones

Mahayana Buddhism was responsible for a great many doctrinal innovations that mainstream Buddhism in India rejected. Among these was the controversial but ultimately influential idea that all sentient beings, across their successive lives, possess at all times the nature of a buddha already, but that this is somehow hidden about them, obscured by afflictions or negative characteristics such as ignorance, desire, hatred, pride, and so forth. Forms of Buddha-nature teaching pervade prominent types of Buddhism that developed in Tibet and in East Asia. But, in its original Indian context, Buddha-nature teaching was very radical, in essence because it at least seems to reimagine the purpose of Buddhist practice from the transformation or development of oneself—from a state of affliction to a state of being liberated or "awakened"—to the discovery or disclosure of a nature that is already there, a perspective reminiscent of what is found in other Indian religious traditions such as Brahmanism or Jainism.

Our English term "Buddha-nature" ultimately comes from the Sanskrit *buddhadhātu*, a term that denotes what is "essential" to a buddha, and which can refer also to the relic of a buddha that is supposed to endure, after his death, within a stupa. Most frequently, however, Buddha-nature is taught with reference to the enigmatic expression *tathāgatagarbha*: the "chamber" or "womb," or possibly also "embryo," for a buddha (the term is notoriously multivalent), which every sentient being (depending on the Buddhist text in question) either "has" or somehow "is." Different

Indian Mahayana texts that discuss Buddha-nature—composed, we believe, between the second and fifth centuries CE—present this idea in different ways. Texts that became particularly influential in Indian and then Tibetan Buddhism understand *tathāgatagarbha* to refer to the basic status of the mind, which is sometimes said to be intrinsically pure or luminous, and needs simply to be cleansed of the afflictions that pollute it. Many strands of Buddhism across Asia were influenced by this notion of Buddha-nature, including early masters in the Chan (or Zen) tradition of East Asia.

However, other Mahayana texts are more unorthodox, and teach that the *tathāgatagarbha*, or otherwise a dormant Buddha-nature, is something mysteriously hidden about one's body, and that, although it cannot be seen by anyone apart from a buddha, it is enduringly present across successive lives. Most contentious is the claim in some of these discourses that one's Buddha-nature can be called, explicitly, a self (Sanskrit: *ātman*), which seemingly departs from a central tenet of earlier and wider Buddhist teaching: that nothing within any sentient being is permanent, or of any enduring value with respect to achieving liberation.

Whether or not teaching about Buddha-nature approaches a notion of selfhood, it nevertheless in all cases suggests a different way of imagining liberation from rebirth. Most Buddhist traditions remained committed to the idea that liberation can only occur because sentient beings are constituted by processes that are in constant flux; through diligent practice one "makes oneself" into either an arhat or, as a bodhisattva, into a buddha. But Buddha-nature teaching imagines liberation to be a process of finding out what one truly is, whether this means the original, pure condition of the mind or even something worthy of being called "one's self." A primary intention of this teaching, however and wherever it is found, was perhaps to reassure practitioners that the goal of their practice is immanently achievable, although it is often in delicate tension with Buddhism's sophisticated way of talking about beings, lives, and progress in terms of processes and the causally conditioned nature of our experience.

About the author

Christopher V. Jones is a Bye-Fellow of Selwyn College, and affiliated lecturer and research associate at the Faculty of Divinity, University of Cambridge. A primary focus of his research is the history of Mahayana Buddhist thought in the early centuries of the Common Era, preserved in Sanskrit, Chinese, and Tibetan literature.

Suggestions for further reading

In this book

See Chapters 5 (texts), 10 (buddhahood), 13 (bodhisattva), 19 (what is reborn), 20 (non-self teaching), and 44 (bodhisattva vow).

Elsewhere

Jones, C. V. *The Buddhist Self: On Tathāgatagarbha and Ātman*. Honolulu: University of Hawai'i Press, 2021.

Ruegg, David Seyfort. *Buddha-Nature, Mind and the Problem of Gradualism in a Comparative Perspective: On the Transmission and Reception of Buddhism in India and Tibet*. London: SOAS, University of London, 1989.

Zimmermann, Michael. *A Buddha Within: The Tathāgatagarbhasūtra—The Earliest Exposition of the Buddha-Nature Teaching in India*. Tokyo: The International Research Institute for Advanced Buddhology, Soka University, 2002.

46
What are the meanings of "emptiness" in Mahayana Buddhism?

Christopher V. Jones

Few aspects of Mahayana Buddhism have attracted as much attention as teachings about emptiness (Sanskrit: *śūnyatā*), or otherwise the claim that all phenomena that we experience are somehow empty (*śūnya*). Most traditions of Mahayana Buddhism accept in some fashion the assertion that "all things are empty," even though there are many ways, in India and elsewhere, in which this claim has been developed and expounded. The Yogacara (or Vijñānavāda) school of philosophy understands emptiness in terms of the non-duality of "perceiving subject" and "perceived object," and teaches a mental continuum that only *imagines* these to be separate realities. Some types of Mahayana literature, such as those concerned with Buddha-nature, attempt to square emptiness teachings with their own affirmative claims about what does, ultimately, exist; the true nature of the mind is adorned with positive qualities, but is fundamentally "empty" of any number of unwholesome characteristics that accrue and are "other" to it. The discussion that follows privileges a particularly influential understanding of teachings about emptiness associated with the Madhyamaka school of thought, which interprets emptiness as a "middle" (*madhyama*) between the erroneous view that things exist as we commonly perceive them, and that they are complete fictions that do not exist at all. Although earlier Buddhist teaching did show some interest in declaring things to be empty (for example, in some texts of the Pali Canon, in which phenomena are "empty" of anything that deserves to be called the self), it is in early sources for Mahayana Buddhism that we witness emptiness become a major concern of Buddhist teaching. Particularly significant is literature concerned with the "perfection of wisdom" (*prajñāpāramitā*), a subset of Mahayana discourses that describe how a bodhisattva should orient him- or herself, in thought and in deed, to make progress in the pursuit of awakening. Perfection of wisdom literature states that all things in our experience are "like illusions," or are "dreamlike"; they are not, in other words, as they appear to be. Some influential works of this literature are explicit that emptiness extends even to the Buddha, Dharma, and Sangha, and to teachings such as the Four Noble Truths—declarations which, on face value, suggest a confusing devaluation of the most important sources of Buddhist authority.

The obvious question is "empty of what?" One slightly technical answer is "own being" (*svabhāva*), a term which itself means subtly different things in different Buddhist intellectual contexts. Where perfection of wisdom literature teaches that "all things are empty of own being," a contrast is intended with claims made in a mainstream (i.e., non-Mahayana) Buddhist philosophical enterprise, begun most probably a century or two before the Common Era. This was the documentation, with reference to teachings attributed to the Buddha, of "what things exist" and the manner in which things exist—the central concern of what is called Abhidharma literature. In forms of Abhidharma, such as that which is still studied in Theravada Buddhism, the objects of interest are *dharma*s, meaning something like "phenomena" and referring to basic units of experience (not to be confused with Dharma in the sense of the Buddha's teaching). Mainstream Buddhist philosophers made attempts to categorize the most basic things that make up human experience, to which all concepts (including nameable objects and complex emotions) could be reduced; mostly facets of mental life, i.e., positive or negative states, or otherwise basic categories of experience such as our perceptions of causation or time. These same philosophers, although acknowledging that an occurrence of any *dharma* (other than nirvana) features in our experience only in a transient, ephemeral fashion, took them to be causally conditioned but irreducible events; they have "own being" in the sense of being basic building blocks of reality that resist further analysis, and therefore constitute what is ultimately real in human experience.

Early authors in the Mahayana tradition found this kind of thinking problematic, seemingly because it misrepresented what Buddhist practice was supposedly about. The problem seems to be that in the search for fundamental aspects of our experience, Abhidharma tradition looks for and risks being attached to a model of the world "built from" these *dharma*s. Philosophical interest in "what is essentially real" leaves the introspective philosopher clinging to what he or she takes to be reality at its most basic or "ultimate" level. Where Mahayana Buddhist literature responds that phenomena are "empty" of own being, what is being advised is a remedial approach to this account of our experience; even seemingly basic phenomena come about because of our conceptualizing minds, which is to say that no aspect of our experience should be valued as finally, irreducibly, ultimately real. Just as there is nothing amidst one's person that should be taken to be a permanent self, so too must the bodhisattva understand that all things in our experience are "without self" in the sense that *dharma*s are not only always dependent on prior causes and conditions, but are all products of our constantly conceptualizing minds.

Teaching about emptiness has always been seen to walk a fine line between affirming that our everyday experience is somehow illusory and the more radical position that things "do not exist" at all. That things do not exist in at least *some* fashion is of course nonsense; human life, to say nothing of the aims of Buddhist practice, is premised on there being some reality, albeit perhaps "dreamlike," which the Buddha addresses in his teaching. Although we necessarily experience things, and can interrogate these experiences and how they come about, to say that they are empty means that because all things are dependently arisen—they are caused by other phenomena, never with a reality all of their own—they only appear to be independently "real," and so are like illusions. This neither denies the apparentness of our lived experience, nor seeks to identify some ultimate truth about things as "empty"; it instead endorses an approach to experience that does not cling to any aspect of it as particularly special or valuable, which is better taught by denying things rather than affirming them. The celebrated *Heart Sutra*, for example, concisely negates virtually every core tenet of earlier Buddhist teaching, saying that all of these things are characterized by emptiness. But this remains on-message: to fully grasp the Buddha's teachings about not being attached to anything in our experience, this must extend to the Buddha himself and to his teachings (including those about emptiness).

The bodhisattva who accepts the emptiness of all things must perform a careful, seemingly paradoxical balancing act: always working for their personal liberation together with that of all other sentient beings, yet never taking any of these realities to be entities that he or she might discern as independently real, and so make objects of attachment. To think and act in such a way, Mahayana Buddhism teaches, is to achieve the mind and character of a buddha.

About the author

Christopher V. Jones is a Bye-Fellow of Selwyn College, and affiliated lecturer and research associate at the Faculty of Divinity, University of Cambridge. A primary focus of his research is the history of Mahayana Buddhist thought in the early centuries of the Common Era, preserved in Sanskrit, Chinese, and Tibetan literature.

Suggestions for further reading

In this book

See Chapters 5 (texts), 13 (bodhisattva), 20 (non-self teaching), 21 (Four Noble Truths), 22 (non-attachment), and 38 (early splits in Buddhism).

Elsewhere

Burton, David. *Buddhism, Knowledge and Liberation: A Philosophical Study*. Aldershot, UK: Ashgate, 2004: pages 79–105.

Westerhoff, Jan. *The Golden Age of Indian Buddhist Philosophy*. Oxford: Oxford University Press, 2018: pages 84–216.

Williams, Paul. *Mahāyāna Buddhism: The Doctrinal Foundations* (2nd edition). Abingdon and New York: Routledge, 2009: pages 45–83.

Williams, Paul, with Anthony Tribe and Alexander Wynne. *Buddhist Thought: A Complete Introduction to the Indian Tradition* (2nd edition). Abingdon and New York: Routledge, 2012: pages 98–123.

47
Is Tantric Buddhism just about sex?

Nick Swann

The short answer is "no." Are you still reading? Good. Tantric sex—or more correctly "sexual yoga"—is a real phenomenon but that does not mean that it is practiced extensively, or by all tantric practitioners, or in a literal sense (in contrast to a visualized, imagined, sense in a meditational context), or all of the time. The term "sexual yoga" may conjure a certain image in your mind, but "yoga" here means training to view an activity from a tantric perspective. The words "yoga" and "yoke" share a common root; a practitioner tries to "yoke" or control an activity by viewing it as tantric, and, for a committed yogi or yogini (male or female practitioner), there might be yogas relating to washing, eating, sleeping, and other routine activities.

Tantric Buddhism, also known as Vajrayana Buddhism, is concerned with finding a quick route to awakening, possibly achieving it in one lifetime or at worst within a dozen or so more. However, its practices are demanding and potentially dangerous. It is demanding because a tantric yogi or yogini commits to integrating tantric thought and practice across all aspects of life. For higher Tantras, this can involve considerable daily time commitment and meditational retreats lasting months or years. It is dangerous because slipping up is understood to lead to some terrible rebirths. Today, Vajrayana Buddhism is alive and well in Northern Buddhist areas, perhaps most famously in Tibetan Buddhism, and in the

Shingon Buddhist tradition in Japan. About a thousand years ago there were elements of Tantra in Southern Buddhism, too.

Tantras themselves are teachings and practices concerning specific, powerful, enlightened beings—we can call them deities— and they are practiced with the intention of ripening a deity's qualities within one. In the "outer" Tantras, these qualities might be wisdom, compassion, long life, or protection from illness as found in the outer Tantras of the deities Mañjuśrī, Avalokiteśvara, White Tārā, or Parṇaśabari, respectively (note that these deities appear in "inner" Tantras too). A yogi or yogini is introduced to a deity through initiation rituals in which they are purified and then instructed on how to meditate on the deity, and given permission to recite the deity's mantra (sacred words connected with the qualities of the deity). This is in an effort to identify with the enlightened body, speech, and mind of the deity, and become more like them. Meditating in this way is another yoga: "deity yoga." If a practitioner is diligent, it is thought that they can develop *siddhi*s, "accomplishments" or psychic powers, related to the deity's qualities, in the way that the Buddha is described as having *siddhi*s such as clairaudience, or being able to appear in different places simultaneously. These are some of the common or "mundane *siddhi*s," which can be indicative of progress toward awakening/enlightenment. Awakening itself is the uncommon or "super-mundane *siddhi*" and, if one has achieved that, then all of the common *siddhi*s are thought to ripen at once. The inner Tantras are focused on ripening the uncommon *siddhi* and it is these Tantras that contain the clearest sexual imagery and where sexual yoga can be found.

In inner Tantras, sexual union is used as a metaphor for non-duality (in this case, lack of distinction between *saṃsāra* and nirvana), as well as for the joining-together of perfected wisdom (female) with method (male), "method" here referring to the other five Mahayana perfections of generosity, morality, patience, effort, and meditation. Sexual bliss is also used as a metaphor for the bliss of nirvana, with the qualification that nirvana's bliss is superior and does not fade. This imagery becomes embodied in deities in inner Tantras, who are typically fierce-looking, naked except for bone jewelry, and depicted in sexual union with a consort. Buddhist Tantra also draws on broader Buddhist philosophy with some traditions privileging Yogacara thought, in which nirvana is present in *saṃsāra* but our karma predisposes us to be ignorant of this and to see them as separate. In such traditions, the morally transgressive nature of tantric imagery helps challenge this dualism, and a yogi or yogini's daily practice might include meditations relating to sexual imagery, invoking the metaphors above. Beyond metaphor, sexual and violent emotions are universally powerful and consequently potent in generating the wisdom display. Some may indeed practice physical sexual yoga with a partner, accompanied by meditations and visualizations aimed at transforming the physiological sexual experience so that the bliss of enlightenment actualizes in the body. However, this is generally confined to a retreat context and requires intensive preparatory training, including mastering specific visualizations and breathing exercises.

The prospect of developing special psychic powers is alluring, and some tantric deities are associated with attracting wealth or with having influence over others. As such, Buddhist Tantra has certain checks and balances that attempt to ensure that practitioners do not practice with purely selfish motivations. Most important of these is that they require initiation (as mentioned above) and instruction by a qualified guru. The twilight language of tantric texts includes deliberately misleading sections; they are still effectively oral teachings requiring explanation by a teacher and reading them at face value is of little practical use. A qualified guru is one who is knowledgeable about the Dharma, compassionate, motivated to help their followers, who has himself or herself received the initiation from a qualified guru, and who has signs of benefiting from their practice. Another check is that practitioners of Buddhist Tantra—which falls under the umbrella of Mahayana Buddhism—are required to take the bodhisattva vow. Tantric practitioners take further vows to keep them on their straight and narrow (and quick) path, and breaching a serious vow—the most serious of which is disrespecting one's guru—can lead to a mind-bogglingly long time in the particularly unpleasant Avīci Hell.

About the author
Nick Swann is a Senior Lecturer in Buddhist Studies at University of South Wales, UK. His research interests include Buddhist Ethics, Buddhist Tantra, and Anthropology and Religion.

Suggestions for further reading

In this book
See Chapters 23 (nirvana), 28 (kinds of meditation), 39 (contemporary divisions), 44 (bodhisattva vow), and 48 (celestial beings in Tibetan Buddhism).

Elsewhere
Beer, R. *The Encyclopedia of Tibetan Symbols and Motifs*. Boston, MA: Shambhala Publications, 2014.

Jacoby, S. *Love and Liberation: Autobiographical Writings of the Tibetan Buddhist Visionary Sera Khandro*. New York: Columbia University Press, 2014.

Samuel, G. *Origins of Yoga and Tantra*. Cambridge: Cambridge University Press, 2008.

Thaye, Lama Jampa. *The Essentials of Tibetan Buddhism*. Bristol, UK: Dechen Foundation, 2017.

48
Why are there so many different celestial beings in Tibetan Buddhism?

Cathy Cantwell

Mahayana Buddhism's emphasis on the Buddha not only as a unique enlightened person but as an expression of enlightened wisdom, potentially accessible to all beings in all places, changed the landscape of divine beings in Buddhism. For it meant that the list of buddhas recognized in early Buddhism, and those of the future, could be expanded to innumerable buddhas existing in different times and places. Chapter 11 of the famous *Lotus Sutra*, which gave rise to an important strand of Buddhism in East Asia, includes an episode in which a buddha of another world system, said to have passed away into the final nirvana long ago, appears to praise the teachings expounded by the Buddha Śākyamūni. The *Avataṃsaka Sūtra* develops this Mahayana vision, in speaking of the presence of infinite buddhas and buddha realms contained within every atom, without being diminished.

Specific buddhas of importance throughout the Mahayana world included Amitābha, who was said to have vowed to lead all who call upon him to be reborn in his buddha realm, where they will have the chance to gain liberation. Pure Land Buddhism grew out of this cult of Amitābha (Amida in Japan). Also of significance is the Medicine Buddha, whose series of vows are listed in a short, much-recited sutra. He is said to have vowed to help beings suffering from many kinds of sicknesses and troubles. Moreover, the spiritual path in Mahayana is described in terms of the progress of the bodhisattva. Advanced bodhisattvas gain mastery over the conditions into which they are reborn, and they may be born into a buddha realm and use miraculous powers to help lesser spiritual aspirants. From the perspective of ordinary mortals, bodhisattvas at the higher stages—such as Avalokiteśvara and Mañjuśrī—may be seen as little different from buddhas. Thus, the Mahayana Buddhist world has a wealth of buddhas and bodhisattvas to whom devotions may be directed. Such practices may include meditative exercises in which the practitioner reflects on the spiritual path and aspires to develop the qualities of the buddha or bodhisattva concerned. They may also consist of simple supplications calling on the presence and help of the buddha or bodhisattva.

Some traditional Buddhist communities focused mainly on a particular buddha or group of Buddhist divinities, but there is scope also for individual choice or spiritual requirements. For example, Avalokiteśvara (who transformed into the female Guanyin in East Asia) is associated with compassion, while Mañjuśrī, the bodhisattva of wisdom, may be the choice for aspiring Buddhist scholars. Furthermore, in early Buddhism, spirit beings, already established as part of the landscape in ancient Indian societies, were integrated as helpers into the retinue of the Buddha. As Buddhism spread throughout Asia, followers added their own deities, or equated local deities with Indian categories of spirit beings.

This Mahayana outlook is shared by the Buddhism established in Tibet, but Tibetan Buddhism also inherited tantric Buddhist practices which had the effect of enlarging the pantheon with a further range of tantric deities. These practices seek to transform ordinary sensual and cognitive experiences through the development of "pure vision," such that the true nature of phenomena is recognized directly, and ordinary forms, sounds, and thoughts become enlightened body, speech, and mind. The practitioner may be initiated into a tantric cycle, enabling them to "generate" and then to "accomplish" the tantric deity concerned. Thus, they receive the blessings or even themselves *become* the deity, actualizing the deity's enlightened qualities. Some tantric deities are tantric forms of pan-Mahayana figures such as Avalokiteśvara, while others are specifically associated with Vajrayana or Tantric Buddhism. In each case, the specific qualities of the deity are associated with one aspect of enlightened wisdom, such as clear mirror-like wisdom or equanimity, allocated to a particular "Buddha family." These enlightened qualities are linked to the different emotional defilements, which are seen as unenlightened distortions of their real nature. Thus, a tantric deity associated with the Lotus Buddha family and its discriminating wisdom,

Assembly of Tantric Longevity Deities, wall mural, Zangdok Palri Temple, Kalimpong, West Bengal, India
Cathy Cantwell, 2009

works on transforming passionate attachments. "Peaceful" tantric deities may appear beautiful with attractive ornaments and environments, while "wrathful" deities with the imagery of destruction and violence are thought most effective in the transformation of hatred and aggression. Both may be male or female. As well as their connections with particular types of enlightened expression, some deities are considered to promote longevity or good health, some with enhancing charisma or prosperity etc.

Which tantric deity is chosen will depend in part on the tradition with which a practitioner is affiliated—transmission of these Vajrayana deities runs through lineages of lamas—and in part on an individual's disposition or the context. In some cases, the lama will give a specific deity practice to a student, but often students themselves decide that they feel especially connected with a particular deity. Some practitioners specialize in a single tantric deity, but most practice several, performing practices according to the occasion. Monastic establishments will generally have a large repertoire of deity practices, which they perform according to a calendrical cycle, perhaps monthly or annually, or in response to the needs of the community.

Further expansion of the tantric pantheon is also encouraged by the possibility of new revelations—a lama who is recognized as a tantric master may have a pure vision revelation, and if recorded and transmitted to their disciples, a new tradition of deity practice may start. Generally, the new practices tend only to introduce slight variations to a particular deity's imagery, so that, rather than wholly new deities, one finds numerous slightly different forms of an established deity.

As well as the "yidam" or meditational deities for cultivating enlightened wisdom, there are also other types of tantric deities with particular functions. These may be considered "worldly" or not yet enlightened—often indigenous deities and spirits integrated into the Buddhist world, put to work to protect or help the tantric practitioners and their communities.

Why so many deities? There are Mahayana buddha and bodhisattva figures, as well as tantric deities. There are numerous different lineages for transmission of different tantric deity practices, with the possibility of further creative transformations of the practices in each generation. Furthermore, the many deities have qualities suitable for different practitioners and occasions.

About the author
Cathy Cantwell is an Associate Faculty Member at the Oriental Institute, University of Oxford, and an Honorary Research Fellow at the School of Anthropology and Conservation, University of Kent. She has specialized in Tibetan and Himalayan tantric rituals of all periods from the tenth century CE, including text critical and historical analysis, as well as ethnographic study of contemporary rituals. She was President of the UK Association for Buddhist Studies, 2015–2021.

Suggestions for further reading

In this book
See Chapters 10 (buddhahood), 13 (bodhisattva), 28 (kinds of meditation), 39 (contemporary divisions), 42 (Pure Land Buddhism), and 47 (Tantra and sex).

Elsewhere
Kapstein, Matthew. *Tibetan Buddhism: A Very Short Introduction*. Oxford: Oxford University Press, 2014.

Samuel, Geoffrey. *Introducing Tibetan Buddhism*. Abingdon and New York: Routledge, 2012.

Tenpe Nyima, Kunkyen, and Shechen Gyaltsap IV. *Vajra Wisdom: Deity Practice in Tibetan Buddhism* (translated by Dharmachakra Translation Committee). Boston and London: Snow Lion, 2012.

Part Seven
Buddhist art and material culture

49
What are the main buildings and symbols of Buddhism?

Arjuna C. B. Ranatunga
with a contribution from Cathy Cantwell

Buddhism began as a religion of simplicity and modesty, but as it grew and spread over the centuries its expression became increasingly ornate and elaborate in terms of both buildings and symbols. The simplest of the buildings used in the religion is the individual monk's cell (*kuti*), which, in the early days of Buddhism, was a small hut often made of leaves and branches, according to specified and restricted dimensions.

The next level of complexity in buildings was the communal recitation hall, where monks and nuns would gather on the four quarters of the lunar month to recite their disciplinary rules (Pali: *pātimokkha*) and confess their transgressions. The need for such a hall also stemmed partly from the restrictions imposed by the three months of the rainy season, when the wanderings of monastics were limited.

Based on these essential needs, over time generous donors offered land and property to the monastic Sangha. These things were seen as communal property, and as one of the four basic material requisites that monastics needed in order to lead the spiritual life (namely, food, clothes, medicine, and lodging). The

Stupa, Suvisuddharama Buddhist Temple, Colombo, Sri Lanka
Elizabeth Harris, 2010

gifts of such things were seen as an important way for lay people to make merit (wholesome, fruitful karma).

The nature of these simple monastic premises became increasingly intricate and adorned, as lay people gave more and more, in some instances expanding into monastic and temple complexes, vast in scope. In the early centuries of Buddhism, the monastic university of Nalanda (in present-day Bihar), and the centers of learning and temples in Taxila (in present-day Pakistan) were especially important. In Sri Lanka, Anuradhapura and Polonnaruwa, two ancient Buddhist capitals, became filled with extensive monasteries and temples. Borobudur in Indonesia and Angkor Wat in Cambodia are two other examples and, in more recent times, the Dhammakaya Grand Meditation Stadium in Thailand has been built to accommodate a million people at a time.

These complexes often included a focus for the devotion of the faithful. In South Asia, these included saplings of the original Bodhi tree, under the shade of which the Buddha attained enlightenment. The tree is considered a kind of living relic, a symbol of the Buddha and what he used to gain enlightenment.

Another structure found in temple grounds are shrines containing relic chambers: great mounds of brick and plaster. These are known as stupas or *caitiya*s. They can, in a sense, be seen as continuations of the burial mounds of prehistory. They were built for the sake of the veneration of the bodily relics of the Buddha, saints, and noble disciples. In East Asia, these took the form of often architecturally stunning pagodas.

But what else can we expect to find in such places? How do Buddhists express their faith symbolically? During his lifetime, the Buddha did not allow himself to be represented physically, because he taught that it was only "he who sees the Dharma" who sees the Buddha. Early Buddhists showed their reverence to him through symbols, some of which have been found inscribed on stone pillars at early Buddhist sites in India, such as Sanchi, near present-day Bhopal, the architectural remains of which date from the third century BCE to the first century CE. These included symbols of his (extraordinary) footprint, of the "Wheel of the Dharma," of the Bodhi tree, and of the seat on which he attained enlightenment. These were very basic and unelaborate; the bare minimum is used to represent the Buddha and his teaching.

The earliest images of the Buddha began only in the first century CE. Archaeologists consider that among the first of these was the *Samādhi Pilimi* (meditation statue), to be found in the ancient city of Anuradhapura, in Sri Lanka. It is again very simple and non-ostentatious in design, made of white dolomite marble and monotone, but showing heroic, well-proportioned features. Others include those found in Gandhāra, a Buddhist kingdom that was

WHAT ARE THE MAIN BUILDINGS AND SYMBOLS OF BUDDHISM? 241

Deer and Wheel of the Dharma, Potala Palace, Llasa, Tibet
Nicholas Cope, 2005

located within present-day Afghanistan and Pakistan, of the same period, and which were influenced by Greek culture.

In Northern Buddhism in its tantric form, temples often take the form of the tantric deity's mandala palace, and the outer parts of the building are generally built with the decorative and symbolic features of such mandala palaces. Other commonly found elements pick up on the common Buddhist heritage: two deer may flank an eight-spoked Wheel of the Dharma on the roof above the entrance porchway (a reference to the Buddha's first sermon in a deer park), and a representation of the wheel of existence may be placed in the porchway to remind those entering of the truths of impermanence and suffering.

Occasionally, even the inner layout of the temple will mirror the mandala structure, with a large image of the tantric deity in the center of the main assembly hall. Generally, however, the main assembly hall will be designed so that rows of monastics and practitioners can be seated along each side of the hall, while the main shrine is at the opposite end as one enters. Often, different storys of the temple building have a symbolic structure, reflecting the three bodies of a buddha—the main assembly hall representing the *nirmāṇakāya* level (the form of a buddha), an upper gallery with a library of Buddhist texts embodying the *sambhogakāya* level (the form of a buddha fit for the heavenly realms), and a further smaller shrine-room on the roof to symbolize the *dharmakāya* (the Dharma body).

In Tibetan contexts, stupas or *chörten* are found not only in the precincts of temples and in sacred sites, but also at the entrance of villages or alongside public pathways. Often elaborately designed in structure with symbolic elements such as the thirteen bodhisattva stages represented in the successive levels of the conical spire, such stupas not only serve the purpose of generating merit through circumambulation, but are considered to benefit the

Zangdok Palri Tibetan Buddhist Temple, Kalimpong, West Bengal, India
Cathy Cantwell, 2009

Bhutanese devotee hanging Auspicious Flags in the sacred area of Paro Taktsang, Bhutan
Nicolas Chong, 2013

whole community and environment, stabilizing the elements and pacifying conflict.

Another ubiquitous Tibetan Buddhist symbol is the *maṇi* wheel, named after Avalokiteśvara's mantra. Cylinder-shaped with a central axis on which they spin and popularly called a prayer wheel, *maṇi* wheels contain rolls of paper inscribed with mantras, which are activated by turning the wheel. The hand-held variety can be spun while walking and reciting mantras. Temple complexes will often have a small building featuring a large *maṇi* wheel which can be turned using a lever as one sits nearby performing recitations. Temple buildings generally have rows of *maṇi* wheels set into the outer walls, so that it is possible to turn them while circumambulating the temple

Tantric symbolism pervades everyday ritual practice in Tibet. Practitioners may keep with them their *vajra* and bell, which are used in virtually all tantric rituals. Symbolizing their tantric commitment, the *vajra* embodies the skillful means of indestructible

Lotsawa Lhakang Temple with *maṇi* wheel, Upper Kinnaur, Himachal Pradesh, India
Christian Luczanits, 1994

enlightenment, while ringing the bell activates the sonorous sound of emptiness and wisdom.

Colorful flags printed with mantras and auspicious symbols are often seen in Tibet and the Himalayas, strung up and fluttering in the breeze. Stones and rocks carved with mantras are placed at sacred sites, as well as *tsa-tsa* molded images (images stamped onto clay), so that the environment takes on the visible presence of the Dharma practice.

Lotus flower
Nicholas Cope

Moreover, natural environments may be imbibed with religious meaning. A respected lama may identify a mountainous area as a tantric mandala, various features embodying the tantric deities. Rock formations may be seen as naturally occurring *vajra*s, and indentations in rock caves may be recognized as the footprints or handprints of tantric masters of the past. Thus, Buddhist symbolism may pervade the whole environment.

Two other symbols that are common across Buddhist schools, frequently found in Buddhist iconography, are the previously mentioned Wheel of the Dharma (Sanskrit: *Dharma-cakra*) and the lotus flower. The "wheel," with eight spokes, derives from the

Buddha's first sermon, named the "Discourse on Setting in Motion the Wheel of the Dharma". It evokes the dynamism of a buddha's teaching as it enters the world and is one of the most important symbols of the Dharma in Buddhism. As for the lotus, the mud from which a lotus grows represents the poisons that fuel craving. The purity of the flower represents enlightenment or awakening. It therefore symbolizes purity and the reality of enlightenment, even in the midst of the world's suffering and craving.

About the authors

Arjuna Ranatunga studied Medicine at Cambridge University and studied Buddhism at Peradeniya University in Sri Lanka, as well as at Sunderland University in the UK. He is the administrator of several online Buddhist groups.

Cathy Cantwell is an Associate Faculty Member at the Oriental Institute, University of Oxford, and an Honorary Research Fellow at the School of Anthropology and Conservation, University of Kent. She has specialized in Tibetan and Himalayan tantric rituals of all periods from the tenth century CE, including text critical and historical analysis, as well as ethnographic study of contemporary rituals. She was President of the UK Association for Buddhist Studies, 2015–2021.

Suggestions for further reading

In this book

See Chapters 3 (ritual), 6 (images), 10 (buddhahood), 11 (reading a Buddha-image), 13 (bodhisattva), 14 (devotion), 30 (role of monasticism), 34 (lay Buddhists), 44 (bodhisattva vow), 46 (emptiness), 48 (celestial beings in Tibetan Buddhism), 50 (Buddhist art), and 51 (mandala).

Elsewhere

Beer, Robert. *The Encyclopedia of Tibetan Symbols and Motifs*. London: Serindia Publications, 1999.

Nārada, Ven. *The Buddha and His Teachings* (4th edition). Malaysia: Buddhist Missionary Society, 1988. See Chapter 6 for the Buddha's first sermon.

Harvey, Peter. *An Introduction to Buddhism: Teachings, History and Practices* (2nd edition). Cambridge: Cambridge University Press, 2013: Chapters 4, 6, and 10.

50
Why do Buddhists make art?

Christian Luczanits

There is no term for "art" in Buddhist literature. Instead, the terms used make clear that what we understand as art today was made for a purpose. Buddhist texts also rarely explain this purpose, so the

Repainting a mural at Kelaniya Temple, Sri Lanka
Elizabeth Harris, 2010

information has to be pieced together from scant references and the visual evidence itself. In the following, I focus on the Buddhist art of India and Tibet and consider the purpose of art parallel to the historical development of Buddhism.

From the earliest Buddhist monuments onwards, a primary purpose of art production is to attract visitors, and with it donations. The stone carving of the railings of Bharhut and Sanchi, two early Indian monasteries centered around stupas, are the result of communal enterprise, the making of their parts contributed by different donors who left their names in inscriptions. This suggests that their making was considered meritorious (generating good karmic fruits), and that leaving one's name established a permanent connection of the donor to the stupa and the relic of the Buddha it contains.

Nevertheless, there is also an overall program underlying these carvings. At Bharhut, *yakṣa*—a group of earth-deities popularly worshipped—from all over India are shown worshipping the stupa. They, along with representatives of the entirety of living beings in popular imagination, set an example for the visiting worshipper. This program must have been decided on and coordinated by the monks responsible for their making. Particular art topics can also be interpreted as didactic, such as the stories of the previous lives of Buddha Śākyamuni, their often minimalist depictions serving as reminder of the message behind them, often an exemplary deed that propels the protagonist on his path to awakening.

A major conceptual shift in Buddhist art production is noticeable in the first century CE with the emergence of the Buddha-image. As far as we can tell today, the earliest Buddha-images added a figurative form to what already was present symbolically. For example, an inscription informs us that a standing image donated by a certain Bala at Kauśāmbī in year 2 of the Kanishka era— that is, 128/129 CE—was placed on a so-called *caṅkrama*, a symbol for a path the Buddha walked on.

The Buddha-image is quickly understood as a substitute for the Buddha himself, whose body is now characterized by supernatural qualities that were summarized in roughly contemporaneous

Stupa and Teaching Buddha, Cave 26, Ajanta, India (late fifth century)
Christian Luczanits, 2005

literature as the so-called major and minor marks. The making of a Buddha-image becomes an act of merit and, in some sources, an obligation of Buddhist practice. The image quite literally stands for the Buddha and his qualities, and seeing and worshipping it equals seeing and worshipping the living Buddha. Once images become residents of niches and temples in monasteries, they also serve as foci of worship and recipients of offerings. Śākyamuni is only one of a succession of buddhas in our world, many of which become depicted in art. Equally, buddhas are imagined to exist in different worlds at the same time, literally filling the entire universe. Notions like these underlie the filling of architectural spaces, such as Cave 26 at Ajanta in India, with many Buddha-images. They also lead to elaborate depictions of buddha worlds, such as Sukhāvatī (or Pure Land) of Buddha Amitābha (Japan: Amida).

The temporal and spatial elevation visible of the Buddha soon equally applies to the bodhisattva, who becomes a focus in Mahayana Buddhism. Bodhisattvas increasingly become representative of characteristic qualities supporting the path to awakening. A classic example is the bodhisattva Avalokiteśvara, whose compassion becomes manifest in depictions where he rescues beings from eight dangers.

Merit-making continues to be a primary purpose for having buddhas, bodhisattvas, and buddha-worlds depicted, but in Mahayana Buddhism the merit is dedicated to the liberation of all beings. Images or murals may also serve as prompts for certain contemplative techniques, such as the remembrance of the Buddha or the visualization of a buddha-world. But, against popular imagination, it is doubtful that images were ever made as aids to meditation. More importantly, ideas about the beneficial appearance of the Buddha's body are transposed to the image and depictions more broadly, making the mere seeing of certain Buddhist imagery beneficial to the viewer.

Tantric Buddhism expands Buddhist imagery toward infinity. Besides buddhas and bodhisattvas, goddesses and wrathful deities can also serve as the main focus of both practice and ritual. This multiplication of imagery goes hand in hand with an emphasis on the symbolic quality a deity stands for. For example, Buddha Amitābha now stands for the "knowledge of equality" or "impartial wisdom," and compassion as an antidote of passion. Compassion is also associated with a range of bodhisattvas, goddesses, and wrathful deities, who are now understood as emanations of Buddha Amitābha and comprise his "family." The primary examples for each type of Amitābha's family are the bodhisattva Avalokiteśvara, goddess Tārā and the protector Hayagrīva.

Buddhist practice now means to visualize and to identify with these deities and their qualities, the precise composition of which is expressed in different iconographic forms. This practice may also include the performance of gestures (*mudrā*) and the repetition of spells (mantra) symbolizing the deity. Again, the depictions of the deities may serve as prompts, but they are not the focus of the practice.

The decoration of a tantric Buddhist monument stands for the totality of individual practices considered authoritative and worthy to promote at a given time and place. Since the symbolism of the highest teachings includes sexual and violent imagery, these may or may not be depicted in spaces accessible to the general public.

While this short survey is based on Indian and Tibetan Buddhist art, many of the principles underlying art production are valid throughout the Buddhist world. Buddhist imagery acknowledges the ability of art to communicate the deeds and qualities of the Buddha, as well as more complex Buddhist teachings beyond the written word, and provides a focus for Buddhist practice to all those who cannot fully devote their life to the Buddhist path. Artistic quality matters, as the art has to be a suitable receptacle for the sacred, and the effort put into it has to be proportionate to the ability of the donor. Generating merit on behalf of relatives, often for those who have passed away, and "all sentient beings" is, however, the biggest driving force for art production.

About the author
Christian Luczanits is David L. Snellgrove Senior Lecturer in Tibetan and Buddhist Art at the Department of the History of Art and Archaeology, School of Oriental and African Studies, University of London. His research focuses on Buddhist art of India and Tibet, in particular Gandhāran and early western Himalayan art.

Suggestions for further reading

In this book
See Chapters 2 (faith) 6 (images), 10 (buddhahood), 14 (devotion to the Buddha), 18 (karma), 42 (Pure Land Buddhism), 48 (celestial beings in Tibetan Buddhism), and 49 (buildings and symbols).

Elsewhere
Schopen, G. "What's in a Name: The Religious Function of the Early Donative Inscriptions." In *Unseen Presence: The Buddha and Sanchi*, edited by V. Dehejia, 92–109. Mumbai: Marg, 1996.

Schopen, G. "Art, Beauty, and the Business of Running a Buddhist Monastery in Early Northwest India." In *Buddhist Monks and Business Matters. Still More Papers on Monastic Buddhism in India*, edited by G Schopen, 19–44. Honolulu: University of Hawai'i Press, 2004.

Sharf, R. H. "Art in the Dark: The Ritual Context of Buddhist Caves in Western China." In *Art of Merit: Studies in Buddhist Art and its Conservation. Proceedings of the Buddhist Art Forum 2012*, edited by D. Park, K. Wangmo, and S. Cather, 38–65. London: Archetype, 2013.

51
What is a mandala?

Christian Luczanits

Already in historic Indian literature, the word "mandala," from the Sanskrit, *maṇḍala,* acquires a fairly broad range of meanings, all of them including some notion of roundness, either literally or symbolically. However, none of them equals the modern Western notion of the term as it was coined by C. G. Jung and early-twentieth-century psychology. This modern Western conception of the mandala as a geometric form including a dominant circular element is based on depictions systematized in a Tibetan Buddhist context, without actual consideration of their original purpose and meaning.

In fact, the Tibetan mandala is the result of the development of esoteric or Tantric Buddhism in India and Tibet and the conversion of a ritual tool into a subject of representation through art. In its fully developed form, a mandala is a square palace occupied by deities and surrounded by outer protective circles. Thereby, the geometric form within the palace aligns with the deities occupying it, often providing a distinctive geometry. It is this central "circle" of deities that the term mandala actually refers to. Surveying early tantric Buddhist literature for the usage of the term allows for the reconstruction of this and other key notions underlying the Buddhist mandala, and also explains the differences in Tibetan and East Asian versions.

The mandala is first and foremost a ritual tool. In its simplest form, it consists of a square space marked by protective features and a circle of deities within it. The ground marks a purified space to which deities can be invited during the ritual. A fire pit may be part of the protective features, and the seats of the deities may be marked by flower blossoms. Thereby, the primary function of the mandala is the initiation of a disciple to the religious practice connected with the invited deity. Mandalas may also be constructed for specific ritual purposes, such as pacifying negative situations or increasing life span or prosperity. Ritual altars of different shapes are still used today for these. The temporary nature of many mandalas is also reflected in elaborate communal rituals when mandalas of colored sand are dismantled at the end of the rituals, with additional rites for the disposal of the sand.

With certain mandalas, in particular the main mandalas of the "Tantra for the Purification of All Bad Transmigrations" and the Kālacakra Tantra, the mandala aligns with imaginations of the cosmos. The Kālacakra mandala actually is the direct result of their merger, and it is with this mandala that the exterior of the mandala became round, as the superimposed disks making up the cosmos are also round. By the late eleventh century, the Kālacakra was considered the pinnacle of all esoteric or tantric Buddhist teachings, and thus the outer circles became normative for all mandalas. East Asian mandalas branched off long before that development, and usually retain the original square form.

If we analyze diverse mandala depictions in the Tibetan context, there are common elements shared by many, optional elements, and unique features of particular mandalas. The center of the mandala retains elements of the original ritual altar, a central lotus symbolizing pacification and a wheel standing for prosperity. Except for the Kālacakra mandala, the color scheme of the mandala palace references the five esoteric buddhas, with Vairocana (white) or Akṣobhya (blue) most often occupying the center. The palace has doors in the cardinal directions that are often framed by the prongs of a crossed *vajra* that forms its adamantine foundation. The entire structure is placed within a lotus circle that symbolizes a purified space, which is protected by the fire and *vajra* circles surrounding it. The latter derives from the visualization of the mandala, in which a *vajra* cage is imagined in three dimensions.

Tantric practitioners completing a sand mandala for a Major Practice Session, Pema Yoedling Dratsang, Gelephu, Bhutan (above); and the completed mandala (below)
Cathy Cantwell, 2013

In fact, mandala palaces may also be depicted in three dimensions, and there are elaborate versions of such mandalas in major monuments across Tibet. Accordingly, architecture that likens a mandala palace or has a roughly square layout is often called mandalaic or even a mandala, but usually it goes conceptually beyond it.

Three-dimensional mandalas can be taken as permanent mandalas for initiation, and may thus replace sand mandalas. Painted mandalas, in contrast, usually come in sets that may derive from a single root text or represent a collection of highest esoteric teachings within a tradition. An example for the former are the twelve to fourteen mandalas deriving from the "Tantra for the Purification of All Bad Transmigrations" mentioned above, which are often found in monuments dedicated to the memory of deceased teachers. An example for the latter derives from a trilogy of texts authored by the Indian scholar Abhayākaragupta (d. early twelfth century), the *Vajrāvalī* dedicated to the mandalas. Depending on the interpretation, this set comprises between twenty-six and forty-five mandalas, with the Kālacakra mandala representing the ultimate one. These often were commissioned together to represent the totality of esoteric Buddhist teachings, and have been displayed at special occasions only. Larger sets often consist of 108 mandalas, an auspicious number.

Particular mandalas may be used by practitioners as prompts to support their visualization practice, but mandalas are not made for "meditating on them." The latter is an understanding that is grounded on the modern Western notion that the geometry of the mandala itself has a positive psychological effect, a notion for which there is no evidence in primary Buddhist sources.

About the author

Christian Luczanits is David L. Snellgrove Senior Lecturer in Tibetan and Buddhist Art at the Department of the History of Art and Archaeology, School of Oriental and African Studies, University of London. His research focuses on Buddhist art of India and Tibet, in particular Gandhāran and early western Himalayan art.

Suggestions for further reading

In this book

See Chapters 3 (ritual), 6 (images), 47 (Tantra and sex), 48 (celestial beings in Tibetan Buddhism), and 50 (Buddhist art).

Elsewhere

Luczanits, C. "On the Earliest Mandalas in a Buddhist Context." In *Mahayana Buddhism: History and Culture*, edited by D. Bryant and S. Bryant, 111–136. New Delhi: Tibet House, 2008.

Sharf, R. H. "Visualization and Mandala in Shingon Buddhism." In *Living Images: Japanese Buddhist Icons in Context*, edited by R. H. Sharf and E. H. Sharf, 151–197. Stanford, CA: Stanford University Press, 2001.

Tanaka, K. *An Illustrated History of the Mandala: From its Genesis to the Kalacakratantra*. Somerville, MA: Wisdom Publications, 2018.

52
How is Buddhism influencing contemporary art?

Tim Stephens

Have you seen one of the most iconic art images in the world: Van Gogh's paintings of sunflowers? Painted around 1888, they meant for him, he once said, to be expressions of "gratitude." The thickness of the paint is tangible. The color yellow seems to hold the sunflower's DNA in the paint itself. Now imagine a Buddha statue, of bright yellow gold, or with a yellow robe, embodying a quality of serenity, or perhaps gratitude.

Neither would be called contemporary art, but perhaps for the wrong reasons: 1888 precedes contemporary art in art history books, and religious icons are seen more as temple or museum objects. Both are also seen as straightforwardly representational. Yet both are vivid and valuable contemporary phenomena, with complex institutional systems in place that guarantee their esteemed value as "cultural forms."

Buddhist-inspired, Buddhist-influenced artists, some from Buddhist heritage countries, influenced international contemporary art, not least in the disappearance of the art "object," from the mid-twentieth century onwards. Contemporary art merged with everyday life, using a vast variety of ephemeral materials, performances, actions, words, and events, no longer confined to drawing, painting, sculpture, or film, but including light, sound, energy, "time-motion." This is, generally speaking, an art of immanence.

Minimal sculpture in the 1960s, like conceptual art, is often ascribed to the influences of formalism, phenomenology, and language philosophy. As art works became more "empty," there was less to see, but more to experience. An alternative art history might explain that both emerged against the background influence of Buddhist philosophy. Why? One of the strongest cultural influences was possibly a shift from the Greco-European axis, centered in classical form and rationalism, to a Pan-Asian encounter, centered in embodiment. This was evident at interdisciplinary art schools such as Black Mountain College.

Today we can see this legacy in Taiwanese artist Charwei Tsai (b. 1980), who took the sacred text of the *Heart Sutra*, a key line in which says, "Form is emptiness, emptiness is form," also translated more recently as "This body itself is emptiness and emptiness itself is this body," and wrote it onto different surfaces, such as plane tree trunks and tofu, where it gradually faded or decomposed. She uses her studio to host meditation groups and takes an active interest in working with the indigenous community. She recently made spiral coils of incense on which a hundred-syllable mantra was written, as a "performance," which, if burnt away into that characteristic scent of smoke in a devotional ritual, would leave us asking: what was the artwork exactly?

Zen Buddhism, arguably, made contemporary Western art—that is, *international contemporary art*—possible. How so? Numerous American artists were inspired by D. T. Suzuki's lectures and teachings especially from the 1950s. Buddhist teachers and traffic started to increase between continents. Concepts such as "non-duality" and "emptiness" started to appear in art; a piece by John Cage in 1952 consisted of 4'33" of silence alongside a score, a performer, and an audience. This would not have been conceivable without Buddhist philosophy. Art history books often cite Marcel Duchamp as the first contemporary conceptual artist, radical enough to place objects from ordinary social life, known as "found objects," into the gallery. Well-argued scholarship by Tosi

Lee in 2004 suggests: "Duchamp's contact with Asian culture could have begun as early as 1908–11." The everyday and the means of representation itself redefined the role of the contemporary artist. This is best illustrated by Lucy Lippard's detailed document *Six Years: The Dematerialization of the Art Object from 1966 to 1972*. Zen famously illustrates its highest insights via everyday imagery and experience, and the aesthetics of Zen infused popular culture.

However, some artists such as Richard Long (b. 1945), Hamish Fulton (b. 1946) and Anthony Gormley (b. 1950) were promoted by a gallery system that only retrospectively contextualized their work as inspired by Buddhism. When Gormley says that he wants his sculpture "to be an invitation to mindfulness," but adds that "I don't have a formal sitting regime myself," he reminds us of John Cage's comment: "I have never practiced sitting cross-legged, nor do I meditate." It was a talk by Cage, attended by Richard Long, that inspired his famous "Line made by Walking" sculpture the next year (1967)—a photograph of a line on the ground formed by repeated walking back and forth. Long and Fulton's work strongly influenced the sense-walking movement, or sound walks, often designed by sound artists. The similarities to ancient traditions of walking meditation in Buddhism, pilgrimage, or the yatra (journey, procession) of Indian heritage, are transparent.

If the gallery system had more adequately described Buddhism's place in contemporary art, many Asian artists might have had as much exposure, recognition, or status as their Western counterparts. A pioneering artist such as Thang Kian Hiong (aka Tang Da Wu, b. 1943) is a case in point. A contemporary of Long and Fulton, he returned to Singapore after his British art education and remains far less well known. Yet, by helping to set up the Artist's Village in 1988, he introduced contemporary art into Singapore, and inspired and taught a whole generation of artists.

Kimsooja (b. 1957) is an artist working currently with sowing flax plants into a field surrounding the Wanås Foundation in Sweden during the Covid-19 pandemic, for a project called *Sowing into Painting*. Originally from Korea, her interest in women's labor and stillness, according to the curator, "naturally establishes a dialogue with everything that is going on; the artworks give space for introspection and spirituality beyond religion." She also turns her artist website over to participative conversations on key ethical themes to which anyone can contribute.

Rirkrit Tiravanija (b. 1961) bought some land (in Thailand) with an artist-collaborator, and dedicated this to a meditation-type, communal practice of co-living, rather like Tang's Artist Village. In his words, it is simply "life." Art becomes life and life becomes art in a form of relational mindfulness, and, ironically enough, this acts as a comment to other villages nearby, and the wider country: how do you practice your Buddhism?

Recent contemporary art that is rooted in Buddhism or Buddhist influence seems to share a spirit of collectivity. There is work commissioned by Buddhists, for instance, that is present in new temples in Asia or Buddhist centers in the West. A common theme in the work of Tiravanija, Kimsooja, and Tang Da Wu is this task of building community, a Sangha, an imperative that many artists promote through participative art practices. Contemporary art may have a lot more to do with the influence of Buddhism than art history generally admits.

About the author

Tim Stephens is an Education Developer, with a specialism in Curriculum, at University of the Arts London and a photographic artist. His research interests include embodiment, the relationship between cognitive and non-cognitive experience, equality, and organizational change.

Suggestions for further reading

In this book
See Chapters 28 (kinds of meditation), 41 (Zen), 46 (emptiness), 49 (buildings and symbols), and 50 (Buddhist art).

Elsewhere

Baas, Jacquelynn, and Mary Jane Jacob (editors). *Buddha Mind in Contemporary Art*. Berkeley: University of California Press, 2004.

Sullivan, Michael. *The Meeting of Eastern and Western Art*. Berkeley: University of California Press, 1997.

Charwei Tsai, Taiwanese Artist: http://charwei.com

Kimsooja, Korean Artist: http://www.kimsooja.com

Part Eight
Buddhism and other religions

53
How has Buddhism been influenced by other religious traditions? How has Buddhism influenced other religious traditions?

Sophie Barker

Stories told from the time of the Buddha in the Pali *Tipiṭaka* depict a rich, diverse, and hotly contested religious landscape, where Buddhists and non-Buddhists interact to debate, discuss, and defend their different perspectives. In these encounters, the teachings of the Buddha are brought into dialogue with the beliefs and practices of others, defining what Buddhism is by negotiating what it is not. These narrative encounters reflect a likely reality for the emergence of Buddhism, which, like any religious tradition, did not spring from a vacuum but from a context where other ideas on religion, society, politics, and culture both existed and interacted. As Buddhism spread from its early origins in South Asia, it encountered new contexts and has influenced and been influenced by the traditions of its new followers. Engaging in diverse and context-specific dialogues across Asia and beyond has contributed to the development of the wide diversity of traditions that are today gathered under the label of Buddhism.

Although the questions I am addressing use the term "religion" to refer to Buddhism and those it has encountered, its use is problematic. With this in mind, what I intend to convey through these questions is twofold: (1) that Buddhism itself is a diverse tradition that has encountered a kaleidoscope of influential individuals and groups, advocating competing views and ways of life; and (2) that Buddhism has been shaped and influenced by its interactions with others, while also shaping and influencing those it has encountered.

Buddhism is depicted in the *Sutta Piṭaka* as emerging from a context rich with philosophical thinking and debate. In the first two *sutta*s of the *Dīgha Nikāya* (collection of Long Discourses), the Buddha presents his teaching in opposition to the views of his opponents. In the first, the *Brahmajāla Sutta* ("The Supreme Net"), he talks about what his teaching is not, by stating sixty-two beliefs foolishly held by ascetics. Meanwhile, the second, the *Sāmaññaphala Sutta* ("The Fruits of the Homeless Life"), represents the positions of six influential teachers believed to be the Buddha's rivals. Two of these teachers are recognizable: Makkhali Gosāla, an influential member of an ascetic group called the Ājīvikas; and the Jain founder Nigaṇṭha Nātaputta (Mahāvīra). These first two *sutta*s of the *Dīgha Nikāya* thus place the Buddha in context alongside many deep and diverse philosophical thinkers and practitioners.

Many of the Buddha's rivals in these texts advocated a renunciate path. In fact, it was exposure to a path of harsh austerity with an ascetic group before his awakening that inspired his conceptualization of the Buddhist path as the Middle Way between two extremes. Though the Buddha encountered many such groups, it is his interactions with brahmins and Jains that draw the most attention.

Jainism was founded earlier but in a similar historical period and geographical location to emerging Buddhist traditions, and the two share a number of similarities. Both strive for liberation from the cycle of birth and rebirth, believe in karma, deny the existence of a creator God, promote non-violence (*ahiṃsā*), share a similar community structure (Sangha), and encourage renunciate practice, among other things. On the surface, there are many similarities between Jainism and Buddhism, but delving deeper into any of these resemblances draws out crucial differences. Two of the most notable differences are the extent to which they practice *ahiṃsā*, which is often observed more stringently by Jains, and their opposing beliefs on the permanence of the self.

The Buddha's teachings not only positioned Buddhism in contest with Jainism, but also the beliefs and practices of traditions such as Hinduism that historically or contemporarily have roots in Vedic literature. The Buddha meets numerous brahmins in the Pali *Tipiṭaka*. During their encounters, he repeatedly challenges the authority of the Vedas and is particularly critical of ritual practice.

Many crucial differences in belief between these traditions stem from the Buddha's rejection of *ātman*. This concept is complex and multifaceted, but, in its simplest definition, it denotes a permanent, essential "self" that is passed between temporary bodies through reincarnation. In teaching its opposite, *anattā* (Pali; Sanskrit: *anātman*), the Buddha directly contested *ātman*, teaching instead that this "self" is impermanent and subject to change.

It is from within this teaching that the Buddha also challenged the idea of a permanent birth status, which has come to be associated with the caste system. For the Buddha, any birth status can be affected positively or negatively by action (karma), not merely in the next life but in this life as well. Challenging the supremacy of the brahmins, he taught that people should be judged according to their spiritual and moral attainment and not their birth status. There are stories, therefore, of the Buddha encouraging people from all walks of life onto the monastic path: the impoverished as well as brahmins, and women as well as men.

Buddhism has interacted with and made roots within a diversity of contexts beyond South Asia, stimulating much diversity in the beliefs and practices of Buddhists today. The integration into Buddhism of gods and other significant human or non-human beings has been a common exchange in these encounters, giving rise to local, national, and regional variation in belief and practice. This exchange is evident in the early textual traditions of South Asia: for example, certain gods significant for some Hindus are represented in both Buddhist and Jain stories.

In its Southeast Asian encounters, spirit (*nat*) worship plays a role in the belief and practice of many Burmese Buddhists, and ghosts and spirits (known generically as *phi*) occupy a similar significance for some Thai Buddhists, with both inspiring the celebration of certain festivals. Encounters with pre-Buddhist traditions in a Tibetan context shaped much of Buddhism's unique character in the region, with pre-Buddhist gods of the atmosphere, earth, and underground having become significant for Buddhists.

When discussing the mutual influence between specific traditions, it is important to acknowledge the existence of a wider context of exchange. Buddhism was not the only tradition interacting with Jains and those in Southeast Asian and Tibetan contexts; for example, traditions associated with Hinduism have also been influential in these contexts. And when, at an early date, Buddhist texts trickled east along the Silk Road to China, its encounters with Daoism and Confucianism have also been similarly complex.

Early translations of Buddhist texts in China borrowed Daoist terminology to convey the Dharma for their Chinese audience. Teachings of impermanence, interdependence, and emptiness resonated with existing ideas in Chinese traditions, promoting the spread of Buddhism. Other concepts emerging from its South Asian origins were less familiar and their significance shifted. Such interactions also played a role in the conceptualization of central Mahayana teachings, such as Buddha-nature, which has been variously associated with the Daoist *dao* and Confucian *li*. Historical and contemporary interactions have been complex and varied, but the idea of "the three teachings are one" is noteworthy in the context of popular practice in China. Tracing its roots to as early as the sixth century, it reflects the fact that Daoism, Confucianism, and Buddhism exist as distinct but harmonious influences in the lives of many.

Chan Buddhism emerged as an influential tradition in the context of these Chinese interactions, and spread to Japan as the predecessor of Japanese Zen (Chan) Buddhism. There it interacted variously with local practices, which became known as Shinto in reaction to the emerging influence of Buddhism. Significant mutual influence took place historically: Shinto *kami* (simplistically translated as "spirits") were viewed variously by Buddhists as dwelling in the heavenly realms, as avatars of buddhas, and as bodhisattvas. A legal separation of Shinto and Buddhism took place during the Meiji period, although it is not uncommon to encounter some examples of coexistence in practice today.

The influence of Buddhism's many encounters are far too various to exhaust here, so my examples have been brief. With this brevity, it is crucial to note that in all cases Buddhism, those it has encountered, and their interactions have not been homogeneous. Their interactions have been complex and multifaceted, and their fluctuating dynamic has ranged from amalgamation to suspicion and contest, having a diversity of effects on those involved.

About the author
Sophie Barker is reading for a PhD in Religious Studies at Lancaster University. Her research explores the role of narrative in the transmission of the *Dhamma* in the Pali *Tipiṭaka*.

Suggestions for further reading

In this book
See Chapters 1 (is Buddhism a religion?), 5 (texts), 37 (relations with Brahmanism), 39 (contemporary divisions), 41 (Zen), 48 (celestial beings in Tibetan Buddhism), and 54 (interreligious relations).

Elsewhere
Appleton, Naomi. *Shared Characters in Jain, Buddhist and Hindu Narrative: Gods, Kings and Other Heroes.* Abingdon and New York: Routledge, 2016.

Liu, JeeLoo. *An Introduction to Chinese Philosophy: From Ancient Philosophy to Chinese Buddhism*. Malden, MA: Blackwell Publishing, 2006.

Walshe, Maurice (translator). *The Long Discourses of the Buddha: A Translation of the Dīgha Nikāya*. Boston: Wisdom Publications, 1995.

54
How do Buddhists view other religious traditions, and what kind of interreligious encounters are Buddhists involved in now?

Elizabeth J. Harris

Buddhism, as the last answer stresses, arose in a religiously diverse context, when philosophical debate was robust and sometimes contentious. From the Pali texts, we can deduce that the Buddha generally advocated courteous rather than polemical debate with other religious groups. Yet these texts also show that early Buddhists could rigorously challenge and even ridicule the beliefs and practices of others. They could also subordinate or appropriate these practices, by elevating the teaching of the Buddha above all other teachings. And, if they appropriated practices from other religious traditions, they always changed them so that they became expressions of the Buddha's teaching. At the heart of these approaches was a tension between two positions. On the one hand, the Buddha taught that clinging to the view that "I alone am right" was a hindrance on the path to awakening/enlightenment. On the other hand, the Buddha's disciples were convinced that the

Dharma, taught by a perfectly awakened buddha, was superior to other religious teachings. These strategies—courteous debate, ridicule, subordination, appropriation—were developed and added to as Buddhism moved outside India into other Asian countries and beyond, and as Mahayana Buddhism evolved. Each context was different but two generalizations can be hazarded. First, which strategy gained the upper hand was dependent on socioeconomic factors and the power relationships that Buddhists found themselves within. Second, when courtesy was shown to Buddhism by religious others, courtesy was returned; when opposition to Buddhism was shown, defensive action was taken. China and Sri Lanka can be taken as two examples.

Buddhism reached China in about the first century BCE and met Daoism and Confucianism. There was some intermingling between Buddhism and Daoism at first, with Buddhist vocabulary being translated into Chinese using Daoist and Confucian terms. Eventually, Buddhism diverged from these traditions and a Chinese Buddhist vocabulary less dependent on Daoism emerged. By the fifth century CE, competitive debates were being held between Buddhists and Daoists. In this process, Buddhism in China was greatly influenced by Daoism and eventually the two coexisted, more or less harmoniously.

Later on, Buddhists in China had to negotiate a relationship with Christians. Christianity first arrived in the Tang Dynasty (618–907) through missionaries from the Church of the East, probably from Syria. Archaeological and textual evidence suggests that these Christians and Chinese Buddhists found common ground in such things as an ascetic morality and monasticism, and worked together. In the eighth and ninth centuries CE, the Confucian-dominated government placed them together in state persecutions! Key to this collaboration was the willingness of these Christians to respect Buddhism. When the Jesuits arrived much later in 1582, a different dynamic arose. At first, the Jesuits seemed to respect Buddhism and Chinese culture. Eventually, however, Buddhists realized that this respect was superficial, masking contempt and the wish to proselytize. So Buddhists in some parts of China turned to polemical defense, which led, for example, to the Jesuits being expelled from the province of Fujian.

To move to Sri Lanka, when Buddhism arrived in the island, in the third century BCE according to tradition, it met an indigenous spirituality that recognized deities and demons, sorcery and exorcism. What eventually happened was not condemnation of these beings and practices but incorporation and subordination. For those who became Buddhists, the Buddha moved to the top of the religious hierarchy, as teacher of ultimate truth, and the other beings became servants of the Buddha and continued to be honored. As for exorcist practices, the ritual changed to include the Buddha. This form of hierarchy continues to the present. What happened in Cambodia, Laos, Myanmar, and Thailand was similar.

Later, Sri Lankans endured three colonial powers from 1506 to 1948: the Portuguese, the Dutch, and the British. This brought Christian missionaries to their shores bent on converting Buddhists to Christianity. The story of the encounter between Buddhists and these Christians is complex. Generally speaking, Buddhists would have preferred respectful coexistence, perhaps punctuated by rigorous debate. However, they were forced into defensive mode, when they faced contempt for, and sometimes violence against, Buddhism and Buddhist places of worship. Under the Portuguese and Dutch, Buddhists mounted violent rebellions, crafted popular folk tales that ridiculed Christianity, and consolidated their own identity through religious revival. Under the British, in the nineteenth century, they showed courtesy to scholar civil servants who sought to learn about Buddhism but eventually rose in polemical opposition to the evangelical Protestant missionaries who were linked to independent European missionary societies. Responding to missionary writing that attempted to undermine Buddhism, Buddhist polemic sought to undermine Christianity. Mistrust between Buddhists and Christians going back to this time is still present in Sri Lanka. Similar defensive action occurred in Myanmar under British rule.

In the twentieth century, as European imperialism waned, Buddhists in both Asia and the West were drawn into what is now termed "dialogue" with other religious traditions. At first, this was in response to a change of attitude among Christians. In 1959, for instance, the National Christian Council Center for the Study of Japanese Religions was founded in Japan. Buddhists were invited to contribute to its journal, *Japanese Religions*, and did so. In the same period, Nikkyo Niwano, the founder of the Japanese lay Buddhist organization Rissho Kosei Kai (Establishment of Righteousness and Friendly Intercourse) was relating to other religious traditions internationally. He helped to found the World Conference on Religion and Peace and brought its first conference to Kyoto in 1970. In Sri Lanka, the Christian Ecumenical Institute for Study and Dialogue in Colombo drew Buddhists into conversation through its journal, *Dialogue*.

The destruction by the Taliban in 2001 of the Buddha-images at Bamiyan in Afghanistan was a contemporary turning point in Buddhist engagement with Islam. Buddhist reactions largely fell into two categories. The first was vehement denunciation of Islam's intolerance and violence. The second was to bring Muslims into dialogue with Buddhists, in order to correct their misunderstandings about Buddhism. For instance, the Taiwanese Dharma Master Hsin Tao organized a series of Buddhist–Muslim dialogues post-2001, which kick-started other Buddhist–Muslim dialogue initiatives. In spite of this, mistrust of Muslims continues to exist in majority-Buddhist countries in Asia: for example, Myanmar, Sri Lanka, and Thailand.

In the twenty-first century, Buddhists are engaging with people of other religious traditions at different levels. Inter-monastic dialogue started in the 1970s, giving Christian monastics the opportunity to live in a Buddhist monastery and Buddhists the opportunity to experience Christian monastic life. This led to some Buddhist and Christian monastics jointly leading Buddhist-Christian retreats. For instance, Amaravati Buddhist monastery in England hosts at least one Buddhist-Christian retreat annually. Other Buddhists have collaborated with people from other religious traditions in socially engaged projects. For instance, the International Network of Engaged Buddhists (INEB), founded in 1989, has always sought collaboration with non-Buddhists. At an academic level also, Buddhists are meeting people of other religions to discuss issues of practice and belief through bodies such as the U.S.-based Society for Buddhist-Christian Studies and the European Network of Buddhist-Christian Studies.

Through these dialogical processes, Buddhists are also revisiting what their texts and their traditions say about religious others. Most attempt to hold together the conviction that the Dharma represents ultimate truth with an attitude of respect, tolerance, and openness toward people from other religious traditions. Mahayana Buddhists, for instance, have utilized the concept of skillful means to incorporate other religious traditions into a Buddhist framework. A few Buddhists, the American Buddhist Rita Gross, for instance, have gone further, embracing what has been termed pluralism: namely, a willingness to recognize that more than one religion may possess liberating truth. And at the level of meditation and contemplative experience, convergences between Buddhism and other religious traditions are being found.

Buddhists today are not united in their attitude to other religions. Generally, though, Buddhists prefer coexistence to confrontation with people of other religions and have only turned to defensive action when they have seen a threat to Buddhism. They have also relished rigorous, but respectful, interreligious debate.

About the author

Elizabeth J. Harris is an Honorary Senior Research Fellow within the Edward Cadbury Centre for the Public Understanding of Religion, University of Birmingham, UK. Her research interests include Theravada Buddhism, religion and conflict, and interreligious studies.

Suggestions for further reading

In this book

See Chapters 30 (role of monasticism), 37 (relations with Brahmanism), 43 (Dalai Lama), 53 (influence of other religions), 60 (engaged Buddhism), and 61 (Buddhism and politics).

Elsewhere

Duckworth, Douglas, Abraham Vélez de Cea, and Elizabeth J. Harris (editors). *Buddhist Responses to Religious Diversity: Theravāda and Tibetan Perspectives.* Sheffield and Bristol, CT: Equinox, 2020.

Lai, Whalen, and Michael von Brück. *Christianity and Buddhism: A Multi-Cultural History of their Dialogue.* Maryknoll, NY: Orbis, 2001.

Schmidt-Leukel, Perry (editor). *Buddhist Attitudes to Other Religions.* St. Ottilien, Germany: EOS, 2008.

Part Nine
Buddhism and ethics

55
What vows do Buddhists take?

Nick Swann

Buddhists tend to talk in terms of "precepts" (guiding rules) or "trainings" rather than "vows" (solemn promises), as this gives a sense of making an effort to change behavior rather than entering into a pact to behave a certain way. Say, for example, you decide that you want to run a marathon. The very thought of it might be quite exciting in itself, as you daydream about crossing the finish line and the feeling of achievement. However, you are unlikely to finish unless you train. You will need to develop the discipline to run a few times each week, in ever-increasing distances, regardless of the weather or how tired you feel after a busy day. You may need to moderate your diet and eat healthier food. Similarly, if a Buddhist wishes to get closer to nirvana, then they might have to make certain adjustments to their lifestyle to help them unpick attachments to *saṃsāra* (the cycle of repeated births and deaths). Of course, if a trainee marathon runner skips a training session and spends an evening on the sofa eating ice cream instead, then that does not mean that they will never reach the finish line on race day, but it might make for harder work further down the line. Similarly, if a Buddhist slips up, it does not mean that they will never reach nirvana, but it will probably delay progress to a greater or lesser extent. Furthermore, as you make progress you start to feel benefits and the training itself becomes enjoyable and fulfilling.

It is not necessary to take any precepts in order to be a Buddhist ("taking refuge" in the Buddha, the Dharma, and the Sangha is enough for this) but many Buddhists do, voluntarily. The number of precepts and the attitude toward them varies across different Buddhist cultures and also depends on whether one is a lay Buddhist or a monk or nun. The focus of this "answer" is on lay precepts.

The five basic precepts for lay people are:

- avoid killing (onslaught on living beings);
- avoid taking what is not given;
- avoid sexual misconduct;
- avoid wrong speech;
- avoid intoxication.

The term "avoid" can bring to mind the term "thou shalt not," but the precepts are not commandments; and, as well as avoiding these negative activities, Buddhists are encouraged to cultivate their opposites. So, while avoiding killing, one also cultivates loving-kindness and compassion toward living beings; while avoiding taking what is not given, one cultivates generosity and non-attachment to material things. While three of these precepts are pretty self-explanatory, sexual misconduct and intoxication need a little clarification. The definitive act of sexual misconduct is cheating on your partner. Sex itself is not considered intrinsically "wrong"; but the pain that infidelity causes the wronged party is. All Buddhist cultures agree on this, but beyond infidelity what constitutes sexual misconduct varies. Avoiding intoxication is different from the other precepts and is not considered such a serious downfall if breached. The purpose is to keep the mind clear, but there is also a sense that if one is intoxicated there is a risk of breaching other precepts, too. Typically, this relates to alcohol consumption but it can extend to psychotropic drugs.

Some devout lay people opt to take extra precepts on special days such as when there is a full or new moon (the days when monks and nuns gather to recite their *vinaya* rules).

These extra precepts are:

- avoid singing and dancing (i.e., trivial entertainment) and adornments such as perfumes and garlands (including jewelry and makeup);
- avoid sleeping on high or luxurious beds, or sitting at the head of a table without invitation;
- avoid eating at an inappropriate time (usually this means fasting after the midday meal).

The extra precepts last until dawn the following day. If you add

- avoid handling money

to the above eight precepts, and split singing/dancing and adornments into two separate precepts, then effectively you have the ten rules of a novice monk or nun. Note that *any* intentional sexual act constitutes "sexual misconduct" if one has become a monk or nun.

As well as the above precepts, Mahayana Buddhists—lay and monastic—take the bodhisattva vow. This is a vow proper and the only one that is considered to last from one birth to the next: a solemn promise to delay entering final nirvana (Sanskrit: *parinirvāṇa*) while there are still beings suffering in the round of birth and rebirth (*saṃsāra*).

In addition to the bodhisattva vow, Vajrayana practitioners—again, lay and monastic—take tantric vows referred to as *samaya*s (Sanskrit; "binding promise"). There are a bewildering number of these—up to 10,100,000. However, there are fourteen main (root) *samaya*s, the four most important of which are:

- to maintain respect and trust in one's guru;
- not to contradict the Buddha's teachings;
- to respect one's fellow tantric practitioners (one's "*vajra* brothers and sisters");
- not abandoning love and compassion.

The eleventh-century Bengali monk Atiṣa reportedly said that he never broke the precepts but at least once a day he thought or did something that broke his bodhisattva vow, after which he was quick to repair it. However, while he no doubt had little trouble keeping the root *samaya*s, he described trying to keep all of the many tantric vows as like trying to keep a plate free of sand during a sandstorm. Nevertheless, Atiṣa saw the benefits of tantric practice as being worth the challenge, and it is possible to repair breaches of the lesser vows by meditating on the deity Vajrasattva and reciting his hundred-syllable mantra at least twenty-one times daily. Beyond that, it is hard to make generalizations regarding tantric vows because with many of the outer Tantras a practitioner can choose how much commitment to make to the practice at the time of the initiation. Inner Tantras, on the other hand, will typically involve daily commitments in terms of prayers, visualizations, and mantra practice.

About the author
Nick Swann is a Senior Lecturer in Buddhist Studies at University of South Wales, UK. His research interests include Buddhist Ethics, Buddhist Tantra, and Anthropology and Religion.

Suggestions for further reading

In this book
See Chapters 32 (monastic rules), 34 (lay Buddhists), 39 (contemporary divisions), 44 (bodhisattva vow), 47 (Tantra and sex), 58 (marriage and family life), 62 (compassion), and 64 (attitudes to sex).

Elsewhere
Bhikṣuni Heng-Ching Shih (translator). *The Sutra on Upāsaka Precepts*. Berkeley, CA: Numata Center for Buddhist Translation and Research, 1994.

Harvey, Peter. *An Introduction to Buddhist Ethics*. Cambridge: Cambridge University Press, 2000: Chapter 9.

Kalu Rinpoche. *Secret Buddhism*. San Francisco: ClearPoint Press, 1995.

56
Are Buddhists pacifists?

Peter Harvey

In line with the key Buddhist ideal of loving-kindness and compassion for all beings, including those who might be seen as "enemies," one of the four most serious rules that Buddhist monks and nuns are required to follow is to avoid intentional killing of a human being. To break this rule entails permanent exclusion from the monastic order, apart from any legal repercussions. There have, though, been some examples of going against the rule, as I will explain. It is also an offense for monastics to watch army activities and there are various lesser rules on not killing any animal or insect.

For lay people, the first of the ethical commitments known as the five precepts is: "I undertake the rule of training to abstain from onslaught on (i.e., killing) living beings," often chanted on a daily basis. All Buddhists are expected to undertake this precept, and aim to live by it. To intentionally kill a human or other sentient being is seen to break this precept, which then needs to be reflectively acknowledged, and the precept retaken. It is also seen to have unpleasant karmic results for the person who does, or orders, such an action. To kill a human is, of course, more serious than to kill another kind of sentient being, and it is seen as worse to kill a (genuinely) good person than a bad one.

These facts naturally set up the expectation that Buddhists are pacifists. But while complete non-violence is the ideal, Buddhists vary in the extent to which they live at this level. While it is true that aggressive warfare is greatly discouraged, all majority

Buddhist countries have armies and, while the preferred way to avoid a threat to a country is by diplomacy, wise alliances, and intelligence-gathering—as found in various *Jātaka* stories on past lives of the Buddha such as the *Mahā-Ummaga Jātaka* (no. 546)—many lay Buddhists have been willing to fight to defend their country and family. The risk to themselves includes the bad karmic results that they may generate in doing so.

Killing in war still breaks the first precept, and has bad karmic consequences. But if the motive is to protect the country's population, and not for personal benefit, this makes the action less bad—though in civil wars and/or ethnic conflicts, motives become much more complex and mixed, and attachments can narrow a person's circle of sympathies. Of course, actions such as looking after the wounded and treating prisoners well are good actions, which will help dilute the bad karma entailed by killing, as do any generous or kind actions. Acts of personal self-sacrifice in armed conflict may be good in this respect, although if they involve killing or injuring someone, this remains a bad aspect.

We also see that the influential scholar-monk Vasubandhu (330–400 CE) is very clear that, when an army kills, all the soldiers are as guilty as the ones who directly do the killing; for, by sharing a common goal, they mutually incite one another. Even a person forced to become a soldier is guilty, unless he has previously resolved "Even in order to save my life, I shall not kill a living being."

To die in combat is certainly seen as karmicly problematic. Once, the Buddha was asked by a professional soldier whether a combatant who falls in battle is reborn in a special heaven. In response, the Buddha is silent, but when the man persists in his questioning, he explains that such a person is actually reborn in a hell or as an animal, especially when dying with a wish to kill.

That said, while the Theravada school aligns itself with such principles of early Buddhism, there was a long-running civil war (*c.* 1983–2009) in Sri Lanka, in which there was conflict between the Sinhalese majority, which is mainly Buddhist, and the Tamil minority, who happen to be mainly Hindu. And in Myanmar

(Burma), the politically influential army has been accused of ethnic cleansing in 2016–2017 against the Rohingya minority, who are Muslim.

In the Mahayana tradition, there is a range of attitudes to the use of lethal force. The *Brahmajāla Sūtra*, influential in China, holds that monastics or lay people who take the bodhisattva vows should not take any part in war. Its first precept is that they should not be spectators of battles, nor should they kill, make another kill, procure the means of killing, praise killing, or approve of those who help in killing. Some texts, however, justify killing a human, on the grounds of compassion in dire circumstances. The *Upāyakauśalya* ("Skill in Means") *Sūtra* tells of the Buddha in a past life as a bodhisattva sea captain who regretfully kills a passenger who is plotting to kill five hundred passengers, both to save these and save the man from the bad karma of killing them. He is willing to himself go to hell for this, but due to this compassionate self-sacrifice, he avoids this and only suffers a lesser karmic result.

A less guarded justification of killing is found in the fourth-century *Mahāparinirvāṇa Sūtra*, which says that in a previous life the Buddha was a king who executed several brahmins for slandering Mahayana teachings, to save them from the bad karma entailed in this (!), and to protect Buddhism—an idea later used in Japan to justify killing those who opposed one's own sect of Buddhism. But such attempts to justify Buddhist involvement in violence are not really convincing in terms of Buddhist principles and have been rare.

In China, the fighting monks of the famous Shaolin monastery practiced a kind of kungfu (*gongfu*), probably developed to defend traders, travelers, and wandering monks against bandits in remote places. They were taught to use their skills only in legitimate self-defense, and not to show off. In the fifteenth and sixteenth centuries, they fought Japanese pirates infesting a coastal region of China.

In Japan, between the tenth and sixteenth centuries, there was a feudal society with no central government and social unrest— political power was up for grabs, and there were strongly drawn sectarian differences between different Buddhist traditions. Monasteries were centers of power, and donated land and defended their interests with armed irregular monks known as *sōhei*. Rinzai Zen monks also began to teach some of the *bushi* warrior-knights how to be calm, self-disciplined fighters, with no fear of death, although Zen monks did not take part in armed conflicts, and their temples were havens of peace, culture, education, and art.

In the Tokugawa era (1603–1867), Japan was unified under a military dictatorship, administered by aristocratic warrior-knights, now known as samurai. Zen became one of the influences on the warrior-ethic known as Bushido, the "way of the warrior," which also drew on previous warrior values and Confucianism, and emphasized such qualities as loyalty to one's feudal lord, self-sacrifice, upholding the honor of one's family name, strength, skill, fearlessness, self-control, equanimity in the face of death, and generosity of mind.

In the early twentieth century, a modernizing Japan, on a wave of Shinto-inspired nationalism, fought wars with Korea, Russia, and China and then, in the Second World War, America and Britain. Buddhists, having been criticized and persecuted at the start of the Meiji era (1878–1912), came to actively support the government. In the Second World War, most Buddhist schools agreed to support the nation in its efforts, this being seen as both fighting Western imperialism and "civilizing" China. In Bushido, the Zen contempt for death was still present, and this was drawn on in the training of kamikaze pilots in the closing phases of the Second World War, when the Japanese were getting desperate. There were, however, some examples of resistance to the war on Buddhist grounds, such as by the Soka Gakkai, even if these were relatively small in effect.

So, while Buddhist ideals are certainly non-violent, and many have stood up for this and worked for peace, the urge to protect others, and sometimes lesser motives, have also led to Buddhists taking part in armed conflicts.

About the author

Peter Harvey is Professor of Buddhist Studies (retired), University of Sunderland, UK, and co-founder of the UK Association for Buddhist Studies. He researches on Buddhist ethics, meditation, and early Buddhist thought.

Suggestions for further reading

In this book
See Chapters 18 (karma), 32 (monastic rules), 41 (Zen), 44 (bodhisattva vow), and 55 (vows/precepts).

Elsewhere
Harvey, Peter. *An Introduction to Buddhist Ethics: Foundations, Values and Issues,* Cambridge: Cambridge University Press, 2000: pages 239–285, 135–136.

Harvey, Peter, et al. "Reducing Suffering During Conflict: The Interface between Buddhism and International Humanitarian Law." *Journal of Contemporary Buddhism.* Forthcoming.

Jerryson, Michael K., and Mark Juergensmeyer (editors). *Buddhist Warfare.* Oxford: Oxford University Press, 2010.

King, Winston L. *Zen and the Way of the Sword: Arming the Samurai Psyche.* Oxford and New York: Oxford University Press, 1993.

57
Are Buddhists vegetarian?

Dhivan Thomas Jones

As a matter of fact, many Buddhists are not vegetarian, and neither was the Buddha a vegetarian. But, as an ethical principle, vegetarianism does follow from the Buddhist principle of non-harming (*ahiṃsā*), and many Asian and Western Buddhists forego meat eating out of compassion for farmed animals.

In the *Jīvaka Sutta* ("Discourse to Jīvaka") in the *Majjhima Nikāya*, the Buddha's physician, called Jīvaka, is said to have asked the Buddha what he thinks of the accusation that "the ascetic Gotama knowingly eats meat specially prepared for him." In response, the Buddha denies the accusation, and explains his ethical reasoning. Meat may be eaten if the ascetic has not (1) seen or (2) heard or (3) suspected that an animal has been slaughtered specifically for them, but not otherwise; a teaching later known as the "threefold purity" of alms-food. The context for this teaching is important. The Buddha's accusers would have been fellow ascetics like the Jains, strict vegetarians who were in competition with the Buddhists for the support of lay people, and who believed that the principle of non-harming (*ahiṃsā*) implied refusing to eat meat. By contrast, the Buddha distinguished meat-eating, which is ethically neutral, with involvement at any level with active harm to animals, which is ethically unwholesome and leads to suffering both for animals and, as a karmic consequence, for the one who harms animals. Not only was the Buddha not a vegetarian, but he disallowed his followers to practice strict vegetarianism even optionally, since such asceticism would undermine a good relationship with lay people. In the "Discourse to Jīvaka," the Buddha, having explained his ethical reasoning, goes on to explain that his followers should cultivate an immeasurable attitude of friendliness (*mettā*), compassion, joy, and equanimity toward those householders who offer alms-food, accepting what is given without greed. The Buddha's attitude is therefore a practical ethics of minimizing any harm to animals, and maintaining an attitude of love and gratitude to supporters. One imagines that the Buddha and his disciples would have mindfully accepted leftover meat placed in their begging bowls.

As a consequence of this practical attitude, mainstream Indian Buddhists were not vegetarian, and today Buddhists in Theravada lands tend to eat meat, although they tend to prefer fish and chicken and avoid beef, while admiring vegetarianism as the full expression of *ahiṃsā*. But the non-vegetarian attitude of mainstream Buddhism came under criticism from Mahayana Buddhists of the early centuries CE. In the chapter on meat-eating from the *Laṅkāvatāra Sūtra*, the literary character of the Buddha teaches Mahāmati that a bodhisattva should not eat any kind of meat. He explains that his earlier teaching, for instance in the *Jīvaka Sutta*, was only a first step, and that he did not in fact approve of meat-eating. Now, in the higher teaching of the Mahayana, he explains that a bodhisattva sees all living beings as having been family members in previous existences, and he or she has no desire for their harm just for the sake of gratifying carnivorous desire. This strongly pro-vegetarian ethic was taken up by Buddhists in China, and many Buddhists in East Asia continue to be vegetarian today.

Contemporary Buddhists, in both Asia and the West, are faced with the fact that modern methods of factory farming imply large-scale, profit-driven animal suffering, so that it is impossible to eat meat and to live by the principle of *ahiṃsā*. For this reason, even the Fourteenth Dalai Lama, who, like many Tibetan Buddhists, is accustomed to a diet involving meat, now promotes vegetarianism. The same logic would in fact strongly favor ethical veganism as the contemporary implication of *ahiṃsā*, since the dairy industry is, generally speaking, no less cruel than the meat industry. Nevertheless, strictly speaking, the Buddha's teaching is that it is not wrong to eat meat (or cheese), though it is wrong to harm living beings. Some Buddhists might eat roadkill, or leftover meat that would otherwise go to waste, although for many Buddhists this would collide with their sense of compassion. Ethical vegetarianism is a way of living out the principle of non-harming rather than an end in itself.

About the author
Dhivan Thomas Jones is a Lecturer in Philosophy and Religious Studies at the University of Chester. His research is mainly in the area of early Buddhist philosophy and he has been an ethical vegetarian since 1985.

Suggestions for further reading

In this book
See Chapters 13 (bodhisattva), 18 (karma), 39 (contemporary divisions), 44 (bodhisattva vow), 55 (vows/precepts), and 58 (marriage and family life).

Elsewhere
Bodhipaksa. *Vegetarianism: A Buddhist View* (3rd edition). Cambridge, UK: Windhorse Publications, 2016. A contemporary defense of Buddhist vegetarianism and veganism.

Ñāṇamoli, Bhikkhu, and Bhikkhu Bodhi (translators). "Discourse to Jīvaka." In *Middle-Length Discourses of the Buddha: A New Translation of the Majjhima Nikāya,* 474–476. Boston, MA: Wisdom Publications, 1995. Other translations available at https://suttacentral.net/mn55.

Śraddhāpa (translator). "The Chapter on Meat-Eating." *Laṅkāvatāra Sūtra.* https://www.sraddhapa.com. This is the primary Mahayana witness to a vegetarian ethic.

Stewart, James. "The Question of Vegetarianism and Diet in Pāli Buddhism." *Journal of Buddhist Ethics* 17 (2010): 100–140. A defense of vegetarianism as an ethical principle in early discourses.

58
Does Buddhism have rules for marriage and family life?

Alice Collett

The monastic life in Buddhism, as with other religions, is generally a celibate one, and part of the renunciation that monks and nuns commit to, when ordained, is the renunciation of family ties. Generally speaking, monastics should not marry and have children but rather live within a community of fellow monks or nuns. Within monastic codes, there are rules governing this aspect of life: for example, on abstention from sexual activity, on loosening ties to one's family, on not ordaining women who are pregnant. The idea behind this lifestyle is that family ties can create attachment, and part of the Buddhist path is to let go of attachments to the world. There is evidence, however, that the rules on this were not always strictly adhered to throughout the history of the tradition, and that some monastics did remain married after ordination, continue relationships with relatives outside of the monastic community, give birth while nuns, and care for children within monasteries.

In some countries and traditions of Buddhism, non-adherence to prescribed celibacy was concealed, in contrast to other times when it was an open, acknowledged choice. The latter has been the case, historically, for Buddhist monastics in Japan. This is thought to have begun with the Pure Land Buddhist monk Shinran

(1173–1262), although non-adherence to monastic celibacy, even when regulated by the Japanese state, is in evidence earlier than this. The reason for this seems to be that abstention from sexual activity has not been a factor by which the worthiness of monastics was judged in Japan, the laity instead considering a monastic worthy by virtue of their abilities to effectively execute rituals, their scholarly training, and their skills in chanting and preaching. This being the case, monastics could openly marry, and live with their families outside of the monastic compound.

A monk or nun can, any time they wish to, leave the monastic community, disrobe, and marry and start a family. This is what happened with the well-known Tibetan monk Chöygam Trungpa. Trungpa was a Tibetan monk who migrated to the West, living initially in the UK, and who co-founded Kagyu Samye Ling Monastery in Scotland; he was a charismatic leader, and well known for his unconventional behavior. Many of Chöygam Trungpa's teachings and practices have come under scrutiny, renewed in recent years in the context of grave allegations against his son and successor. Trungpa married an Englishwoman, Diana Mukpo (born Pybus) in 1970, but continued to be a Buddhist leader, eventually setting up Shambhala International in the U.S.A. It is well known that both he and his wife engaged in extramarital affairs. While this is unconventional, it is not universally considered unacceptable among Buddhist communities.

Buddhist ethics are based on the principle of *ahiṃsā*, or non-harm, and this is the governing principle for all aspects of both monastic and lay life, thus equally for marriage and family life. Unlike monastics, lay people are not governed by rules for marriage and family life. There are, however, sections of Buddhist texts and canons that provide what has been interpreted as guidance for living a lay life. The best known of these is a dialogue between the Buddha and a lay disciple, Sigala, in which the Buddha offers advice on lay life, including on marriage. Although at other times Buddhist texts reveal that monogamy was not always the order of the day in Buddhist societies down the centuries, one aspect of the Buddha's advice to Sigala is concerned with being faithful within marriage. The desire for extramarital affairs can involve a breach of several ethical precepts. The pleasure-seeking involved can be understood as a breach of the first precept, in that desire for sensory experience can lead to harming others, and as affairs are usually conducted in secret, involving deception, lies, and a breach of trust, they can more broadly be considered unethical. If they are done with the initial consent of both parties, and done openly without deception, in such a way that all those involved enter into their liaisons with full awareness and deem it to be what they want then, in theory, it is possible to make a case that one's adherence to the Buddhist ethical code has been barely impacted. In addition, jealousy can and does rear its head in such circumstances so whether, overall, such relationships can be engaged with in a way that does no harm is a moot point. Also, it is not the case that if a Buddhist is discovered to be engaging in extramarital affairs that they can—after the fact—profess that they did not believe it would cause harm. All actions need to be engaged in with mindful awareness of one's own behavior. Each choice made, especially those with potential to cause harm, require careful and responsible forethought.

Non-harm should also be the guiding principle with regards to child-rearing and parenting. As monastics renounce family responsibilities, there are no specific rules in the monastic codes on parenting, and for a lay person, parenting should be governed, as with other aspects of their life, by adhering to the five (lay) precepts. These are guidance, not rules. The modern Buddhist teacher Jack Kornfield has a chapter in his book *Bringing Home the Dharma* on parenting, which reflects on learning how to be a conscious, mindful parent, and modern Buddhist magazines publish essays by parents on their experiences of practicing Buddhism while being a parent. Children do feature both within Buddhist texts and in the history of Buddhism; they have lived at monasteries to receive an education, as well as being reared there by monastic parents. The Buddha famously left his wife with a newborn child in the legendary account of his life, and children feature in other texts and narratives on renunciation. In some Buddhist traditions, children are recognized as incarnations of important teachers, and familial relations can be used as metaphors for relations within the monastic community, such as followers of the Buddha being called the sons and daughters of the Buddha. Vanessa Sasson's edited volume explores many of these aspects of Buddhism's relationship with children and childhood, and includes a chapter by Elijah Ary who was himself, at age seven, recognized as the reincarnation of an important Tibetan teacher (tulku).

About the author

Alice Collett is Director of The South Asia History Project, University of Wolverhampton, UK. Her research focuses on the religious history of ancient India, especially the history of women.

Suggestions for further reading

In this book
See Chapters 30 (role of monasticism), 32 (monastic rules), 42 (Pure Land Buddhism), 47 (Tantra and sex), and 55 (vows/precepts).

Elsewhere
Clarke, Shayne. *Family Matters in Indian Monastic Buddhism*. Honolulu: University of Hawai'i Press, 2013.

Sasson, Vanessa, R. (editor). *Little Buddhas: Children and Childhoods in Buddhist Texts and Tradition*. New York: Oxford University Press, 2013.

"Sigalovada Sutta: The Discourse to Sigala" (*Dīgha Nikāya* 31), translated from the Pali by Narada Thera. *Access to Insight (BCBS Edition)*, 30 November 2013. http://www.accesstoinsight.org/tipitaka/dn/dn.31.0.nara.html

Wilson, Liz (editor). *Family in Buddhism*. Albany: State University of New York Press, 2013.

59
How do Buddhists view suicide and self-immolation?

Peter Harvey

While Buddhism emphasizes that there is much mental and physical suffering in life, this can, paradoxically, help Buddhists not to give in to despair. If suffering is to be expected, then there is less reason to take particular problems *personally*, as the world conspiring against one. As nothing is truly "I," "me," or "mine," this can help Buddhists avoid being dragged down by unpleasant experiences. Reflection on the key Buddhist teaching that everything is impermanent indicates that all bad things come to an end, sooner or later. And, if an unpleasant experience may be the karmic result of one's past bad actions, one can be more willing to patiently live with it, until it changes, rather than sow the seeds of future suffering by new, rash actions.

In the face of some weighty suffering, a person might try to kill themselves hoping for something less intolerable after death; yet there is no guarantee that matters may not be made worse by this act. The next rebirth might be as an animal preyed on and eaten by others, as a frustrated ghost, or in a hell: so suicide may lead on to something *more* "intolerably painful" than the present life. Even in the case of a human rebirth, there are many possible forms of severe suffering.

Buddhism teaches that craving impels one through the round of rebirths, and one form of craving is for non-being—to be without unpleasant situations—and *in extremis*, this might lead to suicide. Yet this craving will lead on to yet another rebirth, along with its problems. So, as an attempted escape from the sufferings of life, suicide is, according to Buddhist principles, totally ineffective. Moreover, as dying in an agitated state of mind is seen as leading to a bad transition into the next life, suicide is seen as likely to lead to a bad rebirth next time. In the Tibetan tradition, the consciousness of one who commits suicide is seen as anguished and weighed down with negative karma, so as to need rituals to aid it.

Now Buddhism sees being born as a human as a rare and precious opportunity for spiritual development, as well as for the pleasures that are also part of human life. Suicide both wastes this opportunity for oneself and also deprives others of benefits that one may bring to them. Moreover, suicide is an act that will bring grief to friends and relatives, and so, if for no other reason, is to be avoided.

Suicide and the ethical precepts

Is it the case that suicide is seen as breaking the first precept, against killing a living being? As Buddhism sees acts that harm either others or oneself as morally unwholesome, and suicide can be seen in this way, one would expect so, although this is rarely explicitly said in the texts. In Tibet, while the first precept only applies to killing others, suicide is nevertheless seen as one of the gravest bad actions, as serious as murder.

The seriousness with which the Buddha in fact viewed suicide can be seen from the following monastic precept from the *Vinaya*, one of the few entailing "defeat" in the monastic life, i.e., permanent expulsion:

> Whatever monk should intentionally deprive a human being of life, or should look about so as to be his knife-bringer, or should praise the beauty of death, or should incite (anyone) to death, saying, "Hullo there, my man, of what use to you is this evil, difficult life?

Death is better for you than life", or who should deliberately and purposefully in various ways praise the beauty of death or should incite (anyone) to death: he is also one who is defeated, he is not in communion.

This rule clearly concerns murder, assisting someone in suicide, or inciting or praising suicide. While this does not say that suicide itself is a "defeat" offense, it would be odd to do so, as a dead person cannot be expelled from the monastic order. That said, one monastic code says that suicide is not an offense, and another that it is a grave offense but not quite a "defeat" one.

Is an unsuccessful suicide attempt a monastic offense, though? In the Theravadin *Vinaya*, an account is given of a monk who, "tormented by dissatisfaction"—which seems to relate to sexual desire—throws himself off a precipice, clearly in an attempt to kill himself. Though he survives, he kills someone else by landing on him. His action is not seen by the Buddha as an offense entailing defeat, but as a lesser offense, due to culpable carelessness, as with unintentionally causing a death by throwing a rock down a cliff.

The commentary on this story extends the prohibition on throwing oneself off a cliff to any method of suicide, even a "passive" method such as self-starvation, as used by Jain saints. It does, however, allow that some instances of self-starvation are acceptable: when a monk has no time to collect food when intently seeking to attain a particular meditative state, and when there is a severe, long-lasting illness and a monk does not want to be a burden on those caring for him, or if further eating would be futile.

Early Buddhist literature also includes discussions of a few cases of those whose illness was frustrating their meditative practice, leading to them killing themselves, but who were seen to have died as enlightened beings, arhats. The Theravada commentaries see them as not arhats prior to their death, but as attaining arhatship at the last minute by insight arising as they watched the process of dying, perhaps accompanied by remorse at their unwise act. Some, though, see these monks as arhats even before killing themselves.

There are also *Jātaka* stories of the Buddha in a past life, as a bodhisattva, giving his life to benefit others—heroic self-giving, rather than "suicide." The Theravada has the story of a hare who wishes to feed a holy man, and gives his own body as he does not wish to harm anything else, and a favorite Mahayana story is of the bodhisattva giving himself to be eaten by a starving tigress and her cubs.

Self-immolation

Self-immolation is literally "self-sacrifice" but is often applied particularly to burning oneself to death. Chapter 23 of the *Lotus Sutra* of the Mahayana refers to mythical heroes burning themselves alive as an act of worship—a rather unguarded way of urging the complete dedication of one's life to a higher ideal, though a few in China took it literally. Another devotion-related motive for self-immolation was the hope of gaining rebirth in the Pure Land of Buddha Amitābha (Japan: Amida).

The Chinese tradition also includes examples, influenced by Confucianism, of a person killing himself as an act of protest, to try to compassionately bring about an improved situation in society. The Vietnam War period saw some famous examples of Buddhists burning themselves to death that broadly fit into this tradition. Distinguishing such acts from "suicide" per se, the Vietnamese monk Thich Nhat Hanh says:

> The monk who burns himself has lost neither courage nor hope; nor does he desire non-existence. On the contrary, he is very courageous and hopeful and aspires for something good in the future. He does not think that he is destroying himself; he believes in the good fruition of his act of self-sacrifice for the sake of others (*Vietnam: The Lotus in the Sea of Fire*, pages 118–119).

In a similar way, since 2009, there have been over 150 self-burnings in Tibet, by both monastics and lay people, in the context of Chinese oppression of Tibetans and their Buddhist culture. These are intended as acts of compassionate self-giving, appealing to the heart of the oppressors so as to bring benefits to other Tibetans and to the oppressors themselves.

About the author

Peter Harvey is Professor of Buddhist Studies (retired), University of Sunderland, UK, and co-founder of the UK Association for Buddhist Studies. He researches on Buddhist ethics, meditation, and early Buddhist thought.

Suggestions for further reading

In this book

See Chapters 18 (karma), 20 (non-self teaching), 32 (monastic rules), 42 (Pure Land Buddhism), 55 (vows/precepts), 61 (Buddhism and politics), 62 (compassion), and 63 (non-attachment and compassion).

Elsewhere

Benn, James A. *Burning for the Buddha: Self-immolation in Chinese Buddhism*. Honolulu: University of Hawai'i Press, 2007.

Harvey, Peter. *An Introduction to Buddhist Ethics: Foundations, Values and Issues*, Cambridge, Cambridge University Press, 2000: pages 286–292.

Keown, Damien. "Buddhism and Suicide—the Case of Channa." *Journal of Buddhist Ethics* 3 (1996): 8–31.

Nhat Hanh, Thich. *Vietnam: The Lotus in the Sea of Fire*. London: SCM Press; New York: Hill & Wang, 1967.

60
What is engaged Buddhism?

Manu Ato-Carrera and Tim Stephens

The Vietnamese Zen monk Thich Nhat Hanh (b. 1926) coined the term "engaged Buddhism" in the 1960s to stress the necessity of an active involvement with social suffering in the context of the Vietnam War. The notion of engaged Buddhism focused the awareness and compassion of Buddhist practice on the conflict, organized monastic and lay Buddhists in networks of peace activism and welfare aid, and proposed concrete ways for ending the war.

Since then, the term "engaged Buddhism" has referred to a plurality of Buddhist movements profoundly informed by different forms of "grassroots" civic engagement, starting from the late nineteenth century to this time. It accounts for a trend that emerged, in parallel, in different regions of Asia and across the major Buddhist traditions, as a way of interpreting Buddhism as socially committed and adapting to the modern world's social needs. As such, engaged Buddhism is sometimes described as one of the modern forms of Buddhism, although others emphasize that Buddhism has always been socially engaged, because of its encouragement of compassionate action.

Instead of deciding whether or not Buddhism is "essentially" socially engaged, engaged Buddhists are more likely to say that Buddhism in the modern world needed to show itself as active in public life, because of the popular view that Buddhist practice was all about "withdrawal" or non-involvement.

Engaged Buddhists draw on resources that lie deep within Buddhism: for instance, embodiments of compassion (Pali and Sanskrit: *karuṇā*) such as Guanyin or Avalokiteśvara, probably the most popular of the Buddhist pantheon of bodhisattvas. She/he is sometimes represented with many heads, many eyes, or many arms, or an open helping hand, which indicate and embody the trait of hearing and seeing the suffering of others as well as a willingness to help. When a sangha, or a collective group of Buddhists, act in unison, this could be seen as an embodiment of this spirit of compassion. Engaged Buddhist action always seeks to join the individual to the collective and finds this in the concept of interdependence—a modern interpretation of the social dimension of the doctrine of dependent origination or *pratītyasamutpāda* (Sanskrit). Linked to it is the term coined by Thich Nhat Hanh and used by many engaged Buddhists, "interbeing," which articulates that social experience in the globalized world is profoundly interconnected: among citizens, between humans, and between all sentient beings and nature.

The Sri Lankan monk Walpola Rahula (1907–1997) was an early pioneer of modernist engaged Buddhism through his book *The Heritage of the Bhikkhu*, which was published in 1946 and argued that the monastic Sangha should not stay within their monasteries but should follow the example of the Buddha, a champion of social reform. This was immediately after the Second World War (1939–1945), when Buddhists were emphasizing the core Buddhist message of *ahiṃsā* (non-harming, or non-violence). This tradition of pacifism, mentioned earlier in the American context of the 1960s, has ancient roots in Buddhism. The Emperor Aśoka (*c.* 268–*c.* 232 BCE), an Indian ruler converted to Buddhism, famously proclaimed that the sound of "war drums had been replaced by the rule of Buddhist law." The first step of engaged Buddhists today has not changed from ancient times in that they would refrain from causing "injury" and not add to, nor create further suffering in their social context. Going beyond the principle of non-harming, Sulak Sivaraksa, a renowned Thai social activist, conceives peace as a highly proactive process that avoids the extremes of doing nothing on the one hand and responding with violence on the other.

Sometimes Buddhist "engagement" limits itself to one core issue, such as gender equality. For instance, the establishment of the Geshema Degree for Tibetan nuns during the past decade, which was led by engaged Buddhist women linked with Sakyadhita ("Daughters of the Buddha")—an international association of Buddhist women founded in 1987—is a remarkable example of the pursuit of gender equality in Buddhist communities.

Anālayo, a contemporary and well-known Buddhist practitioner and scholar, finds an interrelatedness in early Buddhism between *karuṇā*, as the meditative quality of compassion, and *anukampā* ("trembling along with"), as active compassion, where cultivating one strengthens the other. Engaged Buddhists, then, draw on two important aspects of Buddhist heritage: ethics and meditation. Significant figures in engaged Buddhism emphasize again and again the importance of meditation practice. Meditation is at the heart of how Buddhists act mindfully, with awareness and insight. Engaged Buddhists do not simply passionately "take sides," passively "retreat" or indifferently "surrender." They seek wise action. One highly vivid example of wise action is the "peace walks" in Cambodia in the 1990s, which, among other things, led refugees back to the reconstruction of their country after Buddhists had arranged shelter for them and encouraged reconciliation and forgiveness. The practice of meditation itself is seen by both traditionalists and reformists alike as the prerequisite to compassionate and wise action such as this. Engaged Buddhism begins by bringing the practice from the meditation hall into everyday life.

The civic commitment to improve social conditions and the welfare of communities in Buddhist countries tells a story of the complex ways in which monastic and lay communities, adherents and followers, have lived and worked side by side for millennia. Buddhist rulers, such as Aśoka mentioned earlier, offer an example of how Buddhism has featured in governance. The spread of

Buddhism across Asia was often very dependent on rulers' favor and state sponsorship. Today, organizations like the Tzu Chi Foundation in Taiwan, initiated by the Buddhist nun Cheng Yen in 1966, and the U.S.-based Global Buddhist Relief, initiated by the Venerable Bhikku Bodhi in 2007, carry out remarkable work at home and abroad.

Present in engaged Buddhism is also an overtly political stance against social abuse and oppression, denouncing the culture of consumerism, corporate greed, and political corruption, and offering alternatives for a social order aligned with Buddhist and secular values. Every aspect of this social and political agenda is integrated in the aspiration of the International Network of Engaged Buddhists (INEB)—the largest organization of its kind to date, founded in Thailand in 1989, based on the vision of Sulak Sivaraksa working with Thich Nhat Hanh.

Engaged Buddhism contributes a profoundly positive vision to the world, and strives to attain a better future on a collective level.

About the authors
Manu Ato-Carrera is a PhD student at SOAS, University of London, and a researcher and former Coordinator of the Center for Oriental Studies at the Pontifical Catholic University of Peru. He researches Engaged Buddhism.

Tim Stephens is an Education Developer, with a specialism in Curriculum, at University of the Arts London and a photographic artist. His research interests include: embodiment, the relationship between cognitive and non-cognitive experience, equality, and organizational change.

Suggestions for further reading

In this book
See Chapters 13 (bodhisattva), 28 (kinds of meditation), 33 (nuns), 35 (gender equality), 54 (interreligious relations), 56 (pacifism), 59 (suicide

and self-immolation), 61 (Buddhism and politics), 62 (compassion), and 70 (ecological movements).

Elsewhere

King, Sallie B. *Socially Engaged Buddhism*. Honolulu: University of Hawai'i Press, 2009.

Queen, Christopher, Charles Prebish, and Damien Keown (editors). *Action Dharma: New Studies in Engaged Buddhism*. London: Routledge, 2003.

Surpin, Jacob (editor). *True Peace Work: Essential Writings on Engaged Buddhism*. Berkeley, CA: Parallax Press, 2019.

Watts, Jonathan S. (editor). *Rethinking Karma: The Dharma of Social Justice*. Bangkok: International Network of Engaged Buddhists (INEB), 2014.

61
What is the relationship between Buddhism and politics?

Brian Black

According to traditional Buddhist sources, when the Buddha was born, the court priests told his father that he would either become a great political leader or a great religious leader. His father, who was a king, did everything he could to steer his son in the direction of politics, but, alas, when the Buddha came of age and confronted suffering in the world, he rejected politics for the spiritual life. This anecdote from the traditional story of the Buddha's life points toward the tension between religion and politics that appears in various ways throughout the Buddhist tradition. On the one hand, many Buddhist teachings tend to discourage engagement with politics in favor of a monastic life. On the other hand, throughout its history, Buddhist institutions have relied on government support for its survival and have actively sought the patronage of politicians, aristocrats, and merchants.

Buddhism and Politics in ancient India
In the Pali Canon there are several texts that explicitly discuss the duties of the king. In the *Cakkavatti-Sihanada Sutta* (The Lion's Roar on the Turning of the Wheel; *Dīgha Nikāya* no. 26), for example, the Buddha portrays the ideal king as the *cakravartin*

(Sanskrit)—the wheel-turning monarch, who rules according to the Buddhist Dharma. The *cakravartin* is characterized as refraining from violence and ruling according to the counsel of his royal sage, whose advice is based on Buddhist teachings. In the *Aggañña Sutta* (On Knowledge of Beginnings; *Dīgha Nikāya* no. 27), the Buddha offers a slightly different account of the ideal king. Here, he traces the origins of political power to a state of nature, in which people observed that lying and stealing were prevalent when there was no central authority to administer punishment. The people then appointed a pleasant and capable person among them to be king, a form of social contract.

The most famous monarch from the ancient world to support Buddhism was King Aśoka, who ruled most of what is now north and central India, Pakistan, and Afghanistan from 265–232 BCE. Aśoka's empire was the largest in South Asia until the height of the British Empire. According to his inscriptions, he converted to Buddhism after his excessively violent conquest of Kalinga (modern-day Orissa) in the ninth year of his rule. After his conversion to Buddhism, King Aśoka declared that he would rule according to the Dharma, not the sword. Aśoka did not make Buddhism the official religion of his empire, but his support both strengthened its position in India and initiated its spread abroad.

In addition to contributing to the spread of Buddhism during his lifetime, Aśoka has been regarded as an ideal king throughout much of the Buddhist tradition, especially in Theravada Buddhist countries. Many activities performed by Aśoka continued to be imitated by kings throughout Asia for the next two thousand years, such as: contributing lavishly to the monastic Sangha, convening councils, sponsoring new redactions of Buddhist texts, establishing medical centers, building roads, and constructing rest-houses and wells.

Buddhism and politics in Southeast and East Asia

Between the first and tenth centuries CE, Buddhism expanded across almost all of Southeast Asia and East Asia. As Buddhism spread, much of its ability to adapt to new cultures was because of its success in gaining support from royalty, as well as aristocrats and merchants. Buddhism was important to governments for a variety of reasons, including its rituals and symbolic power, as well as its popularity with the laity. In Southeast Asia, for example, many of the region's most well-known historical sites, such as Borobudur in Indonesia, the temples of Ayutthaya in Thailand, and the pagodas of Bagan in Myanmar are reminders of the glories of Buddhism's regal past. Buddhism was a major religion of the Khmer Empire in Cambodia (802–1431), was the official religion of the Kingdom of Bagan in Burma (849–1297), and was the state religion in Thailand during the Ayutthaya period (1351–1767).

Similarly, in East Asia, Buddhism has been closely linked with some of the region's most powerful dynasties throughout its history. In China, Buddhism played a key role in unifying the empire of the Sui dynasty (581-618 CE) and during the Tang dynasty (618–907 CE), Buddhism became a major influence on Chinese culture. In Korea, Buddhism became the state religion during the Goryeo period (918–1392). And, in Japan, Buddhism flourished during the Heian period (794–1185) and maintained close ties with the royal court throughout the Kamakura (1185–1333) and Muromachi (1336–1573) periods. In Central Asia, Buddhism became the state religion in Tibet, Mongolia, and Manchuria. Tibetan Buddhism was adopted as the official state religion of the Yuan Dynasty (1271–1368) and the Manchu Qing Dynasty (1644–1912), both of which ruled China.

Buddhism and politics in modern Asia

As the prominence of Buddhism in pre-modern Asia was often directly related to its support from royalty, in the twentieth century Buddhism went through radical changes throughout the region due to its often fraught relationship with modern political regimes. In the nineteenth and twentieth centuries, most of Asia was colonized: India, Myanmar, Sri Lanka, Hong Kong, and parts of China were ruled by Britain; Vietnam, Cambodia, and Laos by France.

Meanwhile, Japan colonized Korea, Taiwan, Manchuria, and parts of China. In countries that were ruled by Western powers, colonial regimes tended not to support Buddhist institutions formally, while they often actively encouraged widespread Christian missionary activity. Colonialism changed Buddhism throughout Asia, but the effects were different in each context.

In addition to colonialism, another political development that changed Buddhism dramatically in the twentieth century was the emergence of many communist regimes throughout Asia. In China, Buddhism suffered severely during the Cultural Revolution (1966–1976). Not only were many Buddhists persecuted, but also monasteries were closed down and all ordinations of monks were banned. In Cambodia, during the communist revolution under Pol Pot, the Khmer Rouge government (1975–1979) destroyed Buddhist monasteries and killed an estimated 25,000 Buddhist monks. Buddhists have also been persecuted in Tibet since the Chinese occupation.

Whereas Buddhists have been the victims of persecution in some countries, Buddhism has been the religion of the persecutors elsewhere. In Sri Lanka, Buddhist monks and institutions have contributed toward a majoritarian politics that discriminates against Hindu and Muslim minorities. During the civil war (c. 1983–2009), many monks supported military action and some were actively involved in the conflict, often opposing opportunities for a peaceful solution. Similarly, in Myanmar, Buddhists have contributed toward the persecution of the Rohingya, a Muslim minority population. Since 2012, the Burmese military have killed over 10,000 Rohingya and about 700,000 live in exile in Bangladesh and India. Buddhist monks and institutions have repeatedly offered religious justifications for the violence against Muslims.

Meanwhile, in India, a new form of Buddhism emerged in the twentieth century which promised liberation from caste discrimination. This form of Buddhism, called Navayana ("New Vehicle") Buddhism, was founded by Bhimrao Ramji Ambedkar (1891–1956), who was a leading member of the Indian independence movement and main author of India's constitution. Ambedkar was a dalit (untouchable) and suffered caste discrimination throughout his life. In 1956 he converted to Buddhism and initiated about 500,000 of his own followers. Today there are more than seven million followers of Navayana Buddhism in India.

The future of Buddhism and politics in Asia

Whereas Buddhism had declining numbers and dwindling political support throughout much of the twentieth century, in the twenty-first century there are signs of Buddhist revivals across Asia. As with its relationship with politics throughout history, Buddhism's re-emergence is complex and takes different forms in different contexts. In some cases, Buddhism's resurgence is in the form of a militant nationalism that is violently exclusive toward other religions. In other cases, Buddhists speak as a subjugated community expressing resistance toward an oppressive majority. In some cases, governments use Buddhism to initiate intercultural dialogue and pursue soft power. In still other cases, Buddhism is presented as a global movement for peace, justice, and protecting the environment.

About the author

Brian Black, originally from California, earned his doctorate at SOAS (University of London) and now teaches at Lancaster University. His research interests include the Upaniṣads and the *Mahābhārata,* and the narrative relationships between Hindu and Buddhist texts.

Suggestions for further reading

In this book
See Chapters 5 (texts), 30 (role of monasticism), 43 (Dalai Lama), 55 (vows/precepts), 60 (engaged Buddhism), and 62 (compassion).

Elsewhere

Aggañña Sutta and *Cakkavatti Sīhanāda Sutta*. In Maurice Walshe (translator). *The Long Discourses of the Buddha: A Translation of the Dīgha Nikāya*. Boston, MA: Wisdom Publications, 1987: pages 395–405, 407–415.

Harris, Ian (editor). *Buddhism, Power and Political Order*. Abingdon, UK: Routledge, 2007.

Jerryson, Michael. *If You Meet the Buddha on the Road: Buddhism, Politics, and Violence*. Oxford: Oxford University Press, 2018.

Moore, Matthew J. *Buddhism and Political Theory*. New York: Oxford University Press, 2016.

62
How important is compassion in Buddhism?

Pyi Phyo Kyaw

Compassion (Pali and Sanskrit: *karuṇā*) is central to Buddhism, even to its very existence. Buddhism was founded when the Buddha decided to teach the Dharma, the truth that he had realized, out of compassion for all sentient beings caught in *saṃsāra*, the cycle of rebirth and inevitable suffering. Because understanding the Dharma is key to liberation from *saṃsāra*, the Buddhist tradition, which extols generosity, regards the gift of the Dharma as the highest gift of all. A buddha therefore epitomizes the combined virtues of wisdom, in realizing the truth, and compassion, in making it available. Developing compassion is also an integral part of the spiritual transformation of a bodhisattva (future Buddha), perfected over many lifetimes. The future Buddha's great acts of compassion in previous lifetimes are recounted in narratives called *Jātaka*. In several of these, the Buddha sacrifices his own life for others, most famously for a starving tigress so that she can feed herself and her hungry cubs on his flesh.

The rise of Mahayana Buddhism sees a broadening-out of the bodhisattva path, with the aspiration to become a buddha regarded as the ideal for all practitioners. The Mahayana Buddhist pantheon includes advanced bodhisattvas regarded as embodiments of compassion, such as Tārā and Avalokiteśvara (Chinese: Guanyin), who in East Asia may take female form. Avalokiteśvara's compassionate intervention to protect supplicants from every conceivable danger, from shipwreck to lawsuits, and to fulfill their needs and wishes, are described in Mahayana sutras, most famously in Chapter 25 of the highly influential *Lotus Sutra*. Such stories may have assisted the transmission of Buddhism across Asia along the often perilous maritime and land silk routes. Inspiring much Buddhist iconography, including the cave paintings at Dunhuang in China, the Pure Land is another Mahayana concept related to compassion. Pure Lands are created by bodhisattvas and buddhas to provide realms free from suffering in which practitioners can easily hear the Dharma and attain liberation. This concept gave rise to Pure Land Buddhism in China and Japan.

In Tibetan Buddhism, the role of the guru in providing tantric initiation is also attributed to compassion. In tantric symbolism, awakening is sometimes depicted through the coupling of wisdom (*prajñā*), represented by a female bodhisattva, and compassion, in the form of a male bodhisattva or buddha. This coupling may be visualized or enacted. Compassion in this depiction and in most Mahayana traditions is linked with the concept of skillful means, which endorses the use of whatever compassionate means are deemed appropriate to ensure the spiritual progress of others. The concept developed from the Buddha adapting his teaching to the needs of his audience and led to the idea that even proscribed actions, such as lying and killing, may be permissible if they lead to the spiritual progress of others. The renowned *Upāyakauśalya* (Skill in Means) *Sūtra* contains illustrative narratives, including the famous story of the bodhisattva as sea captain. The sea captain, on learning that a murderer on board his ship intends to kill five hundred of his passengers, realizes that he must pre-emptively kill the would-be murderer to save him from hell and the passengers from death. In doing so, he accepts his own likely rebirth in hell for committing such a deed. The purity of his motivation, compassion, results in him avoiding this and only suffering a lesser karmic result.

Some non-Buddhist philosophical traditions discuss criteria such as intelligence in assessing the appropriateness of compassion for any given category of living being, such as domestic animals.

In contrast, Buddhism advocates compassion on the basis of our shared sentience, especially shared suffering, and our interdependence, connected as we are through the complexities of causality and multiple rebirths. Compassion should be developed for all sentient beings including animals and other non-humans. This concern to eliminate suffering, regardless of whose, leads to a direct relationship between compassion and the Four Noble Truths, which stress the universality of suffering, its causes, and how to end it. The result is that compassionate action is informed by sensitivity not only to the actual suffering of oneself and others but also to the conditions that have led to it.

All the above shows that compassion in Buddhism is about action to aid others. Buddhaghosa, a fifth-century-CE commentator on the Pali Canon, defined three modes of compassion in Buddhism: being moved by the suffering of others; combating and demolishing the suffering of others; and scattering it on those who suffer. These combine practical action with developing positive mental states. Buddhist philosophy, ethics, and meditation, therefore, identify not only practical reasons for developing compassion but also methods for doing so. The early discourses state that compassion is directly opposed to the wish to harm others. They also distinguish between awareness of others' suffering and the concern for others to be free from suffering, because, if one becomes fixated on the former, one could fall prey to unwholesome states of mind such as anger, sadness, self-righteousness, and conceit. If we rather focus on the wish for others to be free from suffering, the mind takes the vision of others being freed from suffering as its mental object. This positive state of mind offers an important condition for clear discernment of suffering and its causes so that one is able to respond to suffering with a compassionate attitude. One's compassionate responses in turn strengthen the compassionate disposition of one's own mind. Therefore, such cultivation of compassion transforms the way one thinks, speaks, and acts, and is beneficial for both oneself and others. Merit (the fruit of good action) is also gained through good, compassionate actions, and transferring such merit to outcomes that benefit others is a further act of compassion found throughout the Buddhist world. The cultivation of compassion is the second of a widespread set of meditation practices called the *brahma-vihāra*—divine abodes. Because compassion is often concerned with those who are less well-off than oneself, there is a potential pitfall in that one may perceive others as inferior in status. This is counterbalanced through the cultivation of the other three *brahma-vihāra:* namely, loving-kindness (*mettā*), sympathetic joy at others' success (*muditā*), and equanimity (*upekkhā*). These methods for cultivating cooperative, empathic dispositions toward oneself and others have come to influence compassion-based therapeutic techniques and programs in a broad range of secular contexts.

About the author
Pyi Phyo Kyaw is Dean of Academic Affairs and Lecturer in Theravada Studies at Shan State Buddhist University, Taunggyi, Myanmar. She is also a Visiting Senior Research Fellow at King's College, London, UK. She specializes in Burmese Buddhism, Abhidhamma (Theravada analytical philosophy), Theravada meditation, Buddhist business practices, and Buddhist ethics.

Suggestions for further reading

In this book
See also Chapters 7 (narrative), 13 (bodhisattva), 21 (Four Noble Truths), 22 (non-attachment), 42 (Pure Land Buddhism), 55 (vows/precepts), 60 (engaged Buddhism), 63 (non-attachment and compassion), and 73 (secular Buddhism).

Elsewhere
Anālayo, Bhikkhu. *Compassion and Emptiness in Early Buddhist Meditation*. Cambridge, UK: Windhorse Publications, 2015.

Jenkins, Stephen. "On the auspiciousness of compassionate violence." *Journal of the International Association of Buddhist Studies* 33(1–2) (2010 [2011]): 299–331.

Makranksy, John. *Awakening through Love: Unveiling Your Deepest Goodness.* Boston, MA: Wisdom Publications, 2007.

63
Is non-attachment compatible with compassion?

Elizabeth J. Harris

Both non-attachment and compassion are important qualities in Buddhism; but, to the outsider, they can seem to pull in opposite directions. "Non-attachment" seems to point toward indifference to the world or withdrawal from life. Compassion, on the other hand, seems to speak of active engagement with the sufferings and pain of humanity. In the Buddhist world view, however, the two are utterly compatible with each other. Not only this, both are essential on the Buddhist path toward awakening/enlightenment.

One of the reasons why the two qualities might seem incompatible is that the true meaning of "non-attachment" in Buddhism can be lost in translation. "Non-attachment" or "detachment" are often used to translate the Pali and Sanskrit term, *virāga*. *Virāga*, however, literally means "without lust" (*rāga*) or without strong craving. It has nothing to do with indifference to the world. Rather, it refers to a state of being in which there is no lust or desire for such things as material possessions, riches, status, and sensual pleasures, and no clinging to fixed, inflexible views. The non-attachment that Buddhism encourages leads away from these objects of desire. A person who seriously follows the Buddhist path seeks to lessen craving for them, in the realization that none can give lasting satisfaction because none of them lasts forever.

This involves an internal journey of personal transformation that results in the avoidance of what unchecked *rāga* can lead to, such as possessiveness in relationships, jealousy, competitiveness, and physical violence. The encouraging of this form of non-attachment, therefore, can protect society from the impulses that cause disruption, suffering, and disharmony. It can create citizens who are sensitive and responsive to the needs of others, not aloof.

Non-attachment in Buddhism is also linked to the idea of renunciation. For monks and nuns, renunciation involves leaving their homes and families, and eliminating attachment to or craving for anything connected with their former lives as lay people with family responsibilities. This form of non-attachment is central to the monastic life. Non-attachment for lay people does not involve such radical renunciation but they might nevertheless seek to renounce the desires that have already been mentioned, fostering a mental attitude of non-attachment to material things. This is very different from a lack of compassion for the world.

Compassion (Pali and Sanskrit: *karuṇā*) in Buddhism requires at least two things: an ability to stand in the shoes of others, empathizing with them in their struggles and pain; and a capacity to work actively toward the diminution of suffering in others. In contrast to relationships based on attachment, it is not partial but seeks the well-being of all. The great figures of compassion in Buddhism, the buddhas and bodhisattvas, extend robust and active compassion to all living beings, without distinction. Within them, there is not an ounce of the attachment that would privilege one living being over another.

Non-attachment is necessary for this kind of compassion. Indeed, developing the kind of non-attachment that is present in the term *virāga* leads to the arising of compassion. As Buddhists are quick to point out, when we are concerned only about promoting ourselves through possessions, the gaining of status or our inflexibly held viewpoints, empathetically standing in the shoes of others is almost impossible. Our minds can be so imprisoned by our attachments and desires that we cannot even see let alone help to alleviate the suffering of others. But when we seek to lessen our attachment to self-promotion, the ability to see and respond to the suffering of others increases. And, as we become aware of this suffering, so our attachments lessen further. In a two-way process, compassion becomes the fruit of non-attachment and also the antidote to attachment.

In Buddhism, therefore, non-attachment and compassion intertwine at a deep level. Buddhists are encouraged to withdraw for the purposes of inner moral purification and meditation. The fruits of this should be the lessening of attachment to the objects we crave for and the increase of compassion for all. The right expression of compassion, therefore, is dependent on a form of non-attachment that is not indifference but rather the absence of egotistical self-seeking and attachment to impermanent material objects.

About the author
Elizabeth J. Harris is an Honorary Senior Research Fellow within the Edward Cadbury Centre for the Public Understanding of Religion, University of Birmingham, UK. Her research interests include Theravada Buddhism, religion and conflict, and interreligious studies.

Suggestions for further reading

In this book
See Chapters 22 (non-attachment), 26 (why Buddhists meditate), 30 (role of monasticism), and 62 (compassion).

Elsewhere
Aronson, Harvey B. *Love and Sympathy in Theravāda Buddhism*. Delhi: Motilal Banarsidass, 1980.

Harris, Elizabeth J. *Detachment and Compassion in Early Buddhism*. Kandy: Buddhist Publication Society, 1997. https://www.accesstoinsight.org/lib/authors/harris/bl141.html

Part Ten
Buddhism and contemporary issues

64
What do Buddhists think about sex?

Amy Langenberg

In August 2018, an American Buddhist Insight organization called Against the Stream Meditation Society sent a letter to its members revealing the results of an investigation into sexual assault allegations against its founder, Noah Levine. The investigation determined that Levine had caused harm through sexuality with multiple women. While admitting to promiscuity, Levine denied any misconduct. He also made a number of assertions about Buddhist teachings on sexual ethics, including the idea that the Buddha was "pretty liberal" about sex between consenting adults. Levine is not alone in these views. Among its Western converts, Buddhism is assumed to be less sexually repressive than the Abrahamic religions and more accepting of sexual minorities. But was the Buddha "pretty liberal," as Levine claims? Did he, in fact, know and teach sexual consent? What *do* Buddhists, past and present, think about sex?

Narratives about the Buddha's early life emphasize his attractiveness as a young and handsome prince. They tell the story of his marriage to the lovely Yaśodharā and his enjoyment of the women in his harem. The Buddha, in other words, is not depicted as a sexual innocent. These traditional images of the young prince and his bevy of women may have been present for Noah Levine when he remarked that the Buddha was "pretty liberal" around consensual sex. Nonetheless, traditional forms of Buddhism strongly privilege renunciation over the householder life. In fact, if there is any one thing that defines Buddhism across Asian Buddhist cultures, it is the male celibate ideal.

Arguably the most important of the many vows fully ordained Buddhist monks pledge to keep is celibacy. According to monastic legal codes (*vinayas*), which date to the several centuries after the Buddha lived, the origins of this rule involve a sincere and otherwise chaste monk called Sudinna, who had sex with his former wife in fulfillment of a filial duty to produce an heir. When the Buddha hears of Sudinna's mistake, he famously compares penetrative sex with a woman to inserting one's penis in the mouth of a venomous snake. He then formally establishes the rule forbidding monks to participate in sexual intercourse. In the textual traditions that have survived, this rule is accompanied by detailed descriptions of numerous proscribed sexual behaviors.

Although early Buddhist sexual ethics affirm sexual restraint over sexual engagement, they also include articulations of more moderate forms of sexual discipline intended for lay people, formalized as the third precept. The third precept has been interpreted variously over the history of Buddhism in Asia and the West. For instance, the influential Vietnamese teacher and engaged Buddhist Thich Nhat Hanh recommends sexual activity only within committed relationships, and calls for accountability in cases of abuse. In its simplest canonical formulation, however, the third precept simply says to refrain from "improper behavior in matters of desire." The main example of improper behavior given in the early tradition is "going to the wife of another," often glossed in English as "adultery." The implicit moral subject here is male, and what is ethically problematic is not betraying one's own wife but rather trespassing against the sexual rights of another man. Furthermore, the early sources deem unmarried women to be incapable of controlling their sexuality and criticize sexual activity outside of marriage for women as unacceptable and a mark of moral coarseness.

New articulations of the third precept emerged as Buddhist traditions developed in ancient South Asia and beyond. Scholastic treatises associated with the Mahayana begin to characterize sexual misconduct as fourfold: namely, sex in the wrong place, at the wrong time, using the wrong orifice (anything but the vagina), or with the wrong person (paradigmatically, someone else's wife, but also another man). Such ideas were then taken up by Tibetan scholars and are the reason the Dalai Lama once publicly stated that the Buddhist tradition regards sex between men to be inappropriate.

Traditional articulations of the third precept do not highlight clear communication between individuals enjoying equal agency in a sexual relationship. What is deemed ethical sex for lay people in the classical tradition is heteronormative and sexist, and has little to do with the principle of sexual consent. The monastic legal codes (*vinaya*s), which legislate ethical sexual behavior for monks and nuns, do, however, include something like the concept of consent, primarily in relation to cases involving rape. *Vinaya* authors understood both monks and nuns to be rape-prone. In order to decide if a rape victim could be held responsible for a sexual transgression, they used "consent" as a standard, defining it as giving into or experiencing pleasure during sexual contact. Here, a feminist reading must mark the fact that the *vinaya* authors routinely questioned whether victims of sexual assault were aroused by the experience, or perhaps came to enjoy it after some initial resistance, and equated such feelings with "consent."

Was the Buddha liberal about sex? Not particularly. Did the Buddha define ethical sex as consensual? Not in the contemporary sense. Still, what canonical or other authoritative sources say, and what Buddhists past and present have actually done or thought about sex, often differ. Medieval India saw the emergence of forms of Buddhism in which sexuality was incorporated into Buddhist practice. Referred to as Tantra or Vajrayana, these new forms of Buddhist theory and practice became particularly important in Tibet, where non-celibate Buddhist teachers married, had children, practiced sexual yogas with consorts, and established communities of non-celibate followers. Japan is also known for its married clergy, and for the historical practice of same-sex love between teachers and their young attendants in monastic settings. Many convert communities in the contemporary West are non-celibate and foreground the experiences of married or sexually active lay people, rather than monastic celibates.

More darkly, despite its reputation for centering compassion and nonviolence, Buddhism has had its own #MeToo moment of late. Multiple Buddhist teachers, including Sogyal Lakar of Rigpa, Noah Levine of Against the Stream, and Dagri Rinpoche of the Foundation for the Preservation of the Mahayana Tradition, have faced allegations of sexual misconduct and abuse.

The sexual worlds of Buddhist women and sexual minorities are also difficult to see clearly through abstract doctrines and early texts (which are androcentric and heteronormative as a rule). Still, if a feminist hermeneutic is applied, sources on the early nuns' community afford a glimpse of female intimacies that may sometimes have become sexual. Recent work on early modern Tibetan hagiographies written by women also reveals a world in which female Vajrayana practitioners exercised sexual agency and religious authority, even within the patriarchal institutions of Tibetan Buddhism. Contemporary queer practitioners in North America have begun to make use of Buddhist doctrines such as emptiness and present-time, non-judgmental awareness (mindfulness) to reframe and articulate their experiences as sexual minorities in a Buddhist mode.

What do Buddhists think about sex? The historical and living Buddhist traditions scholars have studied demonstrate that Buddhists inevitably think (and do) many things about sex. They are ascetics but they are also libertines. They are straight but they are also queer. They are ethical but they are also abusers. The thoughts and experiences of less-studied Buddhists—especially the sexually and racially minoritized and the abused—have been far less legible to scholarly observers. But that doesn't make them less Buddhist.

About the author

Amy Paris Langenberg is an Associate Professor of Religious Studies at Eckerd College, U.S.A. Her research interests include female monasticism, gender and sexuality in pre-modern South Asian Buddhism, and, more recently, sexual abuse in American Buddhist communities.

Suggestions for further reading

In this book

See Chapters 9 (what we know of the historical Buddha), 30 (role of monasticism), 32 (monastic rules), 39 (contemporary divisions), 47 (Tantra and sex), 55 (vows/precepts), and 65 (Attitudes to LGBTQI).

Elsewhere

Cabezón, José Ignacio. *Sexuality in Classical South Asian Buddhism*. Somerville, MA: Wisdom Publications, 2017. A comprehensive overview of classical textual tradition on sex.

Gayley, H. "Revisiting the Secret Consort (*gsang yum*) in Tibetan Buddhism." *Religions* 9(179) (2018). Covers Tibetan consort practices and female sexual agency in Buddhism.

Gleig, Ann. "Queering Buddhism or Buddhist De-Queering? Reflecting on Differences amongst Western LGBTQI Buddhists and the Limits of Liberal Convert Buddhism." *Theology & Sexuality* 18(3) (2012): 198–214. Queer interpretations of Buddhist doctrine.

Langenberg, Amy Paris. "Reading against the Grain: Female Sexuality in Classical South Asian Buddhism." *Religion* 49(4) (2019): 728–734. Same-sex intimacy in female communities.

65
What do Buddhists think about those who are LGBTQI?

Sal Campbell

Unlike religious scriptures such as the Christian Bible and some of its interpretations, the many key texts of Buddhism, produced over millennia through oral and written traditions in many languages, have relatively little to say directly about LGBTQI people. Variations in sexual behavior or gender expression were known in the Buddha's time, but the nature of one's gender or sexual desire was seen as largely irrelevant to religious ethics or spiritual practice. From the time of the Buddha, guidelines regarding sexual ethics have centered around the idea of "sexual misconduct" i.e., avoiding causing harm using sexuality, rather than judging LGBTQI people as inherently immoral, or prohibiting them from practicing the Dharma. Overall, Buddhism is not centrally concerned with control of non-normative sexuality or gender identity, and primarily focuses on the mitigation of sexual desire in general, in order to help practicing Buddhists avoid distraction.

This does not mean there are no ethical guidelines for or perspectives on LGBTQI people in Buddhist traditions. For ordained monks and nuns, the basic and absolute rule set out in the *vinaya* rules is celibacy, but this applies as much to heterosexuals as to LGBTQI people, with no moral distinction placed on different sexual behaviors or identities. For lay practitioners, celibacy is not required, but there is still an ethical precept of abstaining from sexual misconduct, usually interpreted according to the practitioner's social norms. Spanning a wide variety of cultures and traditions, there is no overall consensus among all Buddhists regarding LGBTQI people or behavior. A primary divide here is between traditional Asian or "Eastern" Buddhist cultures, which tend to be more conservative in their attitudes toward LGBTQI people, and newer communities of "Western" Buddhists, who are usually more liberal and permissive, much like the societies they reside in. For example, in Sri Lanka, a majority Buddhist country, LGBTQI behavior and transgender identities are still criminalized in laws that remain influenced by the colonial era. So, whereas there are no specific prohibitions on LGBTQI people in Sri Lankan Buddhism, LGBTQI Buddhists are driven underground. In contrast, Western Buddhist movements, having emerged at a time of growing sexual permissiveness and liberalism, are rarely if ever overtly homophobic (though, like contemporary society, still sometimes exclude transgender people), with a growing number of respected LGBTQI teachers emerging.

Buddhists in the West, including LGBTQI people, are more often lay practitioners than monastics, but generally take their pursuit of enlightenment very seriously, so wish to understand how to relate skillfully to doctrinal guidance about lay sexual misconduct. In a historic meeting between LGBTQI Buddhists and the Dalai Lama in 1997, he referred to a fifteenth-century text by Tsongkhapa which stated that sex between men (among other things) was prohibited, but the Dalai Lama also recognized the "possibility of understanding these prohibitions in the context of time, culture and society . . . If homosexuality is part of accepted norms [today], it is possible that it *may* be acceptable." This said, he admitted that he was unable to unilaterally redefine ethical precepts, so the issue would have to remain in dispute. Arguably, then, how strictly the doctrinal guidelines around LGBTQI sexual activity should be interpreted is a matter of debate. Rather than accept or reject the traditional texts in their entirety, it may be both wiser and more compassionate to adopt what José Cabezón calls a "critical Buddhist sexual ethic," examining the presented principles in the light of their scriptural origin, rationale, and whether they support justice to all beings—and if they do not stand up in the light of this examination, respectfully putting them aside.

Variations in sexual behavior (lesbian, gay, bisexual, etc.) tend to be better understood and accepted in Buddhist contexts than alternative gender identities such as transgender, intersex, or gender nonbinary. That said, concepts of personhood in Buddhism have not been limited to rigid binary gender identities, with gender understood as a psychosocial construct which, like other conditioning, can be transcended. There are various examples of Buddhist figures, such as the male bodhisattva Avalokiteśvara, also known as Guanyin and Kannon, the goddess of compassion in China and Japan, who can be understood as transcending fixed, binary gender identity, instead of merely appearing in male or female form to the unenlightened gaze. In a story from the popular Mahayana text the *Vimalakīrti Nirdeśa Sūtra*, an enlightened goddess changes herself into the form of a male, and the arhat Śāriputra (Pali: Sāriputta) into a female and back again, to demonstrate how she has overcome this limited, dualistic understanding, saying to Śāriputra, ". . . the Buddha said, 'In all things, there is neither male nor female.'" The whole sutra demonstrates that concepts connected with time and space are ultimately empty—mere conventions, including any essentialized understandings of gender or sexual identity.

In terms of communities and religious practice, however, Buddhist contexts are often split down binary gendered lines, which complicates how transgender and other gender-variant people interact with Buddhism, and how different Buddhism traditions respond to their presence. This is particularly true of traditional single-sex monastic contexts but is not limited to these. Just as in other contexts like the family, workplaces, and schools, the division of people into rigid gender positions can mean transgender people have found themselves left outside some formal Buddhist institutions. Luckily, however, more inclusive LGBTQI-friendly Sanghas are growing in number, particularly in the West. This said, much like mainstream society, full acceptance of transgender and other gender-variant people in some Buddhist Sanghas still has a long way to go.

Overall, it can be said that Buddhism is not an inherently homophobic or transphobic religion. Religious beliefs have often been used by conservative organizations and governments to label LGBTQI people as immoral, and to justify persecution, ostracism, and harm. It is important not to confuse these negative attitudes with the limits on sexual behavior found in the Buddha's teachings, the Dharma. Following the most basic ethical principle of nonharm, Buddhists should not condone this cruel, harmful treatment of LGBTQI people, recognizing such harm as more immoral than any possible sexual behavior or identity. The Dalai Lama himself has said that, regardless of what certain Buddhist texts might say about same-sex behavior, "it is wrong for society to reject people on the basis of their sexual orientation." If asked how Buddhists should behave toward people who are LGBTQI, the answer would be in the same way as they would behave toward all fellow sentient beings—with dignity, kindness, understanding, and respect.

Being LGBTQI is also no impediment to practicing the Dharma, and, unless one chooses to be a monk or a nun, this includes while being sexually active. Despite the explicit limitations or prohibitions in some traditional texts, Buddhism has never been anti-sex, and acknowledges that sexual behavior, including between queer people, can be life-affirming, pleasurable, and healthy. Fundamentally, non-normative gender identity or sexuality are neither morally wrong nor an obstacle to attaining enlightenment. Another Buddhist teacher, Khandro Rinpoche, has said that "within the Buddha's doctrine itself homosexuality is nothing special, nothing new . . . Each person is responsible for their own mind, own thoughts, emotions, understanding, awakening, realization. It's possible for a homosexual person. It's possible for all sentient beings."

About the author

Sal Campbell is an academic writing specialist at Birkbeck College, University of London. As a nonbinary queer Buddhist, they are concerned with understanding sexuality and gender in the context of Buddhist ethics and practice.

Suggestions for further reading

In this book
See Chapters 19 (what is reborn), 20 (non-self teaching), 46 (emptiness), 55 (vows/precepts), 62 (compassion), and 64 (attitudes to sex).

Elsewhere
Cabezón, J. I. *Sexuality in Classical South Asian Buddhism*. Somerville, MA: Wisdom Publications, 2017. See page 2 for an account of the meeting between the Dalai Lama and LGBTQI Buddhists.

Cabezón, J. *Thinking through Texts: Toward A Critical Buddhist Theology of Sexuality*. 2020. https://info-buddhism.com/Buddhism-Sexuality-Cabezon.html

Peskind, S. *"According to Buddhist Tradition": Gays, Lesbians, and Sexual Misconduct*. Lion's Roar, 2009. https://www.lionsroar.com/gays-lesbians-and-the-definition-of-sexual-misconduct. See this article for the Khandro Rinpoche quote.

Vimalakīrti Nirdeśa Sūtra. https://www2.kenyon.edu/Depts/Religion/Fac/Adler/Reln260/Vimalakirti.htm

66
Should Buddhism be taught in schools?

Denise Cush

Yes! However, it does depend on what sort of school, which country the schools are in, whether the pupils are Buddhist, what you mean by "teaching" and what you understand by "Buddhism."

Schools

There are many different sorts of school even within one country—some publicly funded, some privately funded, some a bit of both—and any of these categories may have a stronger or weaker connection with a particular religious tradition. Religious communities have often pioneered the provision of education for the majority outside the wealthy elite (at least for boys and occasionally for girls) long before the modern state joined in, a notable example being Buddhist monasteries. Whether either the teaching of religions/worldviews or religious practices, dress, or symbols are allowed in schools, varies considerably internationally, as well as by type of school.

Within state-funded education systems, there are three main basic approaches. In some countries, such as the U.S.A., China, or France, the education system is secular in the sense of keeping religion separate from schooling, so that there is no subject called "religious education," and no official teaching of Buddhism or other religions occurs. Elsewhere, the teaching is "confessional" or "denominational," meaning that pupils are nurtured within the religion of their family/community. Either one tradition is deemed to be the national religion and taught to all, or pupils are divided into separate classes of recognized religions. The third option is "non-confessional" or "integrated" religious education, where all pupils are taught together, and a range of religions/worldviews are taught in a way that aspires to be objective, critical, and pluralistic. As might be suspected, classroom reality is somewhat more complex than this threefold division suggests.

Teaching

The name "religious education" is ambiguous, covering both "confessional" and "non-confessional" approaches, and so includes both a class of young Tibetan monks-to-be being nurtured within their own tradition by an older teacher-monk in Nepal, as well as a class of pupils from a variety of religious/non-religious backgrounds taught Buddhism by a non-Buddhist teacher in Sweden. "Teaching" Buddhism in schools, therefore, can mean initiation into a familiar tradition or learning about what for most pupils is something "other people" believe and do.

Case study: teaching Buddhism in English state schools

Non-confessional, multi-faith religious education has been developed since the late 1960s in England. As Buddhism did not focus on God, was perceived as difficult, or only knowable through personal experience, and had less of a visible "ethnic" presence, it tended to be relatively neglected in the curriculum, which is still true to some extent. But, from the 1970s and especially since the mid-1980s, a few scholars and teachers, both Buddhist and non-Buddhist, started to provide both arguments and resources for teaching it.

I do not identify as a Buddhist but have been attempting to teach Buddhism in a non-confessional way at various levels of education since the 1970s. My rationale for teaching Buddhism to mostly non-Buddhist pupils in schools, either secular or religious, in an open way is as follows.

So many different countries and cultures have been influenced by Buddhism, over the millennia and today. As a tradition that does not center on God, the student's concept of "religion" is challenged and widened. Non-Buddhist students' preconceptions of Buddhism tend to be fairly positive and yet their previous knowledge fairly limited, which makes it easier to interest them, as does the fact that Buddhists in the UK are from many different backgrounds, including converts, rather than associated with one particular ethnic group. Many students who would not wish to "become" Buddhists can find some teachings and practices within Buddhism that they can learn from and apply to their own lives, without the teacher straying into "confessional" teaching. Aspects of Buddhism can be taught appropriately to children and young people of *all* ages; as Peggy Morgan pointed out, "Buddhists have children too." Discussion of contemporary issues such as wealth and poverty, gender, climate change, war, and peace can be enhanced with Buddhist insights and perspectives. There are temples and Buddhist centers that can provide visits or speakers to enable students to encounter "real-life" Buddhists. As Buddhism spread into a wide range of cultures, there is a wealth of art, architecture, drama, and dance to appreciate, much of which has had positive resonance in youth culture since the 1960s and still today (walking into Tibetan prayer flags attached to tents is a common hazard at music festivals).

There are challenges for the teacher. For both the Buddhist and the non-Buddhist teacher, it is difficult to provide a balanced picture of the full diversity of the world of Buddhism. Even the specialist tends to know more about some traditions, countries, texts, or teachers than others. It is best simply to acknowledge this. In England, for various reasons, including colonial history and accidents of scholarship, there tends to have been more taught about the Theravada than the Mahayana. Where the Mahayana has been taught, it tends to have been Zen and/or Pure Land from Japan, or forms of Tibetan Buddhism. Thematic categories drawn from a Christian model of religion can be misleading—terms like "worship," "scripture," "faith," and "deity" carry baggage that can hinder understanding. Some textbooks and resources can give partial or misleading portrayals of Buddhism. Gender can be an issue—are all the Buddhists pictured in textbooks male monks in orange robes? One stumbling block for both teachers and students is the mass of non-English terms from Pali and Sanskrit, as well as Chinese, Japanese, and Tibetan, plus Thai, Sinhala, Korean, Vietnamese ... many of these terms are hard to translate, and, to add to the problem, are spelled differently and are impossible to know how to pronounce. Whether to teach meditation in schools is a controversial question, but simple versions of practices such as mindfulness of breathing or developing thoughts of loving-kindness in *mettā* practice may be appropriate in some contexts, with careful planning and the possibility for pupils to opt out.

Pupils from Buddhist families in English state schools may experience some dissonance between what is taught in school and their home life, especially if the teachers lack subject expertise. Researchers such as Morgan and Thanissaro note the lack of time given to Buddhism in comparison with other religions, a focus on doctrines such as the "Four Noble Truths," and concepts such as *anattā* (Pali: non-self), instead of morality and Buddhism as a lived part of everyday life for lay Buddhists. Vocabulary that would have been familiar in the home language might not be recognized in Pali, Sanskrit, or English. Children not obviously from migrant families with roots in Asian Buddhist-majority countries might not be recognized as Buddhists. If taught well as a living tradition, respecting the pupil's knowledge of their own experience of the tradition, and their own personal views, but acknowledging the diverse experience and views of other Buddhists, teaching Buddhism in school can contribute to a Buddhist pupil's religious education in both senses of the term.

My experience and that of many other teachers is that Buddhism can and should be taught in schools of all kinds, to children and young people of any age, as long as the teacher has sufficient subject knowledge, acknowledges the diversity of

Buddhism and differing interpretations, looks at practice as well as teachings, the lives of "ordinary" Buddhist families as well as monks and scholars, women and children as well as men, creative arts and non-verbal forms of communication as well as texts, the transformative experiences of individuals, and the consequences, negative as well as positive, of Buddhist involvement with wider culture and political power.

About the author

Denise Cush is Emeritus Professor of Religion and Education at Bath Spa University, UK. She has taught and written about Buddhism at all levels of education, from primary schools to postgraduate, and also trained teachers of religious education.

Suggestions for further reading

In this book

See Chapters 1 (is Buddhism a religion?), 27 (mindfulness), 39 (contemporary divisions), 50 (Buddhist art), 52 (Buddhist influence on art), 55 (vows/precepts), and 60 (engaged Buddhism).

Elsewhere

Cush, Denise. "Teaching about Buddhism: Some Points to Bear in Mind." *Professional Reflection/REtoday* 35(3) (2018): 60–64.

Dossett, Wendy. "Teaching about Buddhism." In *Religion in Education*, vol. 3, edited by W. Kay and L. Francis, 319–328. Leominster, UK: Fowler Wright, 2000.

Morgan, Peggy. "Buddhists Have Children Too!" In *Shap Mailing*, edited by W. Owen Cole, 25–27. Solihull, UK: Shap Working Party, 1979. Reprinted in: Angela Wood (editor). *Religions and Education*. London: BFSS National RE Centre, 1988: pages 25–27.

Thanissaro, Phra Nicholas. "A Preliminary Assessment of Buddhism's Contextualisation to the English RE Classroom." *British Journal of Religious Education* 33(1) (2011): 61–74.

67
Are alcohol and drugs ever acceptable to Buddhists?

Wendy Dossett

The answer to this question depends in part on whether Buddhism is understood as a lived and changing tradition or whether it is understood through apparently timeless ethical principles. If the former, then there is plenty of evidence that drugs and alcohol have been and are acceptable to Buddhists in different settings around the globe. Tempting though it may be to respond with "it didn't ought to be," thus giving the role of judge to certain written and oral texts, namely the five precepts, it is more productive to explore the role, function, and interpretation of those texts in diverse Buddhist communities over time.

The precepts themselves emerged historically, the first four being familiar among the various ascetic traditions in Greater Magadha (northeast India) in the Buddha's time. As well as appearing in other broadly contemporaneous texts, they appear in the *Vinaya*, the oldest Buddhist texts, firstly as training rules for monastics and later for lay people. The fifth precept which concerns avoiding intoxicants is fairly distinctive to Buddhism.

The fifth precept is open, according to Bhikkhu Bodhi, to two legitimate translations: firstly, "I undertake the training rule to abstain from fermented and distilled intoxicants which are the basis for heedlessness"; and, secondly, "I undertake the training rule to abstain from fermented and distilled liquors and other intoxicants which are the basis for heedlessness." The second translation makes it clear that drugs additional to alcohol are included, and this is the common modern assumption. For Buddhist monks and nuns, a breach is taken as one of the *pācittiya*s (rules entailing confession), i.e., serious, but not leading to expulsion.

The traditional commentary on this rule for monastics explains that for the precept to be violated four factors are required: (1) the intoxicant; (2) the intention of taking it; (3) the activity of ingesting it; and (4) the actual ingestion of the intoxicant. It is notable that intoxication itself is not the problem, but the intoxicant and the intention. The precept may be taken, at least in terms of what constitutes a technical breach, as deonotological, or rule-based, rather than consequentialist (judging the rightness of an action based on its consequences). That said, the precept emerges within a tradition that extols awareness and there are plenty of texts in which the Buddha relays stories about intoxicated monks who compromise their own awareness and bring the Sangha (monastic community) into disrepute.

It is also the case that it is possible to take some intoxicants *without* detrimentally affecting clear awareness. Thus, while on special days of religious observance such as full-moon days, when they formally recite the precepts, Theravada lay people abstain from alcohol, they, along with Buddhists elsewhere in the world, are not obliged to abide by such a strict prohibition on a daily basis. Total abstention is held as an ideal, and some lay people, especially women, do abstain completely, but so long as the use does not result in harm to self or others, it is considered acceptable. This consequentialist view is the dominant and widespread Buddhist attitude to intoxicants. It is a view arguably still based on the precepts because it puts possible harm at the center of decision-making. It also draws on a textual tradition of naming the negative consequences of taking too much intoxicant in terms of karmic demerit, and of increasing the likelihood of breaking the other precepts.

In some tantric Vajrayana traditions, however, entheogens (such as cannabis datura, other psychoactive plants, and even alcohol) are recommended as positively enhancing awareness and insight, if used skillfully and in a ritual setting. In East Asian traditions, especially in Pure Land Buddhism and to some extent in Zen, alcohol use is entirely acceptable. In Pure Land, no amount of precept-keeping can advance the journey to awakening, as attainment is the result of the "other power" of Amida. Thus, eschewing alcohol for religious reasons is subject only to spiritual pride, and therefore worse than needless. In Japan, priests and lay people alike enjoy alcohol, and it forms part of festivals and celebrations throughout the year.

Postwar European and North American interest in Asian religions was characterized, in part, by an association between spiritual practices and psychedelics for the purposes of opening the "Doors of Perception." Thus, countercultural writers such as Jack Kerouac and Alan Watts argued that direct personal insight into impermanence, insubstantiality, and interdependence could be reached as readily through psychedelics, such as mescalin and LSD, as through Buddhism.

As a tradition that frames the human condition in terms of craving, it is not surprising that Buddhist teachings are increasingly drawn upon for the purpose of treating clinical addiction to alcohol and other drugs. From Buddhist interpretations of the Twelve Steps present in some models for recovery from addiction, to mindfulness and a focus on the fifth precept, a variety of approaches have developed. In most of these approaches, however, the focus is not on the substances themselves (unlike in the commentary on the monastic rules) but on the underlying issues that substances are being used to mask.

About the author
Dr. Wendy Dossett is Associate Professor of Religious Studies at the University of Chester, UK. She currently researches Buddhism and spirituality in addiction recovery.

Suggestions for further reading

In this book

See Chapters 32 (monastic rules), 39 (contemporary divisions), 41 (Zen), 42 (Pure Land Buddhism), 55 (vows/precepts), and 58 (marriage and family life).

Elsewhere

Bodhi, Bhikkhu. "Going for Refuge and Taking the Precepts." *Access To Insight*. 2013. http://www.accesstoinsight.org/lib/authors/bodhi/wheel282.html

Dossett, W. "Kleśas and Pretas: Therapy and Liberation in Buddhist Recovery from Addiction." *Implicit Religion: Religion, Spirituality and Addiction Recovery* 22(2) (2019): 215–242.

Siklos, B. "Datura Rituals in the Vajramahabhairava-Tantra." *Curare* 16(2) (1993): 71–76.

Trafford, P. *Avoiding Pamāda: An Analysis of the Fifth Precept as Social Protection in Contemporary Contexts with Reference to the Early Buddhist Teachings*. Master of Studies, Oxford University, 2009. https://www.academia.edu/34976455/Avoiding_pam%C4%81da_An_analysis_of_the_Fifth_Precept_as_Social_Protection_in_Contemporary_Contexts_with_reference_to_the_early_Buddhist_teachings

68
Are human rights compatible with Buddhism?

Damien Keown

Anyone familiar with the speeches and writings of Buddhist leaders like the Dalai Lama would assume the answer to this question was simple. References to "human rights" occur so commonly that the matter seems uncontroversial. Supporters of the "engaged Buddhism" movement frequently call on governments and institutions to respect human rights of the kind guaranteed in charters such as the Universal Declaration of Human Rights (UDHR) of 1948. These include the right to life, liberty, freedom of religion, equality before the law, freedom of assembly, the right to vote, and other such entitlements.

Buddhists who uphold and seek to implement such standards do so presumably because they see them as in harmony with Buddhist teachings. Why, then, might anyone think that the notion of human rights was incompatible with Buddhism?

Here it is important to make a distinction between the *aims* of human rights and the *concept* of human rights. Few (apart from dictators or the leaders of totalitarian states) would object to individuals having the rights and freedoms guaranteed by human rights charters. Some commentators, however, worry that framing objectives in terms of "rights" is inappropriate in the case of Buddhism. They raise objections of two kinds—conceptual and cultural—to Buddhism expressing its values in these terms. Specifically, they are suspicious of the notion of "rights" itself, and what it means for an individual to have and claim them. They also have concerns about whether this quintessentially Western concept can be adopted unproblematically by a religion the roots of which lie in an Asian culture.

In the West, the vocabulary of rights has become the *lingua franca* of political and ethical discourse, and substantive moral claims are made and defended by appeal to them. Thus, the abortion debate is commonly framed as a clash between "the right to choose," and "the right to life." Proponents of euthanasia speak of the "right to die," and minority rights are claimed in a plethora of contexts, such as "gay" and "transgender" rights. Rights of this kind are commonly claimed in situations of conflict, and, in the light of this, some Buddhists feel that "rights talk" only serves to inflame and exacerbate differences. In their view, the emphasis in Buddhist social teachings should be on interdependence, empathy, and reconciliation.

The underlying concern here is that the individualism implicit in the term "rights" is detrimental to both spiritual progress and social stability, because it strengthens the ego and encourages selfish attitudes. Thus the renowned Thai Buddhist teacher, P. A. Payutto has observed that Western notions of rights involve "competition, mistrust and fear." Scholars point out that the idea of rights is not found in traditional Buddhist texts, and there is not even a word for "rights" in any Asian language. Instead, Buddhist social teachings approach such matters from a different perspective and speak instead of *duties* owed by the individual to the community.

Another familiar complaint is that laying claim to individual rights conflicts with the Buddhist doctrine of "non-self" (Sanskrit: *anātman*; Pali: *anattā*): if there is ultimately no self, the argument goes, then who or what is the bearer of the rights in question? This is a complex issue, but a defender of rights might reply that the doctrine of non-self only denies the existence of a transcendental self (*ātman*), not of a phenomenal, empirical self. It does not deny the existence of human individuals with unique self-shaped identities, and if such identities provide a foundation stable enough for the attribution of duties, as the Buddha clearly believed, presumably they also do for rights.

Doctrinal concerns about non-self, it might be added, do not hinder the demands of Buddhists who lay claim to rights: for example, Buddhist refugees who claim a right to asylum or otherwise seek the protection of human rights instruments. It might also be pointed out that human rights protect communities as much as individuals, and, when Buddhist leaders like the Dalai Lama call for freedom of religion, they often do so on behalf of a nation like the people of Tibet.

Apart from these conceptual problems, another concern is the alien cultural provenance of "rights." In the 1990s, the political leaders of a number of Asian states (notably Malaysia, Indonesia, and Singapore, with strong backing from China) began to criticize the idea of human rights on the grounds of its Western intellectual genealogy, seeing talk of such rights as merely a cover for imperialism and neocolonialism. In place of rights, they championed the idea of "Asian values," which they claimed were more community-oriented.

Indian economist Amartya Sen has subsequently challenged the claim that there is anything specifically "Asian" about "Asian values," and the Dalai Lama has repudiated the view that human rights "cannot be applied to Asia and other parts of the Third World because of differences in culture and differences in social and economic development." These authorities highlight commonalities in global ethical standards rather than differences.

Echoing these specifically Buddhist concerns, some secular philosophers also have reservations about the basis for human rights. Skeptics doubt there is any concept of human nature stable enough to provide a foundation for such rights and so dismiss them as fictions dreamed up by well-intentioned politicians. Others, such as relativists, deny that human rights can be *universal*, given the diversity of cultures and moral values across the globe.

The above are simply examples of the arguments deployed by those who would answer our question in different ways. As the discussion shows, we should not simply assume that Western ethical and political concepts can be imported wholesale into Buddhism. They may well find a congenial home, but some reflection is needed if they are to be successfully assimilated. We might need, for example, to create a bridgehead so that Buddhist equivalents for Western notions like human dignity (seen by many as the underpinning for human rights) can be identified. One possibility is that "Buddha-nature"—or the capacity of all beings to attain enlightenment— might fill this role.

Exploratory conversations along these and other lines are continuing, and we shall have to see where they lead. In the meantime, globalization has accelerated the exchange of ideas to such a point that it is hard to imagine there are many Buddhists who would reject the idea of human rights outright. Indeed, the concept is now so central to contemporary ethical, social, and political discourse that it is doubtful we could do without it. Accordingly, we can give a generally affirmative answer to the question posed at the start. It may be helpful, however, when reflecting on this topic, to keep in mind a distinction between the substantive aims of human rights and the conceptual nature of the vehicle chosen to deliver them.

About the author

Damien Keown is Emeritus Professor of Buddhist Ethics at Goldsmiths, University of London. His research has concentrated on contemporary issues in Buddhist ethics and he co-founded the *Journal of Buddhist Ethics* with Charles S. Prebish in 1992.

Suggestions for further reading

In this book
See Chapters 20 (non-self teaching), 43 (Dalai Lama), 45 (Buddha-nature), 60 (engaged Buddhism), and 61 (Buddhism and politics).

Elsewhere
Keown, D., C. Prebish, and W. Husted. *Buddhism and Human Rights*. Curzon Press, London, 1998. The Introduction refers to the Dalai Lama.

King, Sallie B. "Buddhism and Human Rights." In *Religion and Human Rights: An Introduction*, edited by John Witte Jr. and M. Christian Green, 103–118. Oxford and New York: Oxford University Press, 2012.

Meinert, C., and H. B. Zollner (editors). *Buddhist Approaches to Human Rights*. New Brunswick and London: Transaction Publishers, 2010. The article by Martin Seeger refers to Payutto's view.

Sevilla, A. L. "Founding Human Rights within Buddhism: Exploring Buddha-Nature as an Ethical Foundation." *Journal of Buddhist Ethics* 17 (2010): 212–252.

69
What does Buddhism have to say about race?

Tim Stephens

A child leaves home to walk to school in the morning. "Go back to where you came from!" is shouted from across the street. I was a British-born child with one parent from India and one from England, and grew up in an all-white area. This led to many racist insults in 1970s Britain. Do such comments mask the universal dissatisfaction (Pali: *dukkha*) which the Buddha said most people experience? The impact of racism on me was that I did not return to the same house the same person on that day.

There was a global "moment" for the study of race in the 1950s, when UNESCO (United Nations Educational Scientific and Cultural Organization) addressed the "strangest and most disturbing," persistence of racial prejudice that was in stark conflict with the aims of the United Nations. There was a Buddhist contribution, from two Sri Lankan scholars (G. P. Malalasekera and K. N. Jayatilleke), and what they emphasized was the biological and spiritual unity of humankind, together with human dignity and equality.

One of the texts used by the two was a *sutta* named after a brahmin called Vāseṭṭha, in the *Sutta Nipāta*, in which the Buddha took it as self-evident that there is only one human species. All distinctions between humans are "nominal"—in name only—the Buddha stated. For instance, the Buddha cited the diversity of trees and insects, contrasting this diversity with the fact that there is only one type of human. Vāseṭṭha's initial question was an important one in ancient India: Is it "birth" or "deeds" that define a person's status and spiritual accomplishment? In the *Vāseṭṭha Sutta*, the Buddha says that what defines a person is the moral quality of their action, nothing else. We inherit our past actions not our past caste, ethnic, or gender identities.

The Brahmin Vāseṭṭha appears again in the *Aggañña Sutta* of the *Dīgha Nikāya*. At this point, he is living with Buddhist monastics, hoping to become a monk. He shares with the Buddha his experience of being reviled by his fellow brahmins, because he has "gone over" to ascetics of a lower caste, "dark fellows born of Brahma's foot," namely the Buddha's followers. The Buddha then dismisses the racist view of the brahmins through illustrations: for instance, that "both dark and bright ... are scattered indiscriminately among the four castes." He likewise dismisses their inherited high position and purity. The Buddha's reasoning here is distinctly radical and contemporary and in line with modern scientific findings and genetics.

To move to the contemporary world, in July 2013, Black Lives Matter (BLM) was first formed in response to racial injustice and racial violence against people of color. In 2015, a "Buddhists for Racial Justice" website (no longer active) was formed after a delegation of Buddhist teachers and leaders visited the White House. They released an open letter, underlining the Buddhist principles of "suffering, interdependence, non-harming and compassion." It included a significant intention: "We believe it is especially important that as Buddhist teachers and leaders, we encourage the white members of our community to continue to awaken to the history and dynamics of white privilege and the impact of unconscious collective racial bias." This touched the two primary styles of racism that the BLM movement highlighted: the structural, institutional domination of those who are white and the subtle racism present in people's minds.

Some Buddhists in Asia, however, have not put the precept of non-harming (Sanskrit: *ahiṃsā*) and the principle of equality into practice. Sri Lankan Buddhists have shown racism against

Tamils. Myanmar Buddhist racism against the Rohingya Muslims has shocked the world. One of the worst waves of this persecution was in 2017–2018, where state-sponsored evictions took place on a massive scale. The Rohingya were effectively deported to Bangladesh, despite the fact most were indigenous to western Myanmar. Being told to "go back to where you come from" in the country of your birth is an experience of racist nationalism with which I can particularly empathize.

Western Buddhists, however, have not always lived up to these principles either. It is now clear from a range of studies, and courageous efforts, that black and other minority heritage people of color, Asian or indigenous peoples have not always found modern Western convert Buddhist communities either welcoming or open to hearing about their experiences. The publication in 2020 of *Black and Buddhist: What Buddhism Can Teach Us about Race, Resilience, Transformation and Freedom* is the latest example of an admittedly small number of collections such as *Dharma, Color and Culture* and *Making the Invisible Visible*, where we hear the voices of Buddhist practitioners and teachers. For instance, in *Black and Buddhist*, Sebene Selassie, an insight meditation teacher, talks about the complexities of intersectional identity, such as being female and black, and how "Blackness and Buddhism teach me to love my multiplicities, to love myself." This echoes Sharon Smith, who was pioneering in her detailed study born from marginalized and hurtful experiences in a Western convert movement based in London. The wider purpose that the study achieved was in her sharing of what she found valuable in Buddhism, for minorities: namely, creative, engaging, and empowering ways to move beyond narrow definitions of identity. Such publications validate the contribution of people of color to Western Buddhism.

In the Buddha's day there was a bewildering variety of spiritual teachers jostling alongside the Brahman and Jain traditions, not unlike the wide variety of "spiritual" teachers and teachings online today. Black and minority Buddhists are not a distinct or separate cultural group of this kind. Many black and minority ethnic individuals (from non-Buddhist-heritage countries) who are committed to Buddhism join an established Buddhist tradition yet contribute their cultural experiences of embodiment and identity. For instance, angel Kyodo williams, in *Being Black: Zen and the Art of Living with Fearlessness and Grace*, refers to both sermons and rap, and Hilda Gutiérrez Baldoquín to *Ase*, life force, and divine power from Yoruba and her Afro-Cuban heritage, as comfortably as they do to their Zen practice. Such examples reveal the porousness of certain Buddhist traditions and a form of "hybrid" culture that will inform Buddhism. Yet I have been a meditating and practicing Buddhist in the UK for just over twenty-five years and only experienced a black teacher for the first time in 2020! This was the American Gina Sharpe, who, along with Larry Yang, Kate Lila Wheeler, and Rachel Bagby, teaches Dharma leaders in the Spirit Rock Insight Meditation community. For them, 2020 was special in that ninety per cent of their graduates were black indigenous people of color (BIPOC); in 2018 there were only ten such teachers out of more than 350.

T. Liên Shutt, a Vietnamese-born, and later adopted, Asian-American, who is linked with the Spirit Rock community, featured in a publication called "Making the Invisible Visible: Healing Racism in our Buddhist Communities," presented to the Western Teachers' Conference at Spirit Rock in June 2000. It contained voices of minority Buddhist practitioners, many of whom, though very experienced, were not allowed to attend because they were not teachers. The irony was not lost on some of the contributors. Shutt talked about the contradiction of having been born in a Buddhist country and then "americanized," after which he was unable to identify with either migrant Vietnamese Buddhists or the "whiteness" of modern American Buddhist communities, writing that: "For many people of color and mixed-race people, because of our individual and collective histories of disenfranchisement, the need to find Refuge in a Sangha is especially important." "Sangha" is a traditional Buddhist term which encapsulates not only the importance of community but also protection and belonging—in earliest times through shared commitment or kinship.

If American Independence emphasized "individual" rights and freedoms, the French revolution, "collective" rights and freedoms, a type of Buddhist-informed international, anti-racist pluralism would emphasize both acts of individual self-awareness and "external mindfulness." For instance, Paul Gilroy points to the way that W. E. B. Du Bois refers to the "world citizen" as a transcendence of the provincial in American and European thought and describes a unique form of African-American freedom: "a distinctive ... freedom which is won from an experience of suffering, not the redemption of that suffering, but the product of it." We may be witnessing a new Buddhist-informed praxis, born of this distinctive suffering, addressing racial inequality without succumbing to the "illusions" of race, and with the aims of "equality," and "community building," radically liberating Buddhism itself.

About the author
Tim Stephens is an Education Developer, with a specialism in Curriculum, at University of the Arts London, and a photographic artist. His areas of expertise and knowledge are: embodiment, the relationship between cognitive and non-cognitive experience, equality, and organizational change.

Suggestions for further reading

In this book
See Chapters 60 (engaged Buddhism), 61 (Buddhism and politics), 73 (secular Buddhism), and 75 (Western Buddhism).

Elsewhere
Gutiérrez Baldoquín, Hilda (editor). *Dharma, Color and Culture: New Voices in Western Buddhism*. Berkeley, CA: Parallax Press, 2004.

Smith, Sharon, E. *Buddhism, Diversity and "Race": Multiculturalism and Western Convert Buddhist Movements in East London. A Qualitative Study*. Doctorate, Goldsmiths College, University of London, 2009. http://research.gold.ac.uk/id/eprint/2553/1/HIS_Sharon_Smith_2009a.pdf

williams, angel Kyodo, Lama Rod Owens, and Jasmine Syedullah. *Radical Dharma: Talking Race, Love, and Liberation.* Berkeley, CA: North Atlantic Books, 2016.

Yetunde, Pamela Ayo, and Cheryl A. Giles (editors). *Black and Buddhist: What Buddhism Can Teach Us about Race, Resilience, Transformation and Freedom.* Boulder, CO: Shambhala, 2020.

70
Are Buddhists active in ecological movements and protecting the environment to mitigate climate change?

Alex Owens

In 2018 the UN released a statement saying that the tipping point for extreme weather and human displacement was 2030 unless we make some radical global changes. Like every major world religion today, Buddhists have taken a stance on the climate emergency we now face and have developed various movements and initiatives to combat it. Therefore, in short, yes, Buddhists are active in ecological movements. However, the ways in which various well-known Buddhists have reacted to this emergency differ.

Throughout the different textual traditions of Buddhism, a significant amount of attention is paid to how we should engage with the world. For instance, the *Mettā Sutta* of the Pali Canon, which focuses on loving kindness, states:

> Whatever living beings there may be—feeble or strong (or the seekers and the attained) long, stout, or of medium size, short, small, large, those seen or those unseen, those dwelling far or near, those who are born as well as those yet to be born—may all beings have happy minds.

This passage suggests that we should have loving-kindness for all beings, no matter what they are. Loving-kindness is understood by the Theravada school as an opening-up of benevolence or compassion toward others. We can suggest from this that Buddhists must engage in protecting the environment today as our actions, as humans, are negatively impacting the habitats of every single species on the planet, including ourselves.

Similarly, the popular text the *Dhammapada* states: "Even as a bee gathers honey from a flower and departs without injuring the flower or its color or scent, so let a sage dwell in his village" (verse 49). We can see how easy it is for Buddhists today to interpret these texts in a way that supports mitigating climate change. The way in which we, as a species, have treated the planet lies in direct contrast to the image above. Metaphorically speaking, we have gathered the honey, uprooted the flower, and polluted the soil, leaving nothing for those who come after us. Therefore, it has become essential for Buddhists today to engage in ecological movements in order to try and counteract the environmental situation in which we now find ourselves.

From talks presented at "Mind and Life" conferences, writing forewords to books on Buddhism and the environment, and staging interviews with large media corporations, Tenzin Gyatso, the Fourteenth Dalai Lama, has embodied compassion and right action toward the environment. The Dalai Lama's global popularity and his call to action has reached millions of people worldwide. He presents the climate emergency not just as a Buddhist problem but a global one. Through the fame he has acquired, the Dalai Lama has spread the message of environmental action through the language of Buddhism, particularly in terms of interdependence. Interdependence is the notion held by many Buddhists about the interconnected state of the universe and has been adopted as a central idea by many eco-Buddhists today.

An equally important promoter of Buddhism's engagement with ecological movements is the Zen Master Thich Nhat Hanh. Thich Nhat Hanh is perhaps most well known for repackaging "mindfulness," particularly for an American and European audience. However, he is also a significant figure in promoting Buddhists' engagement with protecting the environment. For instance, one of the fourteen precepts of his Order of Interbeing is: Do not live with a vocation that is harmful to humans and nature. Do not invest in companies that deprive others of their chance to live. Select a vocation that helps realize your ideal of compassion." In a similar way to the Fourteenth Dalai Lama, Thich Nhat Hanh links his respect for the environment to an understanding of interdependence. He suggests that Buddhists must aim to protect the environment as, ultimately, we are connected to it on many levels and, similarly, it to us.

Thich Nhat Hanh developed his own understanding of interdependence with reference to the environment through the notion of interbeing. Interbeing can be explained in terms of a piece of paper. The piece of paper that you are reading only exists because of a large interconnected web of events and other entities that helped form it. This paper came from a tree. That tree was reliant on the soil in which it grew, the seed from which it originated, and the rain to provide it with the water it needed to grow. For this page to exist everything needed to be exactly the way it was. This leads Thich Nhat Hanh to explain that every piece of paper contains a cloud within it. This is interbeing. It is because of this innate connection with everything that Thich Nhat Hanh developed engaged Buddhism and promoted active involvement in mitigating the environmental crisis we find ourselves in.

Another way in which Buddhists are protecting the environment today has been developed by Joanna Macy and David Loy. Macy is a well-known environmental activist and writer, and Loy is both a Zen teacher and a founding member of the Rocky Mountain Ecodharma Retreat Center. In his recent book *Ecodharma*, Loy, alongside Macy, has developed what they call the "vows of the ecosattva." The ecosattva builds on the notion of the bodhisattva of the Mahayana tradition but does so specifically with environmentalism in mind. Loy explains that we can all achieve a state of heightened awareness by seeing the knock-on effects of every action we, on a personal level, and as a species, have on the environment around us. The development of the ecosattva vows by Macy and Loy demonstrate that not only are Buddhists active in ecological movements but that they are also constantly innovating ways of engaging with environmental practices to fit with current discourses, outside of the tradition.

The climate crisis is something that affects each and every one of us today. Although environmental concern was present in early Buddhist texts, this concern meant something different when the texts were compiled. It was more localized in scale and far removed from today's global crisis. So, modern Buddhist ecological activists have had to innovate, engaging with debates outside of their tradition in order to create new Buddhist models. To answer the question, then: yes, Buddhists are active in ecological movements, and, through figures such as the Dalai Lama and Thich Nhat Hanh, the tradition as a whole is increasingly seen as "green."

About the author

Alex Owens is a PhD student based at Lancaster University, UK. His work is on Buddhism's engagement with the West, religion, and the environment, and his recent thesis focused on the genealogy of the Indra's Net metaphor.

Suggestions for further reading

In this book
See Chapters 13 (bodhisattva), 27 (mindfulness), 43 (Dalai Lama), 44 (bodhisattva vow), 55 (vows/precepts), 60 (engaged Buddhism), and 62 (compassion).

Elsewhere
Kaza, S. *Green Buddhism: Practice and Compassionate Action in Uncertain Times*. Boulder, CO: Shambhala, 2019.

Loy, D.. *Ecodharma: Buddhist Teachings for the Ecological Crisis*. Boston, MA: Wisdom Publications, 2018.

Order of Interbeing: www.orderofinterbeing.org

71
How do Buddhists relate to the methods of science?

Tim Stephens

Some might see science as providing a type of modern common sense, or set of facts, and religion as offering traditional, commonly held beliefs, or sets of practices, with neither having much to say about the other. After all, the first seems to obtain its authority from math, the second from faith. Yet Buddhists seem to be seen as, and open to seeing themselves as, both religious and scientific. How has this come about?

We all know what it feels like to catch a common cold. The average American apparently gets between one and three per year. Yet a cold is not easy to define, neither are its symptoms. There are at least a hundred different types of virus that might cause a cold in the first place. There are some interestingly consistent treatments: for example, honey. We know wild honey has been harvested for over 10,000 years, and 4,000 years ago Indian Ayurvedic medicine recommended honey as a treatment. Honey's properties are mentioned in the Bible and the Qur'an, so were known to the Jewish tradition. The use of honey is an example of the porous boundaries between religion and science.

Causes, cures, and plausible explanations are often found in science. Defining causality, however, also lies at the heart of Buddhist tradition and is presented in the first sermon of the Buddha, on the Four Noble Truths, which proposes both the cause and remedy for suffering in human life. Science uses methods such as "measuring, questioning, speculating, experimenting, checking, and explaining," all of which can also be found in Buddhist texts and practice, in different periods. Both use these methods for the purpose of in-depth inquiry.

In the late nineteenth century, a Western mathematician produced a proof that arithmetic was a type of "objectively realist logic." It was at a time when scientific rationalism and free thought movements were challenging traditional religion in the West. Buddhists in Asia, particularly those suffering imperial rule in countries such as Sri Lanka, were aware of this and also of the accusation of Christian missionaries in Asia that Buddhism was irrational. In response, they used their own textual resources to present Buddhism as modern and scientific. One well-known event held in 1893 in Chicago, the World's Parliament of Religions, saw Asian Buddhists contributing their own versions of Buddhism, one of whom, Shaku Soyen of Japan, emphasized causation as lying at the heart of Buddhism. Taking illustrations from the natural world, as a scientist might have done, he argued that "there is no effect which is not a cause, so there is no cause which is not an effect."

Often quoted by Buddhists wishing to stress the rationality of Buddhism is the *Kālāma Sutta,* an early story of the Buddha's response to the Kalama clan, who asked him a simple question, after hearing different teachers proclaiming different teachings with equal conviction:

> Which of these [visiting] reverend monks and brahmins spoke the truth and which falsehood?" The Buddha is recorded as replying, "Do not go upon what has been acquired by repeated hearing; nor upon tradition; not upon rumor; nor upon what is in scripture, not upon surmise . . . Kalamas, when you yourselves know, "These things are bad; these things are blamable . . .". abandon them.

Buddhism was thus presented as asking difficult questions of fixed beliefs. Sometimes presented as the "Charter of Free Inquiry," as in the translation recommended in the further reading section of this chapter and used here, this *sutta,* for many Buddhists, confirms the compatibility between Buddhism and scientific methods.

Buddhist inquiry is sometimes described as being pragmatic and empirical, and scientific inquiry as being realist, empirical, and measurable. Both, however, search for "repeatable patterns" if not "natural laws." This can be obscured if Buddhism is stereotyped as only concerned with self-knowledge, as it still can be today. We must remember that Siddhārtha Gautama is recorded as challenging the authority of religion and religious leaders of his time, going far beyond this stereotype. He famously challenged with empirical evidence some of the religious hierarchies of the India of his day, such as those that were present in the caste system.

Yet it is introspective meditative experience and Buddhist analysis of mind that has led to collaboration between Buddhists and some scientists in recent decades, particularly those involved in cognitive science and neuroscience, and contemporary psychologists researching mental health and well-being. Scientists working in these areas have discovered a wealth of new data through Buddhism's analysis of consciousness and the Buddhist practice of meditation. This knowledge has not been knowledge of a world "out there"; it has been knowledge of the mind and how the mind works. It is a type of knowledge that is commonly called "non-dualistic," in some forms of Mahayana Buddhism, neither purely "subjective" and inward-looking nor wholly "objective" and outward-looking.

However, while science can measure most things, and, in spite of this collaboration with Buddhists, it has not yet found adequate ways to measure qualities that Buddhism, in common with many other religious traditions, hold dear, and pay close attention to, such as the cultivation of compassion, equanimity, and serenity. So, there are a series of knowledge conflicts here, not only about what is true in the world but about who holds authority over knowledge, truth, and authenticity in their experience of the world.

The Buddha made an analogy: that a lay disciple should make their livelihood in the same way a bee makes honey, by diligent work and without harming "the source of one's income," namely the flower (*Dhammapada*, verse 49). Just as we can benefit from honey without harming bees, scientific advance should not harm the world it experiments on. One important Buddhist attitude to science, therefore, is that scientific research should be subject to an ethical purpose; it should promote the lessening not the increasing of suffering for all beings and the flourishing of our natural world.

About the author
Tim Stephens is an Education Developer, with a specialism in Curriculum, at University of the Arts London, and a photographic artist. His areas of expertise and knowledge are: embodiment, the relationship between cognitive and non-cognitive experience, equality, and organizational change.

Suggestions for further reading

In this book
See Chapters 5 (texts), 21 (Four Noble Truths), 27 (mindfulness), 54 (interreligious relations), 60 (engaged Buddhism), 72 (modern technology), 70 (ecological movements), 73 (secular Buddhism), and 74 (attitudes to AI).

Elsewhere
Clarke, J. J. *Oriental Enlightenment: The Encounter between Asian and Western Thought.* London: Routledge, 1997.

Kuhn, Thomas S. *The Structure of Scientific Revolutions* (3rd edition). Chicago: University of Chicago Press, 1996.

Wallace, B. Allen. *Buddhism and Science: Breaking New Ground.* New York: Columbia University Press, 2003.

"Kalama Sutta: The Buddha's Charter of Free Inquiry." Translated from the Pali by Soma Thera. *Access to Insight (BCBS Edition)*, November 30, 2013. http://www.accesstoinsight.org/lib/authors/soma/wheel008.html

72
What is the Buddhist attitude to modern technology?

Nick Swann

The standard list of items that a monk or nun is permitted to own includes a set of robes, a belt, a bowl, a razor, a needle, a water strainer, a staff, and a toothpick. In practice, these days the list is longer and might include spare robes, toiletries, a bag, books, and a cell phone and possibly even a tablet computer.

Historically, Buddhists have been comfortable taking available technology and domesticating it to help them be better Buddhists and/or to help preserve and spread Buddhist teachings. We see this particularly with communication technology such as writing and printing, and often at a time of crisis. Sri Lankan tradition has it that Pali texts were first preserved in writing in the first century BCE, when a series of crises in Sri Lanka led to monks fearing that the teachings might not last. The use of stone printing blocks in Buddhist China dates back to the middle of the seventh century, and again these appear to have been carved in order to preserve threatened Mahayana Buddhist teachings. This pattern has repeated itself again with the Buddhist Digital Resource Center (BDRC) and the Asian Classics Input Project (ACIP)—two major projects to digitize Tibetan and Sanskrit Buddhist material for online access. Both projects consistently cited as part of their rationale the risk of losing texts.

There are no Buddhist restrictions on the use of modern technology per se, provided that its use is in line with one's vows or precepts. This can lead to a dilemma with regard to, for example, driving, because in hot weather a lot of insects can get splattered by a car. It can be argued that this is unintentional, and therefore has no karmic "weight" attached to it, but it can also be argued that it is inevitable—if you don't drive, then those insects don't die (at least not on *your* car). Of course, there are also ethical arguments about the environmental impact of driving in general.

Buddhists have benefited as much as anyone from advances in medicine, and a longer life means more time to practice and lay the karmic foundations for future favorable rebirths. However, if a treatment has been developed through the suffering of other sentient beings such as laboratory animals, then for some Buddhists that might not be a karmic price worth paying. After all, in Buddhist thought, all other sentient beings could have been our father or mother in a past life. On a related subject, a tantric Buddhist might be an organ donor but would ask that their body is left for a period of, say, forty minutes after being pronounced dead before organs are harvested. This is because the consciousness is understood to remain in the (physically deceased) body for a time and tampering with the body could disrupt the progression of the consciousness to its next state. For advanced practitioners, this can take hours or even days, but then again such people are typically quite elderly and less likely to be viable donors.

Different Buddhist groups have different attitudes toward the internet as a tool for teaching Buddhism. Treeleaf.org is an online Zen center founded in 2006 (physically based in San Francisco), and even offers Buddhist precepts via an online ceremony. The late Namkhai Norbu Rinpoche (1938–2018), a well-respected lama in the Nyingma tradition of Tibetan Buddhism, would coordinate online retreats and teachings. He even used the internet for a ritual to grant the authority for students to practice what is known as Guru Yoga, a tantric ritual which would usually be conducted face to face. On the other hand, the Sakya tradition of Tibetan Buddhism takes a far more conservative view of the online world, for example not allowing the circulation of esoteric material via email in case an account gets hacked and the material is seen by unauthorized persons.

The 2020 Covid-19 pandemic saw places of worship close down across many parts of the world, and was a catalyst for several Buddhist groups to think of ways in which to move online. Many used social media such as Facebook to livestream activities such as teachings, chanting, and mandala construction, one example being Gaden Shartse Thubten Dhargye Ling in Long Beach, California. The Buddhist Society in London moved its meditation classes to the online platform Zoom. Others, such as Chithurst Buddhist Monastery in Hampshire, UK, increased the frequency of posting videos on their websites.

A feature of the encounter between Buddhist cultures and the West in the past hundred years or so has been a move to present the Buddha's teachings as being entirely coherent with Western scientific thinking, downplaying anything mystical. Note that this has been two-way traffic, with Western spokespersons emphasizing what is rational in the teachings and this being echoed by heritage Buddhist teachers, which then gets amplified by Western readers. Just as significantly, Asian Buddhists mined their own texts for rationalism in the face of Western Christian missionaries insisting that Buddhism was irrational and unscientific. This is a feature of what is known as "Buddhist Modernism." Perhaps an extreme contemporary example of this is neurological research into the effects of meditation on the structure and chemistry of the brain. Volunteer Buddhist monks are common subjects in this kind of research and experiments can involve fMRI scans of monks while they meditate. In this way, modern technology is deployed in an attempt to catch a glimpse of the core of Buddhist meditative experience. However, this research often seeks to reduce meditation to an exercise which simply has a material impact on the brain, and adds to the body of scientific evidence relating to, for example, the effectiveness of mindfulness-based practices. However, at the time of writing the pendulum seems to be swinging back a little and some neuroscientists appear more open-minded about the subtle differences in individual experiences of meditation.

About the author

Nick Swann is a Senior Lecturer in Buddhist Studies at University of South Wales, UK. His research interests include Buddhist Ethics, Buddhist Tantra, and Anthropology and Religion.

Suggestions for further reading

In this book

See Chapters 5 (texts), 18 (karma), 27 (mindfulness), 41 (Zen), 47 (Tantra and sex), 71 (methods of science), and 74 (attitudes to AI).

Elsewhere

Greig, G. *The Pixel in the Lotus: Buddhism, the Internet, and Digital Media*. New York: Routledge, 2014.

Keown, D. *Buddhism and Bioethics*. Basingstoke, UK: Palgrave, 2001.

McMahan, D. *The Making of Buddhist Modernism*. Oxford: Oxford University Press, 2008.

Part Eleven
Emergent Buddhism

73
What is secular Buddhism?

Tim Stephens

Imagine two nineteenth-century anthropologists, the first scientifically minded, also perhaps a collector, and the second a Christian traditionalist and missionary, both men, debating: Is Buddhism actually a religion? This simple question would not have a straightforward yes-or-no answer. The first might say that it obviously is a religion, but a primitive one. It has all the trappings of such: deities, spiritual leaders, monks and nuns, adherents and followers, temples, scriptures, art, rituals, traditions, and fixed beliefs but ones that had yet to fully mature into "organized" religion and, in turn, had yet to evolve into the fine contemporary institutions of law, science, and politics that the present day afforded, without myths and miracles. The second might say clearly: No, Buddhism is not a religion because it has no belief in a God-like creator as present among Jews, Muslims, and Christians. It has no God that possesses duration, transcendence, power, and knowledge.

Secular Buddhism attempts to be neither colonial nor paternalistic. In other words, secular Buddhism is any type of Buddhism that keeps a distance from some or all of the elements that our two fictional characters list above and that define Religious Buddhism with a capital "R." Secular Buddhism finds in the life of the historical Buddha insights into the potential for freedom in a contemporary, egalitarian culture, including less dogmatic forms of both science and spirituality.

There is wide agreement that secular Buddhism is a "modern" and "Western" phenomenon. So, if we take seriously the extent to which the West defined "Buddhism" from its own perspective in the first place—for instance, as a more Protestant and individualistic system distanced from ritual—then we should admit that there is similarly a Western impetus of secularization at work here also. Secular Buddhism cannot be separated from the forces of secularism in modern, democratic, capitalist societies. To state the obvious, secular does not only mean non-religious, although one of its roots is undoubtedly the "Victorian crisis" of science versus religion, or Darwin versus the Bible. "Secular" is an umbrella term for a range of beliefs: secularism, free thought, humanism, and unbelief. For some this privatization, or personalization, of spirituality, or "experience-oriented religiosity" is mystical; yet for others it is part of the long decline known as "disenchantment," the devaluing of the "Religious," described by Weber, which defines rational modernity as such.

There is a strong case to make for the current high profile of secular Buddhism being associated with the work of two Western Buddhist scholars: Martine Batchelor, and Stephen Batchelor in particular. Stephen Batchelor is a well-respected translator, independent scholar, teacher, and ex-monk from both Tibetan and Korean Zen traditions. Martine Batchelor is an ex-nun, translator, and meditation teacher, trained in the Seon (Korean for Chan or Zen) tradition of Korea. Together, they are seen as leading proponents of what is becoming a well-grounded approach which is gaining traction in emergent Buddhisms today.

Secular Buddhism as a contemporary form of Dharma re-emphasizes Buddhist philosophy as pragmatic; the Four Noble Truths are four noble *tasks*. Stephen Batchelor's preamble to his fully formed "secular" position is detailed in three works which, progressively articulated, seem to disown certain Buddhist core beliefs, mainly those related to rebirth and the end goal of enlightenment or freedom from *dukkha* (suffering or unsatisfactoriness), along with maintaining a type of agnosticism. Their titles alone embody this message: *The Faith to Doubt*: *Buddhism without Beliefs* and *After Buddhism*. The clearest statement emerged in his article "A Secular Buddhism" (2012), which replaced a classical Indian "belief-based" Buddhism for a pragmatic approach to Dharma as not actually about any metaphysical "truths" at all. Batchelor's secular Dharma is an attempt to re-engage with the earliest core teachings of the historical Buddha, Gautama, prior to the traditions and orthodoxies that "Buddhism" was about to become. He uses a "modern historical-critical scholarship" for a close reading of the Buddha's first discourse and the earliest texts in particular to do this. However, this is not an attempt to reach historical truth. He states that this reinterpretation of Buddhism is as contingent and imperfect as any other. Secular Buddhism promotes the view that Buddhism is essentially plural.

The contextual groundwork for secular Buddhism is found in the work of many scholars of religion, arts, humanities, and critical theory, broadly influenced by phenomenology and the "crisis" engendered by postmodernism over the last century, reflecting a shift into a post-metaphysical worldview. Some Western scholars similarly resonate with the Greek knowledge or wisdom tradition of "phronesis," found in Aristotle and translated as "practical wisdom." Secular Buddhism is aligned broadly with this Western cultural scholarship, which might also account for its popularity. These positions arise from philosophies of immanence not transcendence.

The secular Buddhist could be thought of as negotiating a position within three overlapping circles: a religious Buddhist heritage, the secular modernity of our age, and a meaningful spiritual life. It is radically "open" and non-denominational, with no centers, no "leaders" and no "followers," and no doctrinal essentialism, although this may be debated. It could be called "rhizomatic." Rhizomes connect across and between other organizations and groups, and proliferate through informal connection and openness to difference. It is a bottom-up, not top-down, form of praxis, perpetuating itself online and internationally across geographic boundaries. And, as its link with Stephen and Martine Batchelor suggests, it appears most popular with Buddhists from non-heritage communities, who seek new ways to be Buddhist in the West.

Secular Dharma, which might even eschew the term "Buddhism" altogether, is ultimately neither textual nor doctrinal but is a living thing. Ethical action realizes a good life through a living practice, and, in the eyes of Martine Batchelor, embraces an holistic approach to creative engagement in the present with awareness and feeling. As a markedly and openly creative project, liberally using the arts, this is a vision very much in tune with our times.

About the author
Tim Stephens is an Education Developer, with a specialism in curriculum, at University of the Arts London and a photographic artist. His research interests include embodiment, the relationship between cognitive and non-cognitive experience, equality, and organizational change.

Suggestions for further reading

In this book
See Chapters 1 (is Buddhism a religion?), 18 (karma), 23 (nirvana), 39 (contemporary divisions), 60 (engaged Buddhism), and 75 (Western Buddhism)

Elsewhere
Batchelor, Stephen. "A Secular Buddhism." *Journal of Global Buddhism* 13 (2012): 87–107.

Batchelor, Stephen. *Stephen Batchelor's Ten Theses on Secular Dharma*. https://secularbuddhistnetwork.org/stephen-batchelors-ten-theses-of-secular-dharma

Higgins, Winton. "The Flexible Appropriation of Tradition: Stephen Batchelor's Secular Buddhism." *Journal of Global Buddhism* 18 (2017): 51–67.

Secular Buddhist Association: https://secularbuddhism.org/us

Secular Buddhist Network: https://secularbuddhistnetwork.org

74
How do Buddhists view artificial intelligence?

Ralph Quinlan Ford

Buddhism is perhaps the best religion to assist the world as it now enters an age of artificial intelligence (AI). The whole idea of superintelligence is not a new phenomenon to Buddhism, as the Buddha has always been viewed as a superintelligent being. This superintelligence, however, was characterized by wisdom and compassion. The same cannot be said of all current forms of AI.

Technologists are predicting that, in 2029, AI will be as good as human intelligence. Most importantly, come the year 2045, AI will surpass human intelligence. This future time in our history has been referred to as "The Singularity" by retired math professor Vernor Vinge. By this time, robots will be doing all, or most of, the manual labor, creating a worldwide existential crisis that could possibly offer an opportunity for the development of spiritual intelligence (SQ)—in Buddhist terms, the development of wisdom and compassion.

For Buddhists, a logical system such as computation, which lies at the heart of AI, is incapable of capturing the whole truth—Dharma. Enlightenment is beyond an intelligence that follows rules, conforms, and calculates. Buddhism is rather about the ending of the emotional roots of unwholesome, harmful states of mind and is as hard to conceive as what The Singularity might actually be.

AI is already scoring your bank loan applications and, in certain U.S. states, influencing how long you will be incarcerated for. So, we are already beginning to be affected by AI as it charts its course to be on a par with human intelligence. AI chooses your music streams and also your internet search results. AI can paint, draw, compose, and even speak. The robots are already outsmarting us in facial recognition tests and diagnostics in medicine. All of this is already leading to information echo chambers, where people are fed information based on the likes and dislikes an AI detects from a person's online activity.

With the wonders of biotechnology using stem cells and genetic technology like CRISPR (clustered regularly interspaced short palindromic repeats), which can edit genes, we already have taken major steps to a state of longevity. Ordinary heart cells can now be turned into pacemaker cells, making mechanical pacemakers obsolete. This is just one example of the marvels taking place. All of humanity is already on its way toward The Singularity. However, current dangerous developments in these technologies include the production of genetically enhanced "Super Soldiers."

Mind, for many, equals "thoughts"—but this is not the case for Buddhists. For Buddhists, mind has a mapped psychological landscape known as the Abhidharma, which defines consciousness as not just one but many different states. In the Abhidharma there are eight consciousnesses, with the intellect being only the seventh of these. AI developers are eager to crack the code of human consciousness, which will allow them to accelerate us all toward The Singularity. One of their blind spots is that, compared to the Buddhist exploration, they have a very limited understanding of what consciousness actually is. AI developers also need to remember that computation is not consciousness. The brain is not the mind and a person with a supercomputer-enhanced brain could be a terrible and indeed dangerous person.

The Buddhist system of both psychology and philosophy is well positioned and profoundly developed in order to help AI developers come to a better understanding of what mind—and perhaps life—actually is. This investigation of Buddhism could have a powerful, positive impact on AI development, if it is also combined with the ethical. For superintelligence is not the same as "super-mind" nor "super-awareness" (and these last two would really impress Buddhists). AI is designed on Western concepts and superficial understandings of what the mind, consciousness, and intellect are. The intellect can model, label, and conceive, but for Buddhists reality can only be perceived—not conceived—by mind.

Buddhist ethics could benefit developers by guiding them to make AI congruent with a peaceful world, in order that it might be developed to help not destroy, and also to have wisdom. Let us not forget that you get out of AI what you put in: how we design the AI determines what it is and what it does. The key point here is that AIs may well be a reflection of who has coded them. Unless the developers know, have, and express human values like fairness, empathy, and compassion, the AIs produced run the risk of being dangerous, potentially leading to wars, famines, environmental disasters, and an erosion of human rights.

The five precepts of Buddhism might also serve AI developers in creating beneficial technology. Many scholars have noted they are in alignment with human rights. *Ahiṃsā*, or non-harming, is a foundational Buddhist ethical principle which reflects the mental positive regard Buddhists must have for the preciousness of life. Buddhist ethics could encourage conscientious objection from AI developers hired to create harmful AIs.

Buddhism can help humanity and world leaders to deal with the existential crisis and ethical debate attached to our journey toward The Singularity. By 2045, we will be living as post-humans alongside cyborgs, mind clones, and digital humans. The guidance Buddhist ethics can bring to the various ethical boards that are being created will be relevant to 520 million Buddhists globally and other world religions, too, as they try to integrate the paradigm shifts emerging from AI advances.

About the author
Ralph Quinlan Forde has an honors degree in Biotechnology from the University of Reading and an MA in Buddhist Studies from the University of South Wales. His research interests include artificial intelligence.

Suggestions for further reading

In this book
See Chapters 24 (enlightenment), 55 (vows/precepts), 60 (engaged Buddhism), 62 (compassion), 71 (methods of science), and 72 (modern technology).

Elsewhere
Bostrom, N. *Superintelligence: Paths, Dangers, Strategies.* Oxford: Oxford University Press, 2014.

O'Neil, C. *Weapons of Math Destruction.* London: Penguin, 2016.

75
Is Western Buddhism a new form of Buddhism?

Sarah Shaw

In 1958, Christmas Humphreys, a Western Buddhist, said "a definitely Western form of Buddhism must in time emerge." Has this happened? People sometimes talk of three varieties of Buddhism: Southern (Theravada), Northern (Mahayana/Vajrayana), and Eastern (Mahayana in China/Japan, etc.). Nowadays, you find discussion of a fourth, Western Buddhism. But we now think more of *Buddhisms*: Buddhism of many kinds. So does category-making through geography still apply? How and why do Buddhisms of different kinds emerge and has a Western Buddhism evolved? Before we look at Western varieties, we need to look at what the others are and how they differ. After the time of the Buddha, the traditions traveled and underwent metamorphoses. Geography is one helpful way of defining them—but not the only one.

Southern Buddhism involves the Buddhisms of Southeast and South Asia, primarily Thailand, Burma/Myanmar, Cambodia, Laos, and Sri Lanka. Often known as Theravada Buddhism, these traditions employ meditations, practices, and doctrines following Pali guidelines, although rich customs and meditation systems have developed alongside, including some based on esoteric strands of meditation and ritual.

Eastern Buddhism emerged in the regions of China, Korea, and Japan (Vietnam could be included here, but its syncretic Buddhism has absorbed many Southern features, too). This refers to diverse Buddhisms that emerged, at first in China, largely on the basis of texts composed in northern India in the second century CE which arrived via Silk Roads from Central Asia. Over centuries, new schools emerged, some from Indian sources, but some from within those regions. Pure Land, Chan/Seon/Zen, Tiantai/Tendai and Huayan are some of these; in Japan, many chanting schools developed, such as those inspired by Nichiren (1222–1282) and offshoots such as Soka Gakkai. Finding unifying factors in the midst of this richness is difficult: but Eastern schools follow a Mahayana path, that of the "Great Vehicle."

Northern Buddhism represents some different strands deriving from early northern India. It emerged in Tibet, Central Asia, and Mongolia after the seventh century CE. Also often termed Mahayana, it has earned a new name: Vajrayana. This too is richly diverse.

This summary has been necessary: it is important to recognize this sense of many diverse "life-forms" of Buddhist practice and doctrine. Buddhisms have developed with great diversities and branches, many of which transcend geographical boundaries. Some elements are common: the Eightfold Path, the doctrine of dependent origination, as well as iconographic and meditative features such as the thirty-two marks of the Buddha/Bodhisattva, found in depictions and buddha figures throughout all regions. But Buddhism has been distinctive in different regions, and even, one could say, directions: it has also never had a centralized supervisory authority, as different regional forms have their own. So the Sangha, the order of monks and nuns, has developed with its own color, styles, and rules in different regions and these have traveled.

To understand Western Buddhism, one needs to know something about all these three. All three major Buddhist traditions have made a deep impact in Europe, America, Australia, New Zealand, and the UK—what we tenuously call the "West." Some have been particularly popular in some regions: the incidence of Chan/Zen in the western parts of the U.S.A., for instance, or the popularity of Theravada, Southern, or Pali Buddhism in the UK. Historical links are important factors here. Many Americans visited Japan, and, importantly, diaspora groups from China and Japan have been emigrating to the western states of the U.S.A. since the nineteenth century, when they formed a large part of the rail-building workforce. The UK's historic links with Burma/Myanmar and Sri Lanka ensured both a large diaspora from those regions, and a sense of a strong cultural connection, too. Generalizations are risky, but it would be fair to say that all the three main types of Buddhism have become popular in varying degrees throughout the world, including the West. They all have different styles and they have all attracted Westerners. Mass communications, the internet, backpack travel among young people searching for spiritual direction, the popularity of the Dalai Lama, Zen "poets" and the modern mindfulness movement: these are just some of the factors that have all had significant influence over the last hundred-and-fifty years. Modernism means people read, discuss, and travel, and, as they do, so all three Buddhist "directional" traditions have found those who are attracted to them. So, for Western Buddhism we can, to a certain extent, say international or global twenty-first-century Buddhism: all schools and sub-schools of Buddhism have some presence in the "West". Feedback from previously non-Buddhist regions has affected practice and understanding in origin areas, too. This has multiple facets, varying from the early Japanese attempts to communicate Zen through German philosophical thinking, which influenced understandings at home, to the way that American and European mindfulness trainings are affecting an understanding of Buddhism in South and Southeast Asia. Buddhism has just proved very popular, in all sorts of ways, by showing the West its meditative traditions, its mindfulness trainings, and its cultural, poetic, and artistic heritage.

Twenty-first-century Buddhism can still in many ways be defined by allegiances or strong links to the three regions: a Zen Buddhist temple in Australia will be a little like one in Japan, and a Theravada temple in the UK feels remarkably like one in Thailand. But those from non-Buddhist backgrounds who have espoused these traditions often do so with particular interests. Meditation and mindfulness have been key attractions for "new"

Buddhists, who did not grow up in a Buddhist background. This focus used to be less paramount for those whose origins were within Buddhist countries. The acceptability of meditation and mindfulness has changed dramatically, however, over the last few decades. Internationalism is affecting all three of the regional Buddhisms. There is also increased interest in so-called secular forms of Buddhism, often influenced greatly by the high impact of the insight meditation schools in the U.S.A., for instance, and by what is called "engaged" Buddhism. As the "West" discovered Buddhism, it has often been the cognitive, the social, and the scientific aspects that have appealed most.

How this plays out, as Buddhisms of different kinds develop in the twenty-first century remains to be seen: there is an increased emphasis on secularism, on rationalism even, and on a Buddhism that is perceived as less devotional than earlier kinds. Lay meditative practice is also becoming more prominent as well as a sense of the individualist search that might not align itself with any particular group. One group, the Triratna Buddhist Community (once Friends of the Western Buddhist Order), was founded in 1967 by Sangharakshita as a consciously syncretic approach involving many Buddhisms. But the appeal of ancient traditions, with their great emotional and spiritual heritage, is deep: lineages of many kinds are finding new roots in new soils. Buddhisms have always traveled and it may be that the Buddhism defined by three "directions" will continue to affect how the West understands and perceives Buddhism well into the next few centuries, too.

About the author
Sarah Shaw is the Khyentse Foundation Reader in Buddhist Studies at the University of South Wales, UK, a fellow of the Oxford Centre for Buddhist Studies, and a member of the Faculty of Oriental Studies, University of Oxford. She researches Buddhist meditation, ritual, narrative, and chant.

Suggestions for further reading

In this book

See Chapters 26 (why Buddhists meditate), 27 (mindfulness), 28 (kinds of meditation), 39 (contemporary divisions), 52 (Buddhist influence on art), 60 (engaged Buddhism), and 73 (secular Buddhism).

Elsewhere

Bluck, Robert. *British Buddhism*: *Teachings, Practice and Development*. London: Routledge, 2008.

Harvey, Peter. *Introduction to Buddhism* (2nd edition). Cambridge: Cambridge University Press, 2012.

Humphreys, Christmas. "Zen comes West." *Middle Way* 32(4) (1958): 126–130.

Index

Page numbers in *italics* refer to images.

Abhayākaragupta 257
Abhidhamma Piṭaka 24, 25, 77–78, 94, 224–225, 371
Afghanistan 78, 241, 275, 308
Africa 348–349
Against the Stream Meditation Society 322, 325
Aggañña Sutta (On Knowledge of Beginnings) 308, 347
ahiṃsā (see: non-harm)
Ajanta Caves, India *250*
Ājīvikas 267
Akṣobhya, Buddha 255
alcohol 337–339
alms-giving 71, 148, 168–169, 289–290
Amaravati Buddhist monastery, UK 275
Ambedkar, Bhimrao Ramji 310–311
Americas 210, 294, 322, 332, 347, 349–350, 375
 art 204, 260
 artificial intelligence 371
 intoxicants 339
 LGBTQI people 325
 online communities 361, 363
Amida (Amitabha), Buddha 43, 144, 207, 208–209, 251
Amida order (see also: Pure Land Buddhism)
Amitabha, Buddha (see: Amida [Amitabha], Buddha)
Amitabha Buddhist Society 210
Anagārika Dharmapāla 177
Anālayo, Bhikkhu 134, 304
Ānanda 14–15, 110, 163
Ānāpānasati Sutta ("Discourse on Mindfulness of Breathing") 137–138
anātman /anattā (see: non-self)
Angkor Wat, Cambodia 240

Aṅgulimāla 15
Aṅguttara Nikāya (Gradual Discourses) 25
anicca (see: impermanence)
animals
 compassion toward 289, 290–291, 314–315, 361
 feeding 63, 313
 images 241
 rebirth 82
anukampā (active compassion) 304
Anuradhapura, Sri Lanka 29, 239–240, *240*
archaeology 19–20, 78, 273
arhats 11, 20, 41, 51, 52, *61*, 112–114, 116–117, 121, 122, 299
art 55, 204, 238–265, 314, 369
artificial intelligence (AI) 370–372
Ary, Elijah 296
asceticism 48, 71, 109, 148, 183, 267, 289, 337
Asian Classics Input Project (ACIP) 360
Aśoka, King 20, 22, 78, 194, 303, 304, 308
astrology 94
atheistic Buddhism 20, 40–43
Atiṣa (monk) 282–283
ātman (see: self)
attachment 100–101, 105, 108, 117, 319–320 (see also: non-attachment)
auspicious numbers 257
auspicious times 17
Australia 174, 210
authenticity 20, 47–48, 76–77, 78–79
authority 20, 21–22, 50–54, 148–151, 194, 224
Avadāna stories 36
Avalokiteśvara (Guanyin) Bodhisattva 43, 70, 143, 213, 234, 243, 251, 313–314, 329

380 INDEX

Avataṃsaka Sūtra ("The Garland Discourse") 26, 38, 66, 232
Avīci Hell 231
awakening 47, 50–54, 82–83, 109, 116–119, 207–209 (see also: enlightenment; nirvana)
awareness 131–134, 338

Bagby, Rachel 349
Bamiyan, Afghanistan 275
banners/flags 30, *169*, 243, 244
bardo (between-lives) period 98
Batchelor, Martine 367, 369
Batchelor, Stephen 367–368
Beat poets 204, 339
Being Black: Zen and the Art of Living with Fearlessness and Grace (williams) 349
bells 33, 243–244
Bharhut monastery, India 249
Bhikkhu Bodhi 305, 337–338
bhikkhus/bhikkhunīs (see: monasticism)
*bhūmi*s 122
Bhutan 243, 256
Black and Buddhist (Selassie) 348
Black Lives Matter (BLM) 347
blessings 15, 17, 66, 234
bliss 111, 114, 208, 229–230
Bodh Gaya, India 29
Bodhi trees 15, 20–21, 29–30, 47, 68, *69*, 240
bodhicitta precepts 218
Bodhidharma (monk) 203
bodhisattva 43, 53, 63–66, 114, 121–122, 138–139, 233, 250–251, 303, 319
bodhisattva path 64–65, 118–119, 191, 213
Bodhisattva Senju (1,000-armed) Kannon 65
bodhisattva vow 154, 208, 217–219, 224, 230, 282–283, 286
body and mind 86–89, 96–97
Borobudur, Indonesia 240
Brahmā 41–42
brahma-vihāra 316
Brahmajāla Sutta ("The Supreme Net") 41, 267, 286
Brahmanism 81, 100, 182–186, 220, 268, 346–347
breathing 131, 137–138, 139, 203, 230, 335
Budai 60–62
Buddha-images 20–21, 29–33, 55–58, 60–62, 71–72, 240–241, 249–250, 275

Buddha-nature 37–38, 50–54, 173, 174, 191, 220–221, 269, 344
Buddha (Siddhārtha Gautama) 10–11, 63, 71, 88, 190–191, 194, 307, 322
  asceticism 183
  compassion 313
  enlightenment 40, *57–58*
  familial relationships 163, 295, 307
  food 289–290
  founds Sangha 153
  historical Buddha 46–48, 50, 368
  meditation 126, 128–129, 136, 137
  parinirvāṇa (final nirvana) 51
  past lives 63, 285, 300
  physical characteristics 12, 51
  preaching 176, 241, 246, 368
  psychic powers 118
  relation to holy texts 27
  relics 15, 17, 19, 20, 21, 47, 51, 240
  Śākyamuni ("sage of the Śākyas") 43, 52, 53, 196, 232, 249
  "three bodies" doctrine 53
  "word of the Buddha" 76–79, 193
Buddhaghosa 138, 315
buddhas 20, 51, 52, 64–65, 69, 122–123, 138–139, 196, 232–233
Buddhism
  categories of people 120–121, 170, 268
  definition 6, 14, 366, 374
  theory vs. practice 172
Buddhist Digital Resource Center (BDRC) 360
Buddhist Modernism 363
Buddhist-Muslim dialogues 275
Buddhist Society, The 363
"Buddhists for Racial Justice" 347
buildings 8, 151, 174, 238–246, 257, 309, 362
Burma (see: Myanmar)
"Burning House" parable 37
Bushido 287

Cabezón, Jose 328–329
Cage, John (composer) 260, 261
Cakkavatti-Sīhanāda Sutta 307–308
calendar
  festivals/holy days 16–17, 71, 177
  monastic rituals 235, 238
Cambodia 149, 158, 193, 240, 274, 304, 309, 310
Caṅki Sutta 82–83

INDEX 381

Caozhi, prince 143
caste system 184, 268, 311, 347
celibacy 151, 164, 166, 282, 293–296, 323, 324–325, 327
ceremonies (see: rituals)
Chan Buddhism (see: Zen [Chan] Buddhism)
chanting 14–15, 17, 43, 141–144, 375
"Charter of Free Inquiry" 357
Charwei Tsai (artist) 260
Cheng Yen (nun) 170, 173, 305
children 71, 84, 87, 96–97, 155–156, 295–296, 323 (see also: education)
Chin Kung 210
China 72, 149, 195, 202, 269–270, 286–287, 290, 332, 375, 376
and Christianity 273–274
Daoism 62, 273
images 60, 66, 314
monks and nuns 154, 169, 286
politics 214, 215, 287, 300–301, 309, 343
printed text 150, 360
texts 4, 26, 76, 77, 142, 192, 194
Chithurst Buddhist Monastery 363
Chöygam Trungpa 294
Christianity 7, 20, 210, 273–275, 310, 335, 357
circumambulation 30, 243
Citta-mātra (see: Yogacara)
clairaudience 229
climate change 352–355
clinging (upādāna) 110–111, 225, 226, 318
cloth bundle (symbol) 60–61
clothing 20, 30, 58, 72, 160, 168, 189
colonialism 207, 274–275, 309–310, 334, 343, 357, 376
Communism 310
compassion (karuṇā) 63, 95, 138, 174, 207, 281, 284, 302–305, 313–316, 318–320 (see also: Avalokiteśvara)
concentration (samādhi) pose 32
conception 87, 96–97, 323
Confucianism 269, 273, 287, 300
consciousness (vinnāṇa/vijñāna) 86–88, 96–97, 203, 218, 358, 361, 371–372
consequences of actions 81–82, 91–94 (see also: karma)
constructive imagination 132–133
conversion 177, 179, 308
cosmology 41, 255
Covid-19 pandemic 72, 261, 362

craving (taṇhā/tṛṣṇā) 96, 97, 98, 105, 110–111, 112, 298
creation of images and art 55–56, 71, 248–252
creator god 40–42, 366
cremation 19, 52

dāgäba (see: stupas)
Dagri Rinpoche 325
Daḷadā Māligāva (Temple of the Tooth Relic), Sri Lanka 21
Dalai Lama, 14th, Tenzin Gyatso 290, 324, 328, 330, 341, 343, 353, 376
Dalai Lamas 43, 119, 151, 212–215
dāna (giving) 70–71, 149, 168–170, 239, 249 (see also: generosity)
dancing 16, 17, 282
Daochup, patriarch 208
Daoism 139, 269, 273
dasa sil mātā (ten precept mothers) 166
death 52, 96, 97, 112, 133, 361 (see also: relics)
of the Buddha 47, 51
grief 36–37, 110, 144, 298
by suicide 297–298
definition of Buddhism 6, 14, 366, 374
Degenerate Age of Dharma (mappō) 202, 208, 209
deities 40–41, 43, 53, 62, 88, 185, 197, 229, 232–236, 249, 254 (see also: bodhisattva)
"deity yoga" 229
delaying nirvana 217
delusion 64, 83, 93, 105, 112, 116
dependent origination (see: pratītyasamutpāda)
devas (see: deities)
devotion 68–72, 300 (see also: Buddha-images; offerings; pilgrimage; rituals)
Dhammakaya Grand Meditation Stadium, Thailand 240
Dhammapada 25, 92, 109–110, 114, 128, 353, 358
Dharma 3, 29, 51, 184, 273, 313
embodiment 53, 197, 244
and secular Buddhism 367–368
Wheel of the Dharma 68, 104
Dharmaguptaka 76, 77, 78–79, 158, 190
Dharmakāra (see: Amida [Amitabha], Buddha)
dharmas 189–190, 224–226

Diamond Sutra 26, 204
Dīgha Nikāya (Long Discourses) 25, 267, 307–308, 347
digital devotion 361
digital technology 22, 72, 150, 176, 360
Dīpaṅkara, Buddha 46, 217
disciples of the Buddha 43, 47, 92, 110, 121, 128–129, 172, 272–273, 294–295
discipline (see: Vinaya Piṭaka)
"Discourse on Setting in Motion the Wheel of the Dharma" 246
Discourses (see: Sutta Piṭaka)
discourses of the Great Vehicle (see: sutras)
divination 94
divine abidings (brahmā-vihāra) 138, 316
Dogen (monk) 202–203
domestic shrines 16, 29, 30, 72 (see also: lay people)
Doṇaloka Sutta 50–51
doubt 208
drug use 337–339
Du Bois, W. E. B. 350
Duchamp, Marcel (artist) 260–261
dukkha/duḥkha 104–105
Dunhuang caves, China 150, 314
duty 342–343
dzogchen (great perfection) 139

Eastern Buddhism 195, 218, 374–375
Ecodharma (Loy) 354–355
Ecumenical Institute for Study and Dialogue 275
education 150, 151, 156, 295, 332–336
Eisai (monk) 202
elements 41, 86
emotions, negative 83, 93, 112, 128, 139
empathy 319
emptiness 26, 223–226, 244, 260, 325
engaged Buddhism 302–305, 341
enlightenment 10, 43, 71, 92, 116–119, 163, 164, 203, 245–246, 370 (see also: awakening; nirvana)
environmental issues 352–355, 361
esotericism 27, 255, 257, 362
European Network of Buddhist-Christian Studies 276
eye-opening ceremony 56

faith 8, 10–12
familial relationships 106, 108, 151, 155, 159, 163, 293–296

fat Buddha 60–62
fatalism 92
Felai Feng grottoes, China 61
festivals/holy days 16–17, 71, 169, 177, 269, 338, 339
fire-lighting 255
flags/banners 30, 169, 243, 244
folk religion 8, 62, 233, 235
footprints (symbol) 29, 32
forest monks 151
Foundation for the Preservation of the Mahayana Tradition 325
Four Noble Truths 104–107, 116, 315, 356, 367
France 309, 332
Friends of the Western Buddhist Order 377
friendship 106, 138, 139

Gaden Shartse Thubten Dhargye Ling, USA 363
Gaṇḍavyūha Sūtra 38
Ganden Monastery, Lhasa, Tibet 214
Gāndhāra, kingdom 240–241
Gāndhārī language 76, 77, 194
Gautama Buddha (see: Buddha [Siddhārtha Gautama])
Géluk order 213–214
gender 66, 229–230, 235, 314, 329
 gender equality 172–174, 268, 323
 gender identity 328, 329
 monasticism 158–159, 163–164, 304
generosity 36, 40, 70, 82 (see also: dāna)
Geshema Degree 304
gestures 32, 38, 57, 204, 251
Global Buddhist Relief 305
Gormley, Anthony (artist) 261
Gotama Buddha (see: Buddha [Siddhārtha Gautama])
"Great Fifth," Dalai Lama 214
"Great Store of Scriptures" 26, 76
grief 110, 144, 298
Gross, Rita 276
Guanyin (see: Avalokiteśvara [Guanyin] Bodhisattva)
Guanyin Sutra 204
Guru Yoga 361
gurus 33, 230–231, 314
Gushri Khan 214
Gutiérrez Baldoquín, Hilda 349
Gyatso, Tenzin (see: Dalai Lama, 14th, Tenzin Gyatso)

happiness 83, 127
happy Buddha (see: fat Buddha)
Hayagrīva 251
health 92–93, 133–134, 143–144, 229, 233, 238, 339, 356, 361
heaps (*skandhas/khandhas*) 100
Heart Sutra 26, 204, 226, 260
heavens 40–41, 43, 46, 53, 91, 121, 270
hells 12, 41, 82, 92, 231, 297, 314
Hinayana 199–200
Hinduism 8, 81, 172, 182–186, 197, 285
homosexuality 322, 324, 325, 327–330
Hōnen (monk) 208–209, 210
Hōtei 60–62
Hsin Tao 275
Huayan school 26, 375
Huike, Patriarch 203
Huineng, Patriarch 26, 38
human rights 302–305, 341–344, 346–349
Humphreys, Christmas 374

identity 100–102, 117, 329, 342–343
idol-worship 31
images 22, 29–33, 36, 229–230, 234–235, 241, 254–255, 303 (see also: Buddha-images)
impermanence (*anicca*) 221, 241
incantations 141, 197
incense 30, 56, 72, 260
India (see also: Theravada Buddhism)
  development of Buddhism 20, 195, 307–308, 309, 310–311, 375
  non-self 99
  origins of Buddhism 50, 137, 172, 173, 182–186, 337
  Pure Land Buddhism 207
  texts 25, 26, 27, 38
indigenous religions 274
individualism 342, 367
Indonesia 149, 240, 309, 343
infidelity 294–295
initiation, Tantric 218–219, 229, 233–234, 255, 257
insight 82–83, 110, 121, 128, 137, 203, 299
intentionality 87, 91, 94, 97, 299, 314
"interbeing" 303, 354
interdependence 353–354, 358–359
interfaith matters 266–270, 272–276
International Network of Engaged Buddhists (INEB) 276, 305
intoxicants 281, 337–339

Islam 149, 275, 286, 310

Jainism 48, 81, 100, 183, 220, 267–268, 269, 289, 299
Japan 65, 71, 72, 195, 229, 270, 310, 357, 375
  and America 210, 375–376
  interfaith interaction 179, 275
  monasticism 151, 155, 169, 174, 178, 293–294, 324
  political power 286–287, 309
  Pure Land Buddhism 208–209
  rituals and symbols 61–62, 66, 142, 144, 339
  Zen Buddhism 202
Jātaka (birth stories) 25, 35–36, 217, 285, 300, 313
Jayatilleke, K. N. 346
*jhāna*s, 81–82, 107, 126–127, 137, 202
Jīvaka Sutta 289–290
Jizō Bodhisattva 71–72
Jōdo Shu and Jōdo Shinshū schools 209
Jung, C. G. 254

Kagyu Samye Ling Monastery, UK 294
Kālacakra Tantra 255
Kālāma Sutta 83, 257, 357
kāma (realm of sense-desire) 43
Kannon (see: Avalokiteśvara [Guanyin] Bodhisattva)
Kanō Kōi (artist) 61
karma 35–36, 91–95, 106, 217, 268, 284–285, 289, 298
  meritorious acts 56, 68, 239, 249
  sharing karma 43
  of women 173
karuṇā (see: compassion)
Kaṭhina 16–17
Kelaniya Temple, Sri Lanka 69, 248
Kevaddha Sutta 42
khandhas (*skhanda*s) 86–87 (see also: heaps)
Khandro Rinpoche 330
Khmer Rouge government, Cambodia 310
Khuddaka Nikāya 25, 112–113
killing 83, 92, 106, 281, 298–299, 314
Kimsooja (artist) 261–262
kindness (see: *mettā/maitrī*)
Kisā Gotamī 36
koans 38, 204

Korea 38, 66, 149, 174, 261, 287, 309, 310, 367
Kornfield, Jack 295
Kosalabimbavaṇṇanā 55

lamas 84, 235, 245, 325, 330, 361 (see also: Dalai Lama, 14th, Tenzin Gyatso)
Dalai Lamas 43, 119, 151, 212–215
Laṅkāvatāra Sūtra 26, 290
Laos 149, 193, 274, 309, 374
laughing Buddha (see: fat Buddha)
lay people 20, 47, 151, 166, 170, 209 (see also: *dāna*; domestic shrines)
  achieving nirvana 114
  familial relationships 294–295
  lay communities 170–171
  LGBTQI people 328
  preaching 178
  precepts 281–282, 284
  Pure Land beliefs 209
  renunciation 319, 323, 338
  rituals 14, 17, 70–71, 155–156, 169, 204
  violence 285
Lee, Tosi 260–261
Levine, Noah 322, 325
LGBTQI people 322, 324, 325, 327–330
light 16, 72
Lippard, Lucy 261
Lokeśvararāja, Buddha 208
Lokottaravādins ("Transcendentalist") 190–191
Long, Richard (artist) 261
Longevity Deities 234
Lotsawa Lhakang Temple, India 244
Lotus Buddha family 234–235
lotus flower 68, 245–246
Lotus Sutra (*Saddharmapuṇḍarīka Sūtra*) 26, 37, 43, 53, 141, 196, 200, 204, 232, 300, 314
Loy, David 354–355
luck 61, 62
Lumbinī, Nepal 47

Machig Labdrön 174
Macy, Joanna 354, 355
maechi 166
Mahāmoggallāna 92
Mahāparinibbāna Sutta 15–16, 19, 286
Mahāprajāpatī/Mahāpajāpatī 163
Mahāsāṃghikas 77, 189, 190, 191
Mahāsthāmaprāpta bodhisattva 143

Mahāvastu 77, 190–191
Mahāvīra 48
Mahayana Buddhism 3, 21, 52, 53, 189, 191–192, 193–197, 199–200, 223–227, 276, 286, 334, 375 (see also: bodhisattva path; bodhisattva vow; Pure Land Buddhism; Zen [Chan] Buddhism; *individual sutras*)
  Buddha-nature 64–65, 70, 118–119, 122–123, 209, 232–233
  enlightenment 143
  identity 102
  kindness 138
  lay preaching 178
  monastic rules 154, 155, 158
  nirvana 114
  non-duality 358
  rebirth 98
  vegetarianism 290
Maitreya (future Buddha) 61
Majjhima Nikāya (Middle-Length Discourses) 25, 132, 289
"Making the Invisible Visible: Healing Racism in our Buddhist Communities" 347, 349
Makkhali Gosāla 267
Malalasekera, G. P. 346
Malaysia 343
mandalas 72, 197, 241, 245, 254–257, 260
maṇi wheel 243
Mañjuśrī Bodhisattva 43, 66, 213, 229, 233
mantras 70, 72, 197, 213, 229, 244, 251, 283
Māra, lord of delusion 32
"marathon monks" 71
marks of the Buddha/Bodhisattva 30, 375
marriage 151, 155, 293–296, 323
martial arts 286–287
materialists 81, 86
meditation 30, 32–33, 106, 118, 126–129, 136–140, 377 (see also: *jhāna*s; *samādhi*)
  compassion 304, 315–316
  memories of past lives 97
  retreats 228, 230
  scholarship 87–88, 358, 363–364
  in schools 335
Tantric Buddhism 229, 230, 283
visualization 138–139
memory 131, 132–133
"mental faults" 117
mental health 297–298

mental states 87–88, 106–107, 109, 138, 143–144, 183–184, 223–226
meritorious acts 22, 70, 249–250, 251, 252, 315–316
mettā/maitrī (loving-kindness) 25, 82, 83, 133, 138, 281, 290, 316, 335, 352–353
Mettā Sutta ("Discourse on Loving-kindness") 133, 352–353
Metteyya/Maitreya, the Friendly One 43
Middle Way 97, 106, 148, 267
mindfulness 130–134, 136–137, 139, 304, 335, 363–364, 376
missionary activity 194, 273–275
monasticism 148–151, 153–156, 159, 163–166, 188–190, 204, 212, 242, 275, 329, 332 (see also: celibacy; *dāna*; Sangha; vinayas)
buildings 169, 238–240
calendar of devotions 235, 238
creating art 249
depictions of 61
etiquette 161
familial relationships 293–296
honorary titles 65
LGBTQI people 328
persecution 310
political power 22, 287
preaching 176–177
precepts 282, 284
questioning 42
renunciation 319, 338, 339, 360
ritual 22, 142
Shaolin monks 286
Mongolia 195, 196, 309, 375
Morgan, Peggy 334, 335
Mount Hiei, Japan 71, 209
*mudrā*s (hand gestures) 57, 316
Mukpo, Diana (born Pybus) 294
Mūlasarvāstivāda *Vinaya* 77, 158
music 16, 17, 141, 143–144, 204, 282
Muttā (nun) 36
Myanmar (Burma) 15, 138, 274, 309, 376
Rohingya people 285–286, 310, 348
women 165, 166, 174

nāma-rūpa 87
Namkhai Norbu Rinpoche 361
narrative (see: stories, importance of)
National Christian Council Center for the Study of Japanese Religions 275

Navayana ("New Vehicle") Buddhism 310–311
Nembutsu (devotional practices towards Amitabha) (see: Amida [Amitabha], Buddha)
Nepal 151, 155, 195, 196
netsuke 62
"New Buddhism" 204
Newari Buddhism 155
Nichiren school 37, 43, 209, 375
Nigaṇṭha Nātaputta (Mahāvīra) 267
nirvana (*nibbāna*) 32, 40, 105, 112–114, 121, 217, 229–230 (see also: awakening; enlightenment)
Niwano, Nikkyo 275
Noble Eightfold Path 82, 106–107, 109, 112, 117, 139–140, 375
Noble Truths (see: Four Noble Truths)
non-attachment 82, 101–102, 108–111, 318–320
non-duality 229, 260, 358
non-harm (*ahiṃsā*) 268, 284–287, 289–291, 294–295, 303, 308, 330, 358–359, 372 (see also: vegetarianism)
non-self 64, 99–102, 111, 184, 297, 342
"nones" 7
Northern Buddhism 195, 218, 241, 375
nuns 36, 154, 158–159, 163–166, 174, 304, 325 (see also: monasticism; vinayas)
Nyingma Gyü-bum 27, 361

offerings 16, 30, 52, 63–64, 218
to Buddha-images 55–56
to deities 185, 197
to monastic communities 70, 71, 149, 168
online communities 361, 362–363
oral tradition 24, 37, 47, 78, 143, 157, 230–231
ordination 149, 153–156, 163–164, 171
organ donation 361
origins 313

pacifism 284–287
*pācittiya*s (rules entailing confession) 338
pagodas (see: stupas)
Pakistan 78, 241, 308
Pali Buddhism (see: Theravada Buddhism)
Pali Canon 3–4, 24, 50–51, 130–131, 184, 190, 193–194, 315, 360 (see also: *Vinaya Piṭaka*; *individual texts*)
paññā/prajñā (see: wisdom)

INDEX

parallel worlds 52, 118–119, 196, 232
parents 106, 108
parinirvāṇa (final nirvana) 32, 47, 51, 58, 217, 282
Parnaṣabari 229
Paro Taktsang, Bhutan 243
Pasenadi, king 55, 132
past lives 51, 63–64, 81–82, 83–84, 92, 97, 217, 290
paṭicca-samuppāda (see: *pratītyasamutpāda*)
Payutto, P.A 342
Pema Yoedling Dratsang, Bhutan *142*, *256*
Perfection of Wisdom in 8,000 Lines 21, *142*
perfection of wisdom (*prajñāpāramitā*) 25, 142, 224, 314
perfections 64, 196, 197, 229–230
persecution
 of Buddhists 310
 of others 285–286, 310
"phronesis" 368
physical work 205
pilgrimage 17, 21, 22, *65*, 70–71, *169*
Platform Sutra 26, 38
pluralism, religious 276
Podae 60–62
poetry 204, 376
politics 9, 22, 151, 194, 202, 307–311, 343, 348
 Dalai Lama 212, 213–215
 engaged Buddhism 302–305
 monasteries 151, 287, 308
 political protest 300–301, 304
Polonnaruwa, Sri Lanka 32, 239–240
postures 56, *57*, 106, 137, 139, 203, 204
Potala Palace, Tibet *241*
Prakrit 27
prātimokṣa/pāṭimokkha 158
pratītyasamutpāda (dependent origination) 77, 96–97, 303, 375
prayer wheel (*maṇi* wheel) 243
preaching 176–179
precepts 218–219, 281–282, 337–338, 354, 372
primordial buddha 52
prophecy 217, 218
prosperity 60–61, 235
prostration 56, 204
protection rituals 14–15, 16, 69, 72, 313–314

psychic powers (*siddhis*) 56–57, 61, 88, 118, 217, 219, 229, 230
Pudgalavāda school 189
pūjas (acts of devotion) 30
"pure abodes" 41
Pure Land Buddhism 26, 52, 143, 207–210, 293–294, 300, 339
"pure vision" 233–234

Qici (monk) 60
questioning mind 11, 12, 42, 48, 357

race/racism 346–350
Rahula, Walpola (monk) 303
Ratana Sutta 15
rationalism 8, 207, 357, 363
reality 64, 116, 189, 225–226
realm of infinite consciousness 41
realm of infinite space 41
realm of sense-desire 43
rebirth 36, 81–84, 86, 96–98, 121, 228 (see also: nirvana; *saṃsāra*)
 based on karma 91, 183
 conception 87, 110
 Dalai Lama 212
 of deities 40–42, 88, 185
 identity 100–101
 intentional 114
 and suicide 297–298
 as a women 173, 174
 of women 164
recital 14, 229, 238
reclining Buddha 32, 58
relics 14, 15, 17, 19–22, 47, 52, 72, 220, 240 (see also: stupas)
religion, a definition 6–8
renunciation 58, 109, 183, 209
 celibacy 164, 166, 323
 monastic rules 154, 160, 168, 170–171, 319
repentance 204
retreats 228, 230, 275, 361
Rewalsar, India *169*
"right view" 82–83
Rinzai school 204, 287
Rissho Kosei Kai movement 178, 275
rituals 14–18, 33, 53, 68–72, 163, 243–244, 338–339 (see also: relics)
 bodhisattva vow 218–219
 Buddha-images 30–31, 56, 61
 chanting 141–144

INDEX 387

circumambulation 30
mandalas 254–257
monasticism 153, 155, 155–156, 204, 205
Tantric Buddhism 197, 228–231, 314
Rock Insight Meditation community 349
Rocky Mountain Ecodharma Retreat Center 354
Rohingya people 286, 310, 348
roshi (Zen teacher) 205
rūpa (material form) 41, 86

Saddharmapuṇḍarīka Sūtra (see: Lotus Sutra)
Saga Dawa 16, 71
saints 15, 65, 120–123, 240
Sakka/Śakra 43
Sakya order 361–362
Sakyadhita ("Daughters of the Buddha") 165, 304
Śākyamuni ("sage of the Śākyas") (see: Buddha [Siddhārtha Gautama])
Śākyas 47, 51
samādhi (concentration) pose 32, 139–140, 240
Samādhi Pilimi (meditation statue) 240
Sāmaññaphala Sutta ("The Fruits of the Homeless Life") 267
samayas (binding promises) 282
sammā-sambuddha/samyaksambuddha (see: Buddha [Siddhārtha Gautama]; buddhas)
saṃsāra 82, 105, 110, 183, 218, 230, 280, 282
Saṃyutta Nikāya (Connected Discourses) 25, 131
Sanchi, India 240, 249
Sangha 10, 70, 123, 153, 172, 188–189, 303, 349 (see also: disciples of the Buddha; monasticism)
Sangharakshita 377
saṅkhāra/saṃskāra (volitional activities) 86
sannā/saṃjnā (perception) 86
Sanskrit 3–4, 21, 25, 27, 76, 77, 191, 194, 360
Śāntideva (monk) 218
Śāriputra/Sāriputta (arhat) 110, 329
Sarvāstivādins ("Pan-realists") 76, 77, 78–79, 189–190, 191
Sasson, Vanessa 296
Satipaṭṭhāna Sutta ("Discourse on the Foundations of Mindfulness") 131, 137

satori 203–204
Sautrāntika school 190
sāvaka buddhas 122
science 99, 356–359, 367 (see also: technology)
artificial intelligence 370–372
ethics 372
scripture (see: texts)
Second World War 287, 303
secular Buddhism 6, 81, 207, 366–369
secularism 130–134, 316, 332, 343
Selassie, Sebene 348
self (ātman) 97, 99, 117, 184–185, 189, 205, 221, 268
self-denial (see: renunciation)
self-immolation 297, 300–301
self-mortification 120
self-sacrifice 36, 63–64, 286, 300, 313
Sen, Amartya 343
senses 96, 128, 131–132
Senyū-ji, Japan 65
Seven Lucky Gods 62
sex 299, 320, 322–326
imagery 252, 314
LGBTQI people 327–330
sexual misconduct 159–160, 281, 282, 322, 323–324, 325, 327
Tantric Buddhism 228, 229–230
Shambhala International, USA 294
Shaolin monks 286
Sharpe, Gina 349
Shenhui (monk) 203
Shingon Buddhism 229
Shinran (monk) 208–209, 293–294
Shinto 270, 287
Shutt, T. Liên 349
Shwedagon Pagoda, Myanmar 31
Siam (see: Thailand)
Siddhārtha Gautama (see: Buddha [Siddhārtha Gautama])
siddhis (see: psychic powers)
Sigala (disciple of Buddha) 294
Singapore 261, 343
Sivaraska, Sulak 304, 305
skillful means (upāyakauśalya) 37, 243–244, 276, 286, 314
Smith, Sharon 348
Snyder, Gary 205
social reform 303–305, 311
Society for Buddhist-Christian Studies 276
Soka Gakkai movement 287, 375

Soto school 127–128, 202, 203
sounds, sacred 56, 244
Southern Buddhism (see: Theravada Buddhism)
Soyen, Shaku 357
Soygal Rinpoche 325
spirit worship 233, 235, 269
spiritual "fetters"/ignorance 116–118
Spiritual intelligence (SQ) 370
spiritual pride 339
śramaṇas/samaṇa 48, 109, 183
śrāvakayāna 199
Sri Lanka
  colonialism 309, 357
  development of Theravada Buddhism 149, 190, 194
  interfaith interaction 273, 274, 275
  LGBTQI people 328
  monastic rules 158
  sacred sites and buildings 20–21, 29, 32, 57, 69, 239–240, 240, 248
  Tamil people 285, 310, 347–348
  women 154, 164, 166
  written texts 24, 55, 360
Sthaviras/Theras 189, 190
stories, importance of 24, 25, 35–39, 47, 57, 158–159, 249, 314
"stream entry" 11
stupas (relic mounds) 19, 20–21, 22, 29–30, 52, 68, 220, 239, 240, 242–243 (see also: relics)
Sudinna (monk) 323
suffering 42, 52, 70, 95, 138, 297–298, 319–320, 361
  causes 83, 100, 110
  Four Noble Truths 104–105
  liberation from (see also: nirvana)
  shared 315
suicide 297–301
Sukhāvatīvyūha Sūtra ("The Land of Bliss [Pure Land] Discourse") 26, 52, 207–208
Sumedhā Buddha 36, 46, 217
susoku-kan (breath-counting meditation) 203
sutras/suttas see individual sutras 24–26, 37, 68–69, 77, 78, 130, 191, 195
Sutta Nipāta 25, 346–347
Sutta Piṭaka (Discourses) 24, 25, 77, 267
Suvisuddharama Buddhist Temple, Sri Lanka 57, 239

Suzuki, D. T. 204, 260
symbolism 29–30, 51, 61, 68, 238–246, 314 (see also: Buddha-images)
syncretic Buddhism 374, 377

Taiwan 60, 151, 210, 260, 275, 310
  nuns 164, 166
  Tzu Chi movement 170, 174
Taliban 275
Tamil people 285, 348
Tāmraparṇīyas (see: Theravada Buddhism)
tangkas (wall hangings) 33
Taniyama, Yozo 144
"Tantra for the Purification of All Bad Transmigrations" 255, 257
Tantric/Vajrayana Buddhism 196–197, 214, 228–231, 324–325, 361, 375
  deities 233–236
  meditation 33, 138–139
  rituals and symbols 218–219, 243–244, 251–252, 254–255, 257, 282–283, 314, 338–339
  temples 241
  texts 27, 158
Tārā 229, 251, 313
tariki (relying on a higher power) 202
tathāgatagarbha 220–221
teachers 173–174, 257, 328
  finding a good teacher 83
  gurus 230
  respect 218, 231, 282
teaching 106
technology 72, 150, 360–363, 370–372, 376
temples 20–21, 29–30, 43, 60, 127–128, 155, 239–240, 243
Tendai Buddhism 71
Tengyur 27
terma (treasure) texts 27
texts see: individual texts 3, 21–22, 24–27, 37, 47–48, 72, 76–79, 150, 165, 172, 360
Thailand 72, 166, 262, 269, 275, 305, 309
  ordination 156
  sacred sites and buildings 32, 60, 151, 240
  spread of Buddhism 149, 193, 274, 374
Thang Kian Hiong (Tang Da Wu) 261, 262
Thanissaro, Phra Nicholas 335
Theragāthā 25
Theravada Buddhism 3, 16–17, 122, 155, 189, 193–194, 199–200, 218, 224–225, 290, 334, 374 (see also: Pali Canon; Vinaya Piṭaka)

INDEX 389

abstinence 338
arhats 118
bodhisattva 64
Buddha-nature 51, 64
chanting 142
enlightenment 118
Four Noble Truths 116
historical Buddha 69
political power 308
preaching 177
rebirth 97-98
ten perfections 64
Therīgāthā 25, 36
Thich Nhat Hanh 300, 302, 303, 305, 323, 353-354
thiláshin 166
"three bodies" doctrine 53
Three Jewels 10, 15, 16, 29, 46, 132-133, 141
Tiantai (Tendai) school 26, 37, 375
Tibet 151, 196, 212, 213-214, 300, 309, 310, 343, 375
Tibetan Book of the Dead 27
Tibetan Buddhism 70, 155, 189, 199, 269, 290 (see also: Dalai Lamas; lamas)
Buddha-nature 220, 221
celestial beings 232-236
compassion 314
meditation 138, 139
non-attachment 101-102
rebirth 84, 98
rituals and symbols 8, 32-33, 71, *169*, 242-244, 254-255, 257, 298, 334
saints 325
Sakya order 361-362
sexual misconduct 324
texts 26, 27, 76, 77, 142, 158, 360, 367
Vajrayana Buddhism 196
women 164, 173, 304, 325
Tiravanija, Rirkrit (artist) 262
tonglen ("giving and taking") 138
touching-the-earth posture 57
tourist attractions 151
transgender people 328, 329-330
translation 3-4, 21, 26-27, 76, 174, 194, 269
Treeleaf.org 361
tripiṭaka/tipiṭaka (three baskets) (see: Abhidhamma Piṭaka; Sutta Piṭaka; Vinaya Piṭaka)
Triple Gem (see: Three Jewels)
Triratna Buddhist Community 170-171, 377

tsa-tsa images 244
Tsongkhapa 328
tulkus 84, 212, 213-214, 296
Tuṣita heaven 46
Tzu Chi movement 170, 174, 305

Udāna 112-113
United Kingdom 174, 348, 375
Buddhist Communities 170-171, 210, 294
colonialism 274, 309
teaching Buddhism 333-336, 349
Upaniṣads 100
Upāyakauśalya Sūtra (Skill in Means) 37, 286, 314
upekkhā/upekṣā (equanimity) 138, 316

Vairocana, Buddha ("he who is radiant") 52, 255
*vajra*s 243-244, 245, 255
Vajrāvalī 257
Vajrayana Buddhism (see: Tantric/Vajrayana Buddhism)
Vāseṭṭha, brahmin 346-347
Vasubandhu (scholar-monk) 285
Vedas 182-184, 268
vegetarianism 289-291
Vesak 16, 71
Vessantara, prince 36
Vibhajyavādins ("Distinctionists") 189, 190
Vietnam 60, 149, 193, 195, 300, 309, 349, 374
Vijñānavāda (see: Yogacara)
Vimalakīrti Nirdeśa ("The Teachings of Vimalakīrti") 170, 329
Vinaya Piṭaka (monastic discipline) 14, 24, 25, 77, 299, 337
vinayas 153-154, 157-158, 165, 188, 190, 298-299, 323, 324, 337
Vinge, Vernor 370
viññāṇa/vijñāna (see: consciousness)
violence 284-287, 310
vipassanā/vipaśyanā (see: insight)
virāga (see: non-attachment)
Visākhā 170
visualization 138-139, 191, 208, 230, 251, 255
vows 153, 154, 280-283 (see also: bodhisattva vow)

walking 71, 127-128, 304

Wanås Foundation, Sweden 261
wandering monks 109, 148, 168–169, 238
Wat Pho, Bangkok, Thailand 32
"way of perfections" 197
Western attitudes
  rationalism 47
  Vajrayana Buddhism 196
Western attitudes and ideas 6, 7–8, 137, 212, 290, 322, 334–335, 339 (see also: colonialism)
  art 259–261
  gender equality 164–165
  human rights 341–344
  LGBTQI people 328, 329–330
  mandalas 254, 257
  mindfulness 130, 353–354, 376
  missionary activity 274–275
  nuns 164–165
  Pure Land Buddhism 210
  race 349–350
  rationalism 357, 363
  scholarship 20, 47, 50, 368
  secular Buddhism 81, 366–369
  self 99, 205
  Zen Buddhism 202, 204
Western Buddhism 46, 150, 204, 262, 325, 348, 374–377
Wheel of the Dharma 68, 104, 240, *241*, 245–246

Wheeler, Kate Lila 349
williams, angel Kyodo 349
wisdom 64, 83, 119, 128, 229–230, 234–235, 244, 314
women 15, 36, 163, 165–166, 172–174, 304, 322, 325 (see also: gender; nuns)
Woodhead, Linda 7
World Conference on Religion and Peace 275
World Fellowship of Buddhists (WFB) 200
"World Religions Paradigm" 7
World's Parliament of Religions 357
writing texts 150, 260, 360

yakṣa (earth-deities) 249
Yang, Larry 349
Yaśodharā 322
yidam (meditational deities) 235
yoga 137, 197, 228–230, 324, 361
Yogacara 89, 223, 230
yogi/yogini 228–231

Zangdok Pairi Temple, India *234, 242*
Zen (Chan) Buddhism 60, 202–205, 270, 334, 339, 349, 367, 375, 376
  art 260–261
  martial arts 287
  meditation 127, 139
  teachers 349, 354
  texts 26–27, 38

www.ingramcontent.com/pod-product-compliance
Lightning Source LLC
Chambersburg PA
CBHW050928240426
43671CB00019B/2950